RABBINIC
LITERATURE

Abingdon Essential Guides

The Bible in English Translation
Steven M. Sheeley and Robert N. Nash, Jr.

Christian Ethics
Robin W. Lovin

Church History
Justo L. González

Feminism and Christianity
Lynn Japinga

Mission
Carlos F. Cardoza-Orlandi

Pastoral Care
John Patton

Preaching
Ronald J. Allen

Worship in Ancient Israel
Walter Brueggemann

RABBINIC LITERATURE

An
ESSENTIAL GUIDE

Jacob Neusner

Abingdon Press
Nashville

RABBINIC LITERATURE
AN ESSENTIAL GUIDE

Copyright © 2005 by Abingdon Press

This book is printed on acid-free paper.

Library of Congress Cataloging-in-Publication Data

Neusner, Jacob, 1932-
    Rabbinic literature : an essential guide / Jacob Neusner.
        p. cm.
    ISBN 0-687-35193-6 (alk. paper)
    1. Rabbinical literature—History and criticism.   2. Jewish law.   3. Aggada—History and
criticism.   4. Bible. O.T.—Criticism, interpretation, etc., Jewish   I. Title.

    BM496.6.N48 2005
    296.1'2061—dc22

                                                                                2004026897

05 06 07 08 09 10 11 12 13 14—10 9 8 7 6 5 4 3 2 1

MANUFACTURED IN THE UNITED STATES OF AMERICA

Contents

CHAPTER 1

What Is Rabbinic Literature?
Why Is It Important?

What Is Rabbinic Literature?

Christians commonly assume that "Judaism is the religion of the Old Testament," and that is at once true and only partially true. It is indeed the religion that derives from the written Torah (the Hebrew Scriptures). But that point of origin is examined in light of the interpretation of Scripture by the oral Torah (the Rabbinic literature).

To gain perspective on Rabbinic literature,[1] we best view it as a coherent reading of and response to Scripture, competing with other responses to the same revealed writings. Various communities of Israelites in the later centuries BCE and the early centuries CE[2] claimed to have inherited the Hebrew Scriptures of ancient Israel. Each of them in its own way applied the story of Scripture to itself and took over for its own community the laws of Scripture. Of these diverse groups, all of them claiming to realize in their own existence the Israel of which Scripture spoke, the one formed by Rabbinic sages enjoys a special position. For that group produced the writings that in time normative Judaism would deem uniquely authoritative. Those writings have formed the foundations of Judaism from antiquity to the present day.

The Rabbinic sages, flourishing in the first six centuries CE, the formative age of Rabbinic Judaism, addressed to the entirety of the people of Israel writings that claimed uniquely to carry forward the heritage of ancient Israelite Scripture. What justified that claim, in the sages' view, was that they read forward from Scripture to their own time, finding in Scripture patterns that govern through all time. On the strength of these enduring paradigms uncovered in Scripture's narratives and laws, the Rabbinic sages proposed to systematize and realize those laws and their theology—to make them the norms for the everyday life of their communities.

This they did by framing a worldview, a way of life, and a theory of who and what "Israel" is that stated in a systematic way what the ancient Israelite Scriptures set forth. These three components—a worldview or ethics, a way of life or ethos, and a theory of "Israel" or ethnos—formed a coherent design for the religious system of the social order the sages wished their Israel to embody. In this way the Rabbinic sages translated Scripture into a design for the life of eternal Israel. They did so by translating Scripture's story—its episodic law, prophecy, wisdom, and theology—into the systematic writings of law and theology that they set forth in their canon. They meant to generalize; for example, from the story of Adam and Eve and the loss of Eden they derived lessons for Israel's repentance and restoration, and from the story of Israel in Egypt they uncovered the pattern of Israel's redemption.

On behalf of Scripture as they interpreted it they claimed the authority of God's Instruction, or in Hebrew, the Torah, which was revealed to Moses at Mount Sinai. But it was not the whole of the Torah. For the Instruction was handed on in two media, writing and oral tradition. This tradition in two parts is called "the dual Torah." The written part of the Torah of Sinai corresponds to what Christianity knows as "the Old Testament." That was joined to a tradition that was orally formulated and orally transmitted until it was committed to writing by the Rabbinic sages in the Rabbinic documents of late antiquity. In chapter 2 we shall encounter the writing that traced that chain of tradition and showed how it extended from Sinai into the very circles of Rabbinic sages responsible for the Rabbinic canon.

Who were these sages of the Rabbinic canon? "Rabbi" was a term of respect, roughly "my lord," and was not unique to the Rabbinic sages of the dual Torah. What made a Rabbinic sage different from all others whom people honored with the same title was mastery of the dual Torah through a process of discipleship. The disciples revered the master as the embodiment of the Torah of Sinai; his deeds exemplified the teachings of the Torah as much as his words transmitted those teachings. Just as Israel, the people, was to realize those teachings in its social order, so the sage's actions and rulings made immediate and concrete the lessons of the oral tradition of Sinai.

The particular books of which the Rabbinic literature of the formative age is comprised divide into two parts, with one set devoted to law and the other to theology and the exegesis of Scripture. All dates are conventions, mere guesses.

The books of the law, or Halakhah, begin in the Mishnah (ca. 200 CE), the "repetition" of the law. The Mishnah was the first document of the Rabbinic literature to reach closure. It set forth the systematic exposition by topics of the heritage of norms of action. The Mishnah is made up of sixty-three tractates, sixty-one of them devoted to particular topics.

The Mishnah is accompanied by a compilation of supplementary rules, the Tosefta (ca. 300 CE), or "supplementary traditions." The Tosefta covers the same topical program as the Mishnah.

A systematic commentary on thirty-nine tractates or topical expositions of the Mishnah is set forth by the Talmud of the Land of Israel (ca. 400 CE).

Another exposition of selected tractates of the Mishnah, the Talmud of Babylonia (ca. 600 CE), joined expositions of law to treatises on theology and scriptural exegesis and became authoritative. The union of law and theology by the second of the two Talmuds won for that Talmud the paramount position in the exposition of Judaism from that time forward.

Systematic commentaries on the legal portions of Scripture located in Exodus, Leviticus, Numbers, and Deuteronomy linked the Halakhah of oral tradition to the Halakhah of Scripture. These are *Mekhilta Attributed to Rabbi Ishmael*, for Exodus, of uncertain date but possibly 300 CE; *Sifra* for Leviticus (ca. 300 CE); *Sifré* to Numbers (ca. 300 CE); and *Sifré* to Deuteronomy (ca. 300 CE).

The books of theology and exegesis of narrative, or Aggadah, encompass the Pentateuch and Ruth, Esther, Lamentations, and Song of Songs (Song of Solomon in the Christian Bible). These are privileged because they occupy a principal position in synagogue liturgy. They are as follows: *Genesis Rabbah* (ca. 400 CE); *Leviticus Rabbah* (ca. 450 CE); and *Ruth Rabbah*; *Esther Rabbah I*; *Lamentations Rabbah*; and *Song of Songs Rabbah*, for none of which a date more specific than circa 500 CE is available.

In addition to the Halakhic works of law and the Aggadic works of theology and scriptural exegesis, a collection of wise sayings and an amplification thereof, tractate *Abot, The Fathers* (ca. 250 CE), and *Abot deRabbi Natan, The Fathers According to Rabbi Nathan* (ca. 500 CE), complete the canon of late antiquity.

Why Is Rabbinic Literature Important?

The religion that the world calls "Judaism" calls itself "the Torah." To Judaism Rabbinic literature is important, therefore, because together with Scripture it affords complete and exhaustive access to the Torah of Sinai.

Why should someone who does not practice Judaism want to know about the Rabbinic literature of the formative age of Judaism? Students of religion include Judaism, and therefore its formative authoritative writings, in their study of the class of religions that are monotheist, along with Christianity and Islam. They furthermore find in Judaism an interesting example of a religion that relies on the study of a body of canonical writings for the preservation of authoritative law and doctrine—a demonstration of how a religion writes down its truths.

But outside of the community of Judaism the greatest interest in the Rabbinic literature derives from the various Christian communions, Protestant, Catholic, and Orthodox, for three closely related reasons.

First, Christians find in Rabbinic Judaism traditions and rules that clearly exercised authority in the time of Jesus, as attested by the Gospels and the Letters of Paul. Rabbinic literature clarifies convictions and practices that enter into the Gospel narratives and Paul's doctrines. So Rabbinic Judaism affords access to background material that is taken for granted in accounts of Christian origins. Knowing the background material sheds light on the context of early Christian writings.

Second, Christians wonder why the majority of Jews from antiquity to the present day have affirmed a view of Scripture and its imperatives different from the Christian one. That puzzlement takes the form of the question, "Why not?"—meaning, why did "the Jews" viewed as a corporate entity not "accept Christ" and join Christianity? Christians understand that Rabbinic Judaism from antiquity to the present day formulated the alternative to Christianity. It is the option that most Jews through the ages have affirmed, in preference to Christianity (and Islam). In the canonical writings of the Rabbinic sages is the affirmative answer to the negative question, "Why not?"

Third, in combination, these two reasons for Christian interest in Rabbinic literature—materials for the Judaic exegesis of the Gospels, and accounts of the Judaic alternative to the Christian reading of the Scriptures shared by Judaism and Christianity—produce a third reason for both Christian interest in Rabbinic literature and Judaic interest in Christian literature. Rabbinic literature affords perspective on Christianity (particularly biblical Christianity, orthodox and catholic) by affording materials for comparison and contrast.

Nothing so illuminates what people do than knowledge of what they have chosen not to do. Rabbinic literature affords a source for alternatives to the Christian way—both alternative modes of expressing doctrines and laws held in common—and different views of issues faced by both communities of Scripture.

This is a two-way street. For the same reason that students of earliest Christianity gain perspective from the Rabbinic literature, so students of formative Judaism grasp matters more clearly in light of Christian alternatives, both in rhetoric (form) and in proposition. An example briefly stated serves to illustrate the process of comparison and contrast made possible for Gospel studies and for the study of Rabbinic literature.

An Example of Comparison and Contrast: The Parable

The exercise of comparison and contrast concerns the parable, called the *Mashal* in the Rabbinic canon. In the Rabbinic literature, the narrative of the *Mashal* recapitulates in other terms the transaction, whether Halakhic or exegetical or theological, that is subject to clarification. In this case the governing language is, "a parable: to what is the matter comparable?" The Hebrew word for parable, *Mashal*, yields a passive, *Nimshal*, resulting in (1) the parable and (2) the base pattern, situation, transaction, event, or proposition that is replicated in the simile constructed by the parable.

In the following composition, the exegetical task is defined in J–K, the *Mashal* is set forth in L, underlined for emphasis, and the *Nimshal*—the explicit articulation of the point of the parable—in M.

TOSEFTA BERAKHOT 1:11*

J. Similarly, "Remember not the former things, nor consider the things of old" (Is. 43:18). Remember not the former things—these are [God's mighty acts in saving Israel] from the [various] kingdoms; nor consider things of old—these are [God's mighty acts in saving Israel] from Egypt.

K. "Behold, I am doing a new thing; now it springs forth" (Is. 43:19)—this refers to the war of God and Magog [at the end of time].

L. They drew a parable, to what may the matter be compared? To one who was walking in the way and a wolf attacked him, but he was saved from it. He would continually relate the incident of the wolf. Later a lion attacked him, but he was saved from it. He forgot the incident of the wolf and would

---

* I have supplied a sentence-by-sentence reference system for the Rabbinic canon of late antiquity. It signals the document, chapter, subdivisions where appropriate, and completed units of thought or sentences. Thus Tosefta *Berakhot* 1:11 J is a citation from the Tosefta, tractate *Berakhot*, chapter 1, the eleventh proposition of that chapter (paragraph), and the eleventh sentence (J) of the paragraph/proposition. Some of the documents in the standard Hebrew editions contain chapter and sentence markings, some do not. The convention for the Talmud of Babylonia is to give the page number, obverse or reverse side of the page; thus *b.* (Bavli/Babylonian Talmud) *Berakhot* 2b would signal the page and the side of the page. My system signals the chapter, the paragraph of the chapter, the subdivision of the paragraph, and the sentence; thus *b. Berakhot* 1:1 I.1A/2A is the first chapter of Bavli tractate *Berakhot*, the first Mishnah paragraph of that chapter (1:1), then I.1 marks the first Talmudic exposition in the exposition of that Mishnah paragraph, the first subset of that exposition, and the A stands for the opening sentence of the exposition. I then give the conventional reference 2A—thus, page 2, obverse side. In this way every unit of thought is signified.

5

relate the incident of the lion. Later still a serpent attacked him, but he was saved from it. He forgot the other two incidents and would continually relate the incident of the serpent.

M. So, too is the case for Israel: the recent travails make them forget about the earlier ones.

Here the *Nimshal*, M, briefly articulates the point of the *Mashal*, L, but in many instances the *Nimshal* is detailed and elaborate. This analytical provocation for the introduction of the *Mashal*, the *Nimshal*, meaning "that to which the parable forms a narrative simile" or "that pattern of actions or events to which the comparison is drawn," is commonly deemed secondary, notional, and occasional. For the specified occasion the *Mashal* is made up to carry out the work of exposition and clarification dictated by the document and its encompassing program, whether that document is the Mishnah or the Tosefta or tractate *Abot* or *Sifra*.

The primary task of the *Mashal* is defined by the *Nimshal*, meaning the Halakhic or exegetical problem governs the formation and functioning of the parable. Numerous cases show that *every single detail* of the *Mashal* captures a component of the Halakhic or the exegetical situation subject to exposition. And the parable succeeds when it is evaluated by the criterion: has the simile left out even one detail of that which is subjected to comparison? Or has it added a detail not generated by that which is subjected to comparison? That exact match in detail of *Mashal* to *Nimshal* is the key. Seldom does the *Mashal* give evidence of constituting a free-standing story or situational simile, exhibiting signs that a prior narrative has been adapted. Commonly, though not always, the *Mashal* in its rich detail shows itself to be the formation of a narrative made up for the distinctive purpose at hand.

Clearly in the Rabbinic canon the union of the *Nimshal* and the *Mashal*—the situation or transaction to be clarified (*Nimshal*) and the abstract rendition of that situation or transaction in narrative form (*Mashal*)—defines the purpose of the parable. It is to render accessible, to clarify the situation or transaction at issue. The parable forms a means to an end. In the context of every Rabbinic document, the parable does not require interpretation but is immediately matched to the situation subject to its illumination. And in no Rabbinic document does the parable routinely require exegesis. It forms a medium of and not a challenge to exegesis.

But in Matthew's Gospel, for example, *the parable itself* is what requires interpretation and explanation. It does not decipher the mystery, it *is* the mystery. Only the disciples know the meaning of the *Mashal*, and there is no articulated *Nimshal* at all. Take for example Matt. 13:3-9, the parable of the sower, which ends, "He who has ears, let him hear." The disciples then make explicit the puzzle of the parable:

"Why do you speak to them in parables?" [They are told,] "To you have been given to know the secrets of the kingdom of heaven, but to them it has not been given.... This is why I speak to them in parables, because seeing, they do not see, and hearing, they do not hear, nor do they understand." (Matt. 13:10, 11, 13)

As if to underscore the obscurity of parables, Matthew proceeds to collect a set of parables of the kingdom of heaven (Matt. 13:24-34), which he then unpacks for the disciples alone (Matt. 13:36-37): "Then he left the crowds and went into the house. And the disciples came to him, saying, 'Explain to us the parable of the weeds of the field,'" which Jesus proceeds to do. Given a parable stripped down to its essential elements and out of all documentary context, we should readily identify a Matthean parable by the (articulated) absence of a *Nimshal* joined to the *Mashal*.

When we realize that the parable in the Gospels carries a different burden from the parable in the Rabbinic literature, we grasp more clearly than before the particular function of parables in the Gospels—and in the Rabbinic literature. People made choices. We see here the alternatives that circulated among heirs of a common Scripture.

CHAPTER 2

The Oral Torah

Tractate *Abot (The Fathers)*

The claim that the Rabbinic literature records an originally oral tradition registers in tractate *Abot, The Fathers* (or *"The Founders"*), a collection of five chapters of wisdom sayings that came to closure circa 250 CE.[1] The Mishnah, the law code of Judaism, which we shall meet in chapter 3, as printed today always includes *Abot* (sayings of the sages), but that document reached closure about a generation later than the Mishnah and is independent of the Mishnah.

While tractate *Abot* serves as the Mishnah's initial apologetic, it does not conform to the formal, rhetorical, or logical traits characteristic of the Mishnah overall. The document forms a handbook for disciples of sages, especially those involved in study, teaching, and administration of the law.[2]

The connection to God's revelation to Moses at Mount Sinai is explicit. The Rabbinic sages whose sayings are collected are assigned positions in the chain of tradition commencing then and there. The chain of tradition is framed in this language:

> Moses received the Torah at Sinai and handed it on to Joshua,
> Joshua to elders, and elders to prophets. And prophets handed
> it on to the men of the great assembly. They said three things: Be
> prudent in judgment. Raise up many disciples. Make a fence for
> the Torah.
>
> *Abot* 1:1

8

What follows are the names of Rabbinic sages assumed to have flourished from the second century BCE to the third century CE. What signals a tradition distinct from Scripture is that the sayings, beginning with the "three things" cited here, do not derive from Scripture. This tractate, then, comprises a tradition external to Scripture that began at Sinai and is represented by sayings of the Rabbinic sages.

What precipitated the need to account for "traditions of the fathers" outside of Scripture was the appearance of the Mishnah a generation earlier, circa 200 CE. The Mishnah, the first document (beyond Scripture) of Rabbinic Judaism to come to closure, is a freestanding law code and only sparingly cites Scripture to prove its propositions. The question therefore arose: What is the standing of the laws of the new code? The answer was that the Mishnah presents traditions of sages who stand in a chain of tradition beginning at Sinai. *The Fathers* presented sayings of sages extending from Sinai to figures named in the Mishnah itself, thus linking the Mishnah to Sinai. The link consists of the chain of tradition handed on through the generations of sages. It followed that, because of the authorities cited in its pages, the Mishnah constitutes part of the Torah of Sinai. By the evidence of the chain of tradition, the Mishnah too forms a statement of revelation, that is, "Torah revealed to Moses at Sinai."

The theological program of tractate *Abot* bears a political proposition as well. It concerns the relationships between the Rabbinic sages, who were qualified by their mastery of traditions of the Torah, oral and written, and the political head of the Jewish community of the Land of Israel, the patriarch, who was supported by the Roman government in the reconstruction after the rebellions of 66–73 and 132–135 CE, and who sponsored the Mishnah itself. The patriarchate, represented by the names of Hillel, Gamaliel, and Simeon ben Gamaliel, is situated in the chain of tradition going back to Sinai alongside the Rabbinic sages of the same period.

How is this political claim of the patriarchate to legitimacy within the Torah, not only by reason of Roman support, expressed? In *The Fathers*, the first chapter's list of names of the sages forms a coherent pattern. The order of the sages exhibits a certain topical coherence, but in substance is random and episodic. Major authorities of the Mishnah stand in a chain of tradition reaching back to Sinai; hence, the Mishnah contains the Torah of Sinai (the patriarchs' names are underlined):

Moses

Joshua

Elders

Prophets

Men of the Great Assembly

Simeon the Righteous

Antigonus of Sokho

1.	Yosé ben Yoezer	Yosé ben Yohanan
2.	Joshua ben Perahiah	Nittai the Arbelite
3.	Judah ben Tabbai	Simeon ben Shetah
	4. Shemaiah	Abtalyon
	5. Hillel	Shammai

Gamaliel
Simeon his son [that is, Simeon ben Gamaliel]
Rabban Simeon ben Gamaliel

Once the pairs end, we find Gamaliel, who is (later on) represented as the son of Hillel, and who is the Gamaliel who was the apostle Paul's master, and then Gamaliel and Simeon, his son, Hillel's grandson, with Simeon ben Gamaliel duplicated. Elsewhere Hillel is represented as patriarch, or ruler, of the Jewish community of the Land of Israel, as are Gamaliel and Simeon his son, prior to the destruction of the Temple and Jerusalem in 70 CE; and Gamaliel II and Simeon II his son and Judah come afterward. In that context the list of tractate *Abot* 1:1ff. takes on significance.

The cogency of the list emerges when we realize that the names Gamaliel and Simeon continued through this same family of primary authorities through Gamaliel II, ruler of the Jewish community after the destruction of the Second Temple in 70 CE, into the second century. His son, Simeon ben Gamaliel, was ruler of the Jewish community after the defeat of Bar Kokhba in 135—and also, as it happens, the father of Judah the patriarch, the same Judah the patriarch who sponsored the Mishnah. Judah the patriarch stands in the chain of tradition going back to Sinai. So both the teachings of the sages of the Mishnah and the political sponsor of the document, who also was numbered among the sages, formed part of this same tradition. The list itself bears the message that the patriarch and sages employed by him carry forward the tradition of Sinai.

The theological proposition that validates the Mishnah is that the Torah is a matter of tradition. The tradition goes from master to disciple, Moses to Joshua. And, further, those listed later in *Abot* include authorities of the Mishnah itself. That fact forms an implicit claim that (1) part of the Torah was, and is, orally formulated and orally transmitted, and (2) the Mishnah's authorities stand in the tradition of Sinai, so that (3) the Mishnah too forms part of the Torah of Sinai.

Tractate *Abot* deals with no single topic, and, it follows, the document also contains no proposition that is argued in detail. But the first two chapters do set forth a proposition, which is to be discerned not from what is said but from the list of names that are set out in those chapters. Specifically, the list of names and the way in which they are arranged contains the claim that the two great pillars of the Mishnah—the patriarch of the Jewish community in the Land of Israel (that is, Judah the patriarch [Hebrew *nasi*], sponsor of the document and the one recognized by the Roman government as ruler of the Jewish ethnic group) and the sages who studied and, where relevant, applied the laws of the Mishnah—stand equally in the chain of tradition going back to Sinai. This union of the patriarch and the sages forms the document's proposition concerning the sponsorship of the Mishnah and the divine authority that is accorded to its sages.

The Fathers According to Rabbi Nathan

Tractate *Abot*, *The Fathers*, thus delivered its message through aphorisms assigned to named sages. A few centuries later—the date is indeterminate but it is possibly circa 500 CE—*The Fathers According to Rabbi Nathan*,[3] a vast secondary expansion of that same tractate, endowed those anonymous names with flesh-and-blood form, recasting the tractate by adding a sizable number of narratives.[4] In this way the later authorship indicated that it found in narrative in general, and in stories about sages in particular, modes of discourse for presenting its message that the earlier authorship did not utilize.

This document exists in two versions. One is printed in the standard editions of the Talmud and consists of forty-one chapters; the other was first published in full in 1887 by Solomon Schechter and comprises forty-eight chapters. Schechter called the standard printed Talmud version A, and the one he published in addition to it he called B. The differences between the two versions involve readings, substance, arrangement, and extent. Judah Goldin states, "A comparative study of the two versions reveals that though in essence both have the same purpose—to interpret *Avot*—each version favors [a] particular emphasis of its own. What contributes to the special interest of ARN [the standard version] is that it has preserved a number of old more or less conservative views unacceptable to later normative tannaitic teaching."[5]

The Fathers According to Rabbi Nathan in both versions presents two types of materials and sets them forth in a fixed order. The document contains (1) amplifications of sayings in *The Fathers* as well as (2) materials not related to anything in the original document. The order in which *The Fathers According to Rabbi Nathan* arranges its types of material becomes immediately clear. First, its authorship presents amplifications of the prior document, and only second does it tack on its own message. Thus the compilers presented their ideas as continuous with the prior document. Where the authorship gives us compositions that are essentially new in rhetoric, logic and topic, it is in that second set of materials that we find what is original to them.

What do the compilers of *The Fathers According to Rabbi Nathan* actually contribute? Given an apophthegm, whether or not that saying is drawn from *The Fathers*, the authorship of *The Fathers According to Rabbi Nathan* will do one of the following:

(1) give a secondary expansion, including an exemplification, of the wise saying at hand;

(2) cite a proof text of Scripture in that same connection;

(3) provide a parable to illustrate the wise saying (as often as not instead of the proof text);

(4) add a sizable composition of materials that intersect with the foregoing, either by amplifying on the proof text without regard to the wise saying served by the proof text, or by enriching discourse on a topic introduced in connection with the base saying; or

(5) tack on a protracted story of a sage and what he said and did, which may or may not exemplify the teaching of the apophthegm at hand.

Where the authorship of the later document has chosen to cite and amplify sayings in the earlier one, that exercise comes first. There may also be parables or other sorts of stories, sometimes involving named sages, that illustrate the same point. Some sequences of unadorned sayings appear here and not in *The Fathers*. These come later in a sequence of discourses in *The Fathers According to Rabbi Nathan*. This general order predominates throughout.

Clearly the authors of the compositions collected in the document find in narrative a fine medium for their message. Narrative here may encompass one of four modes of the concrete portrayal of a message: (1) the parable; (2) the precipitant: the narrative setting for, or formal precipitant of, a saying; (3) the (ordinarily legal, but sometimes moral) precedent; and (4) the story. The story furthermore is divided into two subspecies: (4a) scriptural or Scripture story and (4b) sagacious or sage story.

The Parable. A parable unfolds through resort to narrative. There was a king who had such and so, who said such and such, who did so and so—with the result that such and such happened. The parable is a narrative in that the appeal for cogency is to teleology, and the proposition of the parable emerges (whether made explicit or not) as a self-evident exemplification of the teleology at hand. The parable forms a medium for clarification, and its effect must be transparent.

The Precipitant: The Narrative Setting for a Saying. The formal setting, or "precipitant," for a saying merely portrays a situation to which a setting pertains. Here is an example in tractate *Abot*:

> Also: he [Hillel] saw a skull floating on the water and said to it, "Because you drowned others, they drowned you, and in the end those who drowned you will be drowned."
>
> *Abot* 2:6

"He saw a skull and said ..." hardly adds up to a substantial narrative, let alone a sustained story, since nothing happens to draw out the significance of the event *he saw*, but writing such as this does demand classification as a narrative, because something has happened, not merely been said. Such a formal setting for a saying may prove substantial, but it will not constitute a narrative in the way that a parable or other kind of story does, because not the action but the saying forms the focus of interest, and the potentialities of tension and resolution constituted by the precipitating action ("*one day he saw a skull and said...*") are never explored.

A Precedent or Illustration of a Law. A precedent narrates a case, often in the form of a tale of something done, not merely said. The setting is always discourse on the law, but what marks the narrative as precedent— as distinguished from the narrative as story—is not its setting but the definitive narrative convention that obtains in the precedent but not in the story (sage, scriptural, or other). An example is presented by the opening paragraph of the Mishnah, with its counterparts in *The Fathers According to Rabbi Nathan*:

A. From what time may they recite the Shema' in the evening?
B. From the hour that the priests enter [their homes, having immersed and witnessed sunset as the completion of the purification rite] to eat their heave offering consecrated priestly rations, which must be eaten in a state of cultic cleanness],
C. "until the end of the first watch,"
D. the words of R. Eliezer.
E. But sages say, "Until midnight."
F. Rabban Gamaliel says, "Until the rise of dawn."

Now comes the precedent or illustration of the law:

G. His [Gamaliel's] sons returned from a banquet hall [after midnight].
H. They said to him, "We did not [yet] recite the Shema'."
I. He said to them, "If the dawn has not yet risen, you are obligated to recite [the Shema']."

Mishnah *Berakhot* 1:1A-I

Specifically, the precedent will portray a tableau *of completed action*, in which the tension is established not by the action but by the (sage's) ruling, and in which the resolution of the tension is accomplished solely by the same component, the decision of the sage. In line with this convention that nothing really happen, in the precedent we rarely find a beginning, middle, and end, such as we always find in a parable and a story. The precedent or illustration is concrete and specific, in the way a story is, but not to a distinctive named person and time and place, in the way a story

13

is. The precedent, unlike a story, is paradigmatic and makes a general point, rather than being historical and peculiar to a distinctive situation. A precedent or illustration of the law is like a parable in that it presents no concrete details that allow us to identify a particular place or actor.

The Story (Scriptural or Sage). Among narratives, we may always distinguish a story from any other type of narrative in one fundamental and definitive way. Its importance requires emphasis: while meaning to provide a good example of how one should behave, the teller of a story always deals with a concrete person and a particular incident. The person is concrete in that he (in our document there is not a single story about a woman) is always specified by name. The story concerns a particular incident in that the viewpoint of the narrator makes clear the one-timeness and specificity of the event that is reported. The story always happens in historical time, and the point it wishes to make is subordinate to the description of action, the development of a point of tension, at which the story commences, and its resolution, at which the story concludes—its beginning, middle, and end.

The authorship of *The Fathers According to Rabbi Nathan* clearly found inadequate the modes of discourse and the media of expression selected by the framers of tractate *Abot*. The later writers possessed a message they deemed integral to that unfolding Torah of Moses at Sinai. They resorted to a mode of intelligible discourse, narrative, that conveyed propositions with great clarity. Not only that, but among the narratives utilized in their composition, they selected one for closest attention and development: the sage story.

Accordingly, they found a place for all four types of narrative, and, of greatest interest, they made use of the sage story to convey powerful propositions lacking all precedent in *The Fathers* and that were, in context, therefore of an utterly fresh order. That they made the shift from a document that articulated propositions principally through aphorisms to one that made points through narrative, and particularly through sage stories, is entirely clear.

Three traits define the sage story in *The Fathers According to Rabbi Nathan*:

(1) The story about a sage has a beginning, middle, and end, and it also rests not only on verbal exchanges ("he said to him..., he said to him..."), but on (described) action.

(2) The story about a sage unfolds from a point of tension and conflict to a clear resolution and remission of the conflict.

(3) The story about a sage rarely invokes a verse of Scripture and never serves to prove a proposition concerning the meaning of a verse of Scripture.

What about Scripture stories? The traits of stories about scriptural figures and themes are just the opposite of sage stories:

(1) In the story about a scriptural hero there is no beginning, middle, and end, and little action. The burden of the narrative is carried by "he said to him ... , he said to him ..." Described action is rare and plays only a slight role in the unfolding of the narrative. Often the narrative consists of little more than a setting for a saying, and the point of the narrative is conveyed not through what is told but through the cited saying.

(2) The story about a scriptural hero is worked out as a tableau, with description of the components of the stationary tableau placed at the center. There is little movement and no point of tension that is resolved.

(3) The story about a scriptural hero always invokes verses from Scripture and makes the imputation of meaning to those verses the center of interest.

So *The Fathers According to Rabbi Nathan* systematically enriches *The Fathers* with a variety of narratives, each with its own conventions. When the narrators wished to talk about sages, they invoked one set of narrative conventions, deemed appropriate to that topic, and when they turned to making up stories about scriptural heroes and topics, they appealed to quite different narrative conventions.

The topical program of *The Fathers According to Rabbi Nathan* in particular emerges only as topics are identified that are treated in the successor compilations (collections of comments on a received text, thus *The Fathers According to Rabbi Nathan* comments on the tractate *The Fathers*) but not in tractate *Abot*. Points of emphasis in *The Fathers* lacking all counterpart in restatement and development in *The Fathers According to Rabbi Nathan* are three. First, the study of the Torah alone does not suffice. One has also to make an honest living through work. In what is particular to *The Fathers According to Rabbi Nathan* we find not that point but its opposite: one should study the Torah and other things will take care of themselves—a claim of a more supernatural character than the one in *The Fathers*.

A second point of clear interest in the earlier document to which, in the later one, we find no response tells sages to accommodate their wishes to those of the community at large, to accept the importance of the government, to work in community, and to practice self-abnegation and restraint in favor of the wishes of others. The sage here is less a supernatural figure than a political leader, eager to conciliate and reconcile the other.

The third and most important indicative shift in the later document imparts to the teleological question an eschatological answer altogether lacking in the earlier one. This is a key difference and requires a word of explanation.

If we were to ask the authorship of tractate *Abot* to spell out their teleology, they would draw our attention to the numerous sayings about this life's being a time of preparation for the life of the world to come, on the one hand, and to judgment and eternal life, on the other. The focus is on the individual and how he or she lives in this world and prepares for the next. The category is the individual, and, commonly in the two documents before us when we speak of the individual, we also tend to find the language of "this world" (*olam hazzeh*) and "the world to come" (*olam habba*). The sequence of sayings about this world and the next form a stunning contrast to the ones about this age (*olam hazzeh*) and the next age (*le'atid labo*). In general, though not invariably, the shift in language draws in its wake a shift in social category, from individual to social entity of group, nation, or people. The word *olam* bears two meanings, "world" and "age." In context, when we find the word bearing the sense of "world," the category under discussion is the private person, and where the required sense, in English, is "age," then—as a rough rule of thumb—what is promised is for the nation.

We can tell that the definitive category is social, and therefore national, when the fate not of the private person but of holy Israel is at stake. The concern, then, is what will happen to the nation in time to come, meaning the coming age, not the coming life of the resurrection. The systemic teleology shifts its focus to the holy people, and, alongside, to the national history of the holy people—now and in the age to come. So in the movement from the language of *this world* and *the world to come* to the wording *this age* and *the age to come*, often expressed as *the coming future* (*le'atid labo*), we note an accompanying categorical shift in the definitive context: from the individual and the private life of home and family to society and historical, public life. That shift then characterizes the teleological movement as much as the categorical change. And, as we see, it is contained both in general and in detail in the differences we have noticed between *The Fathers* and *The Fathers According to Rabbi Nathan*.

The national-eschatological interest of the later document, with its focus on living only in the Land of Israel and its contrast between this age, possessed by the Gentiles, and the age to come, in which redeemed Israel will enjoy a paramount position (which has no counterpart in the earlier composition), emerges not only in sayings but also in stories about the critical issue, the destruction of Jerusalem and the loss of the Temple, along with the concomitant matter, associated with the former stories, about repentance and how it is achieved at this time.

Yet a further point of development lies in the notion that study of the Torah combined with various virtues, for example, good deeds and fear of sin, suffices, with a concomitant assurance that making a living no longer matters.

> A. R. Judah b. Ilai says, "Whoever treats the words of the Torah as the main thing and earning a living as trivial is treated as the main thing in the world to come.

B. "... earning a living as the main thing and the words of the Torah as second is treated as trivial in the world to come.

C. "There is the following parable: to what may the matter be compared?

D. "To a path that goes between two roads, one of fire, the other of snow. If one walks toward the fire, lo, he is burned by the fire, and if he walks toward the snow, lo, he is frozen by the cold.

E. "What should he do? He should go between the two and take care not to be burned by the fire or frozen by the cold."

The Fathers According to Rabbi Nathan XXVIII:XII.1

Here too the new medium of the later document—the stories about sages—bears the new message. For that conviction emerges not only explicitly—for example, in the sayings of Hananiah about the power of Torah study to take away many sources of suffering, and Judah ben Ilai's declaration that one should consider words of the Torah as the principal and earning a living as trivial, and so on—but also in the detail that both Aqiba and Eliezer began poor but through their mastery of Torah ended rich.

The Fathers According to Rabbi Nathan differs from *The Fathers* in one aspect so fundamental as to change the face of the base document completely. While the earlier authorship took little interest in the lives and deeds of sages, the later compilers contributed in a systematic and orderly manner the color and life of biography to the named but faceless sages of *The Fathers*. The stories about sages make points that correspond to positions taken in statements of viewpoints peculiar to *The Fathers According to Rabbi Nathan*. *The Fathers* presents an ideal of the sage as a model for the everyday life of the individual, who must study the Torah and also work, and through the good life prepare now for life after death. But *The Fathers According to Rabbi Nathan* has a different conception of the sage—of the value and meaning of the study of the Torah, and of the center of interest—and also has selected a new medium for the expression of its distinctive conception. To spell this out:

(1) the sage is now—in *The Fathers According to Rabbi Nathan*—not a judge and teacher alone but also a supernatural figure;

(2) study of the Torah in preference to making a living promises freedom from the conditions of natural life; and

(3) Israel as the holy people, seen as a supernatural social entity, takes center stage.

And these innovative points are conveyed not only in sayings but also in stories about sages.

What follows is that the medium not only carries a new message but also forms a component of that new message. The sage as a supernatural figure now presents Torah teachings through what he does, not only through what he says. Therefore telling stories about what sages did and the circumstances in which they made their sayings forms part of the Torah in a way that was not true of the earlier document. The interest in stories about sages proves therefore to be not merely literary or formal; it is more than a new way of conveying an old message. Stories about the sages are told because sages stand for a message that can emerge only in stories and not in sayings alone. So we turn to a close reading of the stories themselves to review that message and find out why through stories in particular the message now emerges. For what we see is nothing short of a new mode of revelation—that is, of conveying and imparting God's will in the Torah.

People told stories because they wanted to think about history, and, in an ancient setting, history emerged in an account of what happened, with an implicit message of the meaning of events conveyed in the story as well. They further conceived of the social entity, Israel, as an extended family, children of a single progenitor, Abraham, with his son and grandson, Isaac and Jacob. Consequently, when they told stories, they centered on family history. That generally accounts for the details of what the authorship of *The Fathers According to Rabbi Nathan* have chosen to add to the topical program of *The Fathers*. The sage in the system of *The Fathers According to Rabbi Nathan* was the supernatural father who replaced the natural one; events in the life of the sage constituted happenings in the history of the family-nation, Israel. So history blended with family, and family with Torah study. The national, salvific history of the nation-family Israel took place in such events as the origins of the sage, in other words, his beginnings in Torah study; the sagacity of the sage, the counterpart to what we should call social history; the doings of the sage in great turnings in the family's history, including especially the destruction of the Temple, now perceived as final and decisive; and the death of the sage while engaged in Torah study. And these form the four classifications of story in this document.

CHAPTER 3

The Rabbinic Canon:
Law (Halakhah)

T he Rabbinic literature of the formative age, the first six centuries CE, is divided into two parts, law (Halakhah), organized around the Mishnah, and lore (Aggadah), organized around Scripture. The Halakhah is set forth in the following texts: the Mishnah, a law code (ca. 200 CE); the Tosefta, a supplement to the code (ca. 300 CE); and two analytical commentaries on selected topics (tractates) of the Mishnah and the Tosefta—the Talmud of the Land of Israel (ca. 400 CE) and the Talmud of Babylonia (ca. 600 CE). The Aggadah is presented principally in seven large commentaries to Scripture that we shall meet in chapter 4, but is set forth in episodic compositions in the two Talmuds as well.

The Mishnah

The Mishnah is philosophical in its method and systematically topical in its presentation.[1] It covers topics of both a theoretical and practical character.[2] Produced in about 200 CE under the sponsorship of Judah, who was appointed by the Roman government as the patriarch (*nasi*) or ethnic ruler of the Jews of the Land of Israel, it is comprised of sixty-two tractates (plus tractate *Abot, The Fathers*). It is divided into six divisions (with their subjects).

1.   AGRICULTURE (*Zera'im*): *Berakhot* (blessings); *Pe'ah* (the corner of the field); *Demai* (doubtfully tithed produce); *Kila'yim* (mixed seeds);

Shebi'it (the seventh year); *Terumot* (heave offering or priestly rations); *Ma'aserot* (tithes); *Ma'aser Sheni* (second tithe); *Hallah* (dough offering); *Orlah* (produce of trees in the first three years after planting, which is prohibited); and *Bikkurim* (first fruits).

2.   APPOINTED TIMES (*Mo'ed*): *Shabbat* (the Sabbath); *Erubin* (the fictive fusion meal or boundary); *Pesahim* (Passover); *Sheqalim* (the Temple tax); *Yoma* (the Day of Atonement); *Sukkah* (the festival of Tabernacles); *Besah* (the preparation of food on the festivals and Sabbath); *Rosh Hashanah* (the New Year); *Ta'anit* (fast days); *Megillah* (Purim); *Mo'ed Qatan* (the intermediate days of the festivals of Passover and Tabernacles); and *Hagigah* (the festal offering).

3.   WOMEN (*Nashim*): *Yebamot* (the levirate widow); *Ketubot* (the marriage contract); *Nedarim* (vows); *Nazir* (the special vow of the Nazirite); *Sotah* (the wife accused of adultery); *Gittin* (writs of divorce); and *Qiddushin* (betrothal).

4.   DAMAGES or civil law (*Neziqin*): *Baba Qamma, Baba Mesi'a, Baba Batra* (civil law covering damages and torts, then correct conduct of business, labor, and real estate transactions); *Sanhedrin* (institutions of government; criminal penalties); *Makkot* (flogging); *Shebu'ot* (oaths); *Eduyyot* (a collection arranged on other than topical lines); *Abodah Zarah* (relationships with idolatry and idolaters); and *Horayot* (rules governing improper conduct of civil authorities).

5.   HOLY THINGS (*Qodashim*): *Zebahim* (everyday animal offerings); *Menahot* (meal offerings); *Hullin* (animals slaughtered for secular purposes); *Bekhorot* (firstlings); *Arakhin* (vows of valuation); *Temurah* (vows of exchange of a beast for an already consecrated beast); *Keritot* (penalty of extirpation or premature death); *Me'ilah* (sacrilege); *Tamid* (the daily whole offering); *Middot* (the layout of the Temple building); and *Qinnim* (how to deal with bird offerings designated for a given purpose and then mixed up).

6.   PURITIES (*Tohorot*): *Kelim* (susceptibility of utensils to uncleanness); *Ohalot* (transmission of corpse uncleanness in the tent of a corpse); *Nega'im* (the uncleanness described at Lev. 13–14); *Parah* (the preparation of purification water); *Tohorot* (problems of doubt in connection with matters of cleanness); *Miqva'ot* (immersion pools); *Niddah* (menstrual uncleanness); *Makhshirin* (rendering susceptible to uncleanness produce that is dry and so not susceptible); *Zabim* (the uncleanness covered in Lev. 15); *Tebul Yom* (the uncleanness of one who has immersed on that selfsame day and awaits sunset for completion of the purification rites); *Yadayim* (the uncleanness of hands); and *Uqsin* (the uncleanness transmitted to clean parts through what is connected to unclean parts of the same produce).

In volume the sixth division covers approximately a quarter of the entire document. Topics of interest to the priesthood and the Temple, such as priestly fees, conduct of the cult on holy days, conduct of the cult on ordinary days and management and upkeep of the Temple, and the rules of cultic cleanness, predominate in the first, second, fifth, and sixth divisions. Rules governing the social order form the bulk of the third and fourth. Of the Mishnah's tractates, only *Eduyyot* is organized along other than topical lines, instead collecting sayings on diverse subjects attributed to particular authorities.

The stress of the Mishnah throughout on the priestly caste and the Temple cult points to the document's principal concern, sanctification. When God had completed creation, he sanctified what he had made, so "sanctification" is understood as the correct arrangement of all things, each in its proper category, each called by its rightful name. That is, holiness is portrayed just as at the creation in the Priestly document and just as with the cult itself in Leviticus. Further, the thousands of rules and cases (with sages' disputes thereon) that comprise the document upon close reading turn out to express in concrete language abstract principles of hierarchical classification. These define the document's method and mark it as a work of a philosophical character. Not only that, a variety of specific, recurrent concerns, for example, the relationship of being to becoming, actual to potential, and the principles of economics and politics, correspond point by point to comparable ones in Graeco-Roman philosophy, particularly Aristotle's tradition. This stress on proper order and right rule and the formulation of a philosophy, politics, and economics within the principles of natural history set forth by Aristotle explain why the Mishnah deserves to be classified as philosophy, concerning as it does the order of the natural world in its correspondence with the supernatural world.

The system of philosophy expressed through concrete and detailed law presented by the Mishnah consists of a coherent logic and topic, a cogent worldview and comprehensive way of living. It is a worldview that speaks of transcendent things, a way of life in response to the supernatural meaning of what is done, a heightened and deepened perception of the sanctification of Israel in deed and in deliberation. Sanctification thus means two things: first, distinguishing Israel in all its dimensions from the world in all its ways; and second, establishing the stability, order, regularity, predictability, and reliability of Israel in the world of nature and supernature, in particular at moments and in contexts of danger. Danger means instability, disorder, irregularity, uncertainty, and betrayal. Each topic of the system takes up a critical and indispensable moment or context of social being. Through what is said in regard to each of the Mishnah's principal topics, what the system—expressed through normative rules—wishes to declare is fully expressed. Yet if the parts severally and jointly give the message of the whole, the whole cannot exist without all of the parts, so well joined and carefully crafted are they all. The details will become clear in our survey of the document's topical program.

The Mishnah's sole logic of coherent discourse is philosophical; indeed, it is most commonly syllogistic. It is a logic that rests on the coherence yielded by the classification of things by their intrinsic traits and the formulation of the rules governing things of a given class; one classification is then compared and contrasted to others of a like character, with the object of setting forth the hierarchy of the classifications. This method of scientific inquiry is called *Listenwissenschaft*, that is, natural history: classification of things in accordance with their intrinsic taxonomic traits, and (concomitantly) the hierarchization of the classes of things, that is, species of the same genus.

How this logic of coherent discourse forms groups of facts into coherent propositions is illustrated by Mishnah tractate *Sanhedrin* 2:1-2, in which the authorship wishes to say that Israel has two heads, one of state, the other of cult—the king and the high priest, respectively—and that these two offices are almost entirely congruent with one another, with a few differences based on the particular traits of each. Broadly speaking, therefore, our exercise is one of hierarchical classification, setting forth the genus and the species. The genus is head of holy Israel. The species are king and high priest. Here are the traits in common and those not shared, and the exercise is fully exposed for what it is: an inquiry into the rules that govern, the points of regularity and order of political structure. My outline, set out in boldface type, makes the point important in this setting.

MISHNAH *SANHEDRIN* **Chapter Two**

1.   The rules of the high priest: subject to the law, marital rites, conduct in bereavement

MISHNAH *SANHEDRIN* **2:1**

A.   A high priest judges, and [others] judge him;

B.   gives testimony, and [others] give testimony about him;

C.   performs the rite of removing the shoe [Deut. 25:7-9], and [others] perform the rite of removing the shoe with his wife.

D.   [Others] enter levirate marriage with his wife, but he does not enter into levirate marriage,

E.   because he is prohibited to marry a widow.

2.   The rules of the king: not subject to the law, marital rites, conduct in bereavement

MISHNAH *SANHEDRIN* **2:2**

A.   The king does not judge, and [others] do not judge him;

B.   does not give testimony, and [others] do not give testimony about him;

C.   does not perform the rite of removing the shoe, and others do not perform the rite of removing the shoe with his wife;

D.   does not enter into levirate marriage, nor [do his brothers] enter levirate marriage with his wife.

The philosophical cast of mind is amply revealed in this well-formed and highly formalized essay, which in concrete terms effects a taxonomy through the matching of data of an identical class, a study of the genus, national leader, and its two species, king and high priest: how are they alike, how are they not alike, and what accounts for the differences. The premise is that national leaders are alike and follow the same rule, except where they differ and follow opposing rules. But that premise is also subject to the proof effected by the survey of the data consisting of concrete rules, those systemically inert facts that here come to life for the purpose of establishing a proposition. By itself, the fact that, for example, others may not ride on the leader's horse bears the burden of no systemic proposition. In the context of an argument constructed for nomothetic (lawgiving), taxonomic purposes, the same fact is active and weighty. The logic of coherence undertakes the search for points in common and therefore also points of contrast. We seek connection between fact and fact and sentence and sentence in the subtle and balanced rhetoric of the Mishnah by comparing and contrasting two things that are alike and not alike.

At the logical level, too, the Mishnah falls into the category of familiar philosophical thought. Once we seek regularities, we propose rules. What is like another thing falls under its rule, and what is not like the other falls under the opposite rule. Accordingly, as to the species of the genus, so far as they are alike, they share the same rule. So far as they are not alike, each follows a rule contrary to that governing the other. So the work of analysis is what produces connection, and therefore the drawing of conclusions derives from comparison and contrast: the *and*, the *equal*. The proposition, then, that forms the conclusion concerns the essential likeness of the two offices, except where they are different, but the underlying premise is that we can explain both likeness and difference by appeal to a principle of fundamental order and unity. The high priest and king fall into a single genus, but speciation, based on traits particular to the king, then distinguishes one from the other.

To understand the complete system set forth by the Mishnah, and therefore the Halakhah, we review the six divisions of the Halakhah fully exposed by the Mishnah (the Talmuds would address only selected tractates/topics and omit whole divisions).

THE DIVISION OF AGRICULTURE treats two topics: first, producing crops in accordance with the scriptural rules on the subject; and second, paying the required offerings and tithes to the priests, Levites, and poor. The principal point of the division is that the land is holy because God has a claim both on it and on what it produces. God's claim must be honored by setting aside a portion of the produce for those for whom God has designated it. God's ownership must be acknowledged by observing the rules God has laid down for use of the land. In the temporal context in which the Mishnah was produced, some generations after the disastrous defeat by the Romans of Bar Kokhba and the permanent closure of Jerusalem to Jewish access, the division brought assurance that those

23

aspects of the sanctification of Israel—the Land of Israel, Israel itself and its social order, the holy cycle of time—that survived also remained holy and subject to the rules of heaven.

THE DIVISION OF APPOINTED TIMES carried forward the same emphasis upon sanctification regarding the high points of the lunar-solar calendar of Israel. The second division forms a system in which the advent of a holy day, like the Sabbath of creation, sanctifies the life of the Israelite village by imposing on the village rules on the model of those of the Temple. The purpose of the system, therefore, is to bring into alignment the sanctification of the village and the life of the home with the sanctification of the Temple on those same occasions of appointed times. The underlying and generative logic of the system comes to expression in a concrete way here. We recall the rule of like and opposite, comparison and contrast. What is not like something follows the rule opposite to that pertaining to that something. Here, therefore, since the village is the mirror image of the Temple, the focus is dictated by the analogical-contrastive logic of the system as a whole. If things are done in one way in the Temple, they will be done in the opposite way in the village. Together the village and the Temple on the occasion of the holy day form a single continuum, a completed creation awaiting sanctification. The village is made like the Temple in that during appointed times one may not freely cross the lines distinguishing the village from the rest of the world, just as one may not freely cross the lines distinguishing the Temple from the world. But the village is a mirror image of the Temple. The boundary lines prevent free entry into the Temple, so they restrict free egress from the village. On the holy day what one may do in the Temple is precisely what one may not do in the village.

So the advent of the holy day affects the village by bringing it into sacred symmetry with the Temple so as to effect a system of opposites; each is holy in a way precisely opposite to the other. Because of the underlying conception of perfection attained through the union of opposites, the village is not represented as conforming to the model of the cult, but of constituting its antithesis. The world thus regains perfection when on the holy day heaven and earth are united, the whole being completed and united: the heaven, the earth, and all their hosts. This moment of perfection renders the events of ordinary time, of "history," essentially irrelevant. For what really matters in time is that moment in which sacred time intervenes and effects the perfection formed of the union of heaven and earth, of Temple, in the model of the former, and Israel, its complement. It is not a return to a perfect time but a recovery of perfect being, a fulfillment of creation, which explains the essentially ahistorical character of the Mishnah's division on Appointed Times. Sanctification constitutes an ontological category and is effected by the creator.

This explains why the division in its rich detail is composed of two quite distinct sets of materials. First, it addresses what one does in the sacred space of the Temple on the occasion of sacred time, as distinct from what one does in that same sacred space on ordinary, undifferentiated days, which is a subject worked out in Holy Things (*Qodashim*). Second, the division defines how for the occasion of the holy day one creates a corresponding space in one's own circumstance, and what one does within that space during sacred time. The division as a whole holds together through a shared generative metaphor. It is the comparison, in the context of sacred time, of the spatial life of the Temple with the spatial life of the village, with activities and restrictions to be specified for each upon the common occasion of the Sabbath or festival. The Mishnah's purpose, therefore, is to correlate the sanctity of the Temple, as defined by the holy day, with the restrictions of space and of action that make the life of the village different and holy on that day.

THE DIVISION OF WOMEN defined the role of women in the social economy of Israel's supernatural and natural reality. Women acquired definition wholly in relationship to men, who imparted form to the Israelite social economy. The status of women was effected through both supernatural and natural, this-worldly action. Women formed a critical systemic component, because the proper regulation of women—who were subject to fathers, then husbands—was deemed a central concern of heaven, so that a betrothal would be subject to heaven's supervision (*Qiddushin*, sanctification, being the pertinent tractate). Documents such as the marriage contract or the writ of divorce, which were drawn up on earth, stood also for heaven's concern with the sanctity of women in their marital relationships; so too, heaven may through levirate marriage dictate whom a woman married. What man and woman do on earth accordingly provokes a response in heaven, and the correspondences are perfect. So women are defined and secured both in heaven and here on earth, and that position is always and invariably relative to men.

The principal interest for the Mishnah is interstitial, just as, in general, sanctification comes into play at interstitial relationships, those that require decisive classification. Here the point of concern is that at which a woman becomes, or ceases to be, holy to a particular man—that is, enters or leaves the marital union. These transitions are the dangerous and disorderly points in the relationship of woman to man, and therefore, the Mishnah states, to society as well. The division's systemic statement stresses the preservation of order in transactions involving women and (other) property. Within this orderly world of documentary and procedural concerns a place is made for the disorderly conception of the marriage not formed by human volition but decreed in heaven, the levirate connection. Mishnah tractate *Yebamot* states that supernature sanctifies a woman to a man (under the conditions of the levirate connection). What it says indirectly is that man sanctifies too: man, like God, can sanctify the relationship between a man and a woman, and can also effect the cessation of the sanctity of that same relationship.

Five of the seven tractates of the division of Women are devoted to the formation and dissolution of the marital bond. Of them, three treat what is done by people here on earth, that is, the formation of a marital bond through betrothal and marriage contract and dissolution through divorce and its consequences. The division and its system therefore delineate the natural and supernatural character of the woman's role in the social economy framed by man: the beginning, end, and middle of the relationship. The whole constitutes a significant part of the Mishnah's encompassing system of sanctification for the reason that heaven confirms what men do on earth. A correctly prepared writ of divorce on earth changes the status of the woman to whom it is given, so that in heaven she is available for sanctification to some other man, while, without that same writ, in heaven's view, should she go to some other man, she would be liable to be put to death. The earthly deed and the heavenly perspective correlate. That is indeed very much part of the larger system, which says the same thing over and over again.

THE DIVISION OF DAMAGES comprises two subsystems that fit together in a logical way. One part presents rules for the normal conduct of civil society. These cover commerce, trade, real estate, and other matters of everyday social life, as well as mishaps, such as damages by chattels and persons, fraud, overcharge, interest, and the like. The other part describes the institutions governing the normal conduct of civil society, that is, courts of administration and the penalties at the disposal of the government for the enforcement of the law. The two subjects form a single tight and systematic dissertation on the nature of Israelite society and its economic, social, and political relationships as the Mishnah envisages them. The main point of the first of the two parts of the division is that the task of society is to maintain perfect stasis, to preserve the prevailing situation, and to secure the stability of all relationships. To this end, in the exchanges of buying and selling, giving and taking, and borrowing and lending, it is important that there be an essential equality of interchange. No party in the end should have more than what he had at the outset, and none should be the victim of a sizable shift in fortune and circumstance. All parties' rights to, and in, this stable and unchanging economy of society are to be preserved. When the condition of a person is violated, so far as possible the law will secure the restoration of the person's previous status.

The goal of the system of civil law is the recovery of the prevailing order and balance, the preservation of the established wholeness of the social economy. This idea is powerfully expressed in the organization of the three tractates that comprise the civil law, which treat first abnormal and then normal transactions. The framers deal with damages done by chattels and by human beings, in other words, thefts and other sorts of malfeasance against the property of others. The civil law pays closest attention to how the property and person of the injured party so far as possible are restored to their prior condition, that is, a state of normality. So, for example, attention to torts focuses upon penalties paid by the malefactor to the victim, rather than upon penalties inflicted by the court on the malefactor for what he has done. When speaking of damages, the Mishnah thus takes as its principal concern the restoration of the fortune of victims of assault or robbery. Then the framers take up the complementary and corresponding set of topics, the regulation of normal transactions. When we rapidly survey the kinds of transactions of special interest, we see from the topics selected for discussion what we have already uncovered in the deepest structure of organization and articulation of the basic theme.

The other half of this same unit of three tractates presents laws governing normal and routine transactions, many of them of the same sort as those dealt with in the first half. At issue are deposits of goods or possessions that one person leaves in safekeeping with another. Bailments, for example, occur in both wings of the triple tractate: first bailments subjected to misappropriation, or accusation thereof, by the bailiff, then bailments transacted under normal circumstances. Under the rubric of routine transactions are those of workers and householders, that is, the purchase and sale of labor; rentals and bailments; real estate transactions; and inheritances and estates. Of the lot, the one involving real estate transactions is the most fully articulated and covers the widest range of problems and topics. The three tractates of the civil law together provide a complete account of the orderly governance of balanced transactions and unchanging civil relationships within Israelite society under ordinary conditions.

The character and interests of the division of Damages present probative evidence of the larger program of the philosophers of the Mishnah. Their intention is to create nothing less than a full-scale Israelite government, subject to the administration of sages. This government is fully supplied with a constitution and bylaws. It makes provision for a court system and corresponding procedures, as well as a full set of laws governing civil society and criminal justice. This government, moreover, mediates between its own community and the outside ("pagan") world. Through its system of laws it expresses its judgment of others and at the same time defines, protects, and defends its own society and social frontiers. It even makes provision for procedures of remission, to expiate its own errors. The (then nonexistent) Israelite government imagined by the second-century philosophers centers upon the (then nonexistent) Temple, and the (then forbidden) city of Jerusalem. The Temple is one principal focus. There the highest court is in session; there the high priest reigns.

The penalties for law infringement are of four kinds, one of which involves sacrifice in the Temple. (The others are compensation, physical punishment, and death.) The basic conception of punishment, moreover, is that unintentional infringement of the rules of society, whether "religious" or otherwise, is not penalized but rather expiated through an offering in the Temple. If a member of the people of Israel intentionally infringes against the law, to be sure, that one must be removed from society and put to death. And if there is a claim of one member of the people against another, that must be righted, so that the prior prevailing status may be restored. So offerings in the Temple are given to appease heaven and restore a whole bond between heaven and Israel, specifically on those occasions on which without malice or ill will an Israelite has disturbed the relationship. Israelite civil society without a Temple is not stable or normal, and not to be imagined. And the Mishnah is above all an act of imagination in defiance of reality.

The plan for the government involves a clear-cut philosophy of society, a philosophy that defines the purpose of the government and ensures that its task is not merely to perpetuate its own power. The Israelite government, within the Mishnaic system, is supposed to preserve a perfect, unchanging society; the goal of the system throughout is to create a perfect balance, proportion, and arrangement of the social order, including its goods and services and its responsibilities and benefits. This happens in at least five ways.

First, one of the ongoing principles of the law, expressed in one tractate after another, is that people are to follow and maintain the prevailing practice of their locale.

Second, the purpose of civil penalties, as we have noted, is to restore the injured party to his prior condition, so far as this is possible, rather than merely to penalize the aggressor.

Third, there is the conception of true value, meaning that a given object has an intrinsic worth, which, in the course of a transaction, must be paid. In this way the seller does not leave the transaction any richer than when he entered it, or the buyer any poorer (this is a parallel to penalties for damages).

Fourth, there can be no usury, a biblical prohibition adopted and vastly enriched in the Mishnaic thought, for money ("coins") is what it is. Any pretense that it has become more than what it was violates, in its way, the conception of true value.

Fifth, when real estate is divided, it must be done with full attention to the rights of all concerned, so that, once more, one party does not gain at the expense of the other.

In these and many other aspects the law expresses its obsession with the perfect stasis of Israelite society. Its paramount purpose is in preserving that stasis and ensuring that the perfection of the division of this world is kept inviolate or restored to its true status when violated.

THE DIVISION OF HOLY THINGS presents a system of sacrifice and sanctuary. The division centers upon the everyday and rules always applicable to the cult: the daily whole offering, the sin offering and guilt offering that one may bring at any time under ordinary circumstances; the right sequence of diverse offerings; the way in which the rites of the whole, sin, and guilt offerings are carried out; what sorts of animals are acceptable; the accompanying cereal offerings; the support and provision of animals for the cult and of meat for the priesthood; and the support and material maintenance of the cult and its building. We have a system before us: the system of the cult of the Jerusalem Temple, seen as an ordinary and everyday affair, a continuing and routine operation. That is why special rules for the cult, both in respect to the altar and in regard to the maintenance of the buildings, personnel, and even the city of Jerusalem, will be elsewhere—in Appointed Times and Agriculture. But from the perspective of Holy Things, those divisions intersect by supplying special rules and raising extraordinary (Agriculture: land-bound; Appointed Times: time-bound) considerations for the theme that Holy Things claims to set forth in its most general and unexceptional way: the cult as something permanent and everyday.

THE DIVISION OF PURITIES presents a very simple system of three principal parts: sources of uncleanness, objects and substances susceptible to uncleanness, and modes of purification from uncleanness. So it tells the story of what makes a given sort of object unclean and what makes it clean. Viewed as a whole, the division of Purities treats the interplay of persons, food, and liquids. Dry inanimate objects or food are not susceptible to uncleanness. What is wet is susceptible, so liquids activate the system. What is unclean, moreover, becomes clean through the operation of liquids, specifically, through immersion in fit water of requisite volume and in natural condition. Liquids thus deactivate the system, and water in its natural condition is what concludes the process by removing uncleanness. Water in its unnatural condition, that is, deliberately affected by human agency, is what imparts susceptibility to uncleanness to begin with. The uncleanness of persons, furthermore, is signified by body liquids or flux in the case of the menstruating woman and the *zab* (the person suffering from the form of uncleanness described at Lev. 15:1ff.). Corpse uncleanness is conceived to be a kind of effluent, a viscous gas, that flows like liquid. Utensils for their part receive uncleanness when they form receptacles able to contain liquid.

In sum, we have a system in which the invisible flow of fluid-like substances or powers serves to put food, drink, and receptacles into the status of uncleanness and to remove those things from that status. Whether or not we call the system "metaphysical," it certainly has no material base but is conditioned upon highly abstract notions. Thus, in material terms, the effect of liquid is upon food, drink, utensils, and people. The consequence has to do with who may eat and drink what food and liquid, and what food and drink may be consumed in which pots and pans. These loci are specified by tractates on utensils and on food and drink.

The human being is ambivalent. Persons fall in the middle, between sources and loci of uncleanness, because they are both. They serve as sources of uncleanness; they also become unclean. The *zab* who suffers the uncleanness described in Lev. 15, the menstruating woman, the woman after childbirth, and the person afflicted with the skin ailment described in Lev. 13 and 14—all are sources of uncleanness. But being unclean, they fall within the system's loci, its program of consequences. So they make other things unclean and are subject to penalties because they are unclean. Unambiguous sources of uncleanness never also constitute loci affected by uncleanness. They always are unclean and never can become clean: the corpse, the dead creeping thing, and things like them. Inanimate sources of uncleanness and inanimate objects convey uncleanness *ex opere operato*: their status of being unclean never changes; they present no ambiguity. Systemically unique, people and liquids have the capacity to inaugurate the processes of uncleanness (as sources) and also are subject to those same processes (as objects of uncleanness).

OMITTED DIVISIONS. When we listen to the silences of the system of the Mishnah as much as to its points of stress, we hear a single message. It is the message of a system that answered a single encompassing question, and the question formed a counterpart to that of the Pentateuchal system of the sixth century BCE. The Pentateuchal system addressed the events of the sixth century, especially the destruction of the Jerusalem Temple in 586 BCE. At stake was how Israel as defined by that system related to its land, represented by its Temple, and the Pentateuchal message may be simply stated: what appears to be a given is in fact a gift, subject to stipulations. The precipitating event for the Mishnaic system was the destruction of the Jerusalem Temple in 70 CE; the question turned on obsession with the defeat of Bar Kokhba and the closure of Jerusalem to Jews. The urgent question taken up by the Mishnah was, specifically, What, in the aftermath of the destruction of the holy place and holy cult, remained of the sanctity of the holy caste, the priesthood, the holy land, and, above all, the holy people and its holy way of life? The answer was that sanctity persists, indelibly, in Israel, the people, its way of life, its land, its priesthood, its food, its mode of sustaining life, and its manner of procreating and so sustaining the nation.

The Mishnah's system therefore focused upon the holiness of the life of Israel, the people, a holiness that had formerly centered on the Temple. The logically consequent question was, What is the meaning of sanctity, and how shall Israel attain, or give evidence of, sanctification? The answer to the question derived from the original creation, with the end of the Temple directing attention to the beginning of the natural world that the Temple had embodied. For the meaning of sanctity the framers therefore turned to that first act of sanctification, the one in creation, which came about when, all things in array, in place, each with its proper names, God blessed and sanctified the seventh day on the eve of the first Sabbath. Creation was made ready for the blessing and the sanctification when all things were very good, that is to say, in their rightful order, called by their rightful name. An orderly nature was a sanctified and blessed nature—so dictated Scripture in the name of the Supernatural. So to receive the blessing and to be made holy, all things in nature and society were to be set in right array. Given the condition of Israel, the people, in its land and in the aftermath of the catastrophic war against Rome led by Bar Kokhba in 132–135 CE, putting things in order was no easy task. But that is why, after all, the question was pressing, the answer proving inexorable and obvious. The condition of society corresponded to the critical question that obsessed the system builders.

The Tosefta

A huge supplement to the Mishnah,[3] four times larger in volume than the document it amplifies, the Tosefta (ca. 300 CE)[4] depends upon the Mishnah for its rhetoric, topical program, and logic of coherent discourse, like a vine on a trellis. The Tosefta has no structure of its own but most commonly cites and glosses a passage of the Mishnah, not differentiating its forms and wording of sentences from those of the cited passage. Only seldom—for somewhat under a sixth of the whole of its volume—does the Tosefta present a statement that may be interpreted entirely independent of the Mishnah's counterpart (if any). The Tosefta contains three kinds of writings.

(1) The first consists of verbatim citations and glosses of sentences of the Mishnah.

(2) The second is made up of freestanding statements that complement the sense of the Mishnah but do not cite a Mishnah paragraph verbatim. These statements can be fully understood only in dialogue with the Mishnah's counterpart.

(3) The third comprises freestanding, autonomous statements, formulated in the manner of the Mishnah but fully comprehensible on their own.

The editors or compilers of the Tosefta arranged their materials in accordance with three principles, and these govern the order of the Tosefta's statements in correspondence to the Mishnah's. First come statements that cite what the Mishnah's sentences say, and this ordinarily will occur in the order of the Mishnah's statements. Second, in general Mishnah citation and gloss will be succeeded by Mishnah amplification, which is to say, sentences that do not cite the Mishnah's corresponding ones, but that cannot be understood without reference to the Mishnah's rule or sense. The first two kinds of statements are the ones that cannot be fully understood without knowledge of the Mishnah, which defines their context. Third in sequence, commonly, will be the small number of freestanding statements that can be wholly understood on their own and without appeal to the sense or principle of the corresponding Mishnah passage; in some few cases, these compositions and even composites will have no parallel in the Mishnah at all.

These autonomous statements require attention in their own right. These comprise paragraphs that make their own point and can be fully understood on their own terms. These freestanding materials are of two kinds. First, some autonomous materials address topics important to a passage in the Mishnah and are placed by the Tosefta's framers in a position corresponding to the one in the Mishnah. What marks these materials as autonomous is that, while they intersect with the Mishnah's topic, their interest in that topic bears no point in common with the Mishnah's treatment of the same topic. A second criterion, which is complementary, is that we can understand what follows without referring to the Mishnah. The second type of autonomous materials addresses topics omitted in the Mishnah, and this type is included only because, in the Mishnah, there may be tangential references to the topics treated by the Tosefta's authors. The criterion of classification, then, is even simpler than that governing the first type. The Tosefta's authorship has collected this kind of material from we know not where. It could have been composed in the same period as the writing of the Mishnah.

While these freestanding statements—that could have stood in the Mishnah as well as in the Tosefta itself—may have reached final formulation prior to the closure of the Mishnah, most of the document either cites the Mishnah verbatim and comments upon it, or can be understood only in light of the Mishnah, even though the Mishnah is not cited verbatim. That is sound reason for assigning the formulation of most of the document and the compilation of the whole to the time after the Mishnah was concluded. The first two types of materials certainly were written after the closure of the Mishnah. The Tosefta as a whole, covering all three types, was compiled sometime after the conclusion of the Mishnah circa 200 CE but before the formation of the Talmud of the Land of Israel (ca. 400 CE), which frequently cites materials found in the Tosefta and interprets the Mishnah in light of the Tosefta's complements. The entire compilation, therefore, is a work of the third century, ending circa 300 CE.

But in substance the document's claim proves even stronger. The Tosefta's materials, cogent not of themselves but only in relationship to the Mishnah, serve as the Mishnah's first commentary, first amplification, and first extension. Since both Talmuds read Mishnah passages through Tosefta complements to the Mishnah, the Tosefta forms the bridge between the Talmuds and much of the Mishnah. But that does not mean the Tosefta is a very accessible document; the opposite is the case. And the reason derives from the Tosefta's very character as a document of mediation, expansion, and extension of another piece of writing. The Tosefta makes sense only in relationship to the Mishnah. That is so not only for its program and order, which are defined by the Mishnah, but also for its individual compositions. Each completed unit of thought of the Tosefta is to be understood, to begin with, in relationship with the Mishnah: Is it a citation of and commentary on the Mishnah passage that forms its counterpart? Is the passage fully to be comprehended on its own or only in relationship to a counterpart passage of the Mishnah? Or is the passage freestanding?

One cannot write about the Tosefta's theology or law as though these constituted a system susceptible of description and interpretation independent of the Mishnah's system. At the same time, the exegetes of the Mishnah in the Tosefta and in the two Talmuds stand apart from, and later than, the authors of the Mishnah itself. Accordingly, the exegetes systematically say whatever they wish to say by attaching their ideas to a document earlier than their own and by making the principal document reflect what they wish to contribute. The system of expressing ideas by reframing those of predecessors preserves the continuity of tradition and establishes a deep stability and order upon the culture framed by that tradition. The Tosefta not only depends for structure, order, and sense upon the Mishnah, but, in general, the materials assembled in the Tosefta set forth no viewpoint other than that of the Mishnah's counterpart materials clarified, refined, and improved. No study has as yet shown a sustained tendency in the Tosefta to execute a distinct exegesis of the Mishnah in such a way as to recast the sense or character of the Mishnah's program, though in numerous passages the work of commentary shades over into a fresh reading of a specific problem.

The Two Talmuds

The Halakhah came to full articulation in the two Talmuds: the Talmud of the Land of Israel, also called the Yerushalmi (or Jerusalem Talmud; ca.

400 CE), and the Talmud of Babylonia, also called the Bavli (ca. 600 CE). A talmud—generically defined—is a sustained systematic amplification and analysis of passages of the Mishnah and other teachings alongside the Mishnah, inclusive of the Tosefta, that are accorded equivalent status. The first of the two Talmuds treats the first four divisions of the Mishnah; the second one, divisions two through five. Neither systematically comments on the sixth division, though both attend to one tractate in that division, *Niddah*, on menstrual uncleanness. Throughout, each is independent of the other, the two meeting only at parts of the Mishnah.

But they form species of a common genus. Both proceed by taking up a few sentences of that prior text and paraphrasing and analyzing them. Both ask the same questions, clarifying the language of the Mishnah, identifying the scriptural foundations of the Mishnah's rules, and comparing the Mishnah's rules with those of the Tosefta or other texts of Tannaite status (that is, when presented with attributions of sayings solely to names that occur also in the Mishnah or Tosefta). The two Talmuds furthermore are comparable because they organize their materials in the same way. They take up almost the same topical agenda, in common selecting some divisions of the Mishnah and ignoring others, agreeing in particular to treat the matters of everyday practice, as distinct from theory, that are covered by the Mishnah's divisions of Appointed Times, Women, and Damages. Both documents moreover are made up of already available compositions and composites, which we may identify by reference to the same literary traits or indications of completion prior to inclusion in the Talmuds. So they exhibit traits of shared literary policy.

Not only are the two Talmuds alike, but in their canonical context they also are different from all other documents of Rabbinic Judaism in its formative age. Among Mishnah-centered writings in the canon—the Tosefta, Sifra, the two Sifrés, the Bavli and the Yerushalmi—only the two Talmuds conduct sustained analytical inquiries over a broad range of problems. The Tosefta is not an analytical document; we have to supply the missing analytical program (as the authors of the two Talmuds, but particularly the Bavli, discovered early on). Sifra, as we shall soon see, treats the Mishnah in only a single aspect, while the two Talmuds cover that aspect generously, along with a far more elaborate program. Further, they pursue no encompassing exegetical program. So the two Talmuds are unique in context.

Both Talmuds invariably do one of these four things with the Mishnah: (1) text criticism; (2) exegesis of the meaning of the Mishnah, including glosses and amplifications; (3) addition of scriptural proof texts of the Mishnah's central propositions; or (4) harmonization of one Mishnah passage with another such passage or with a statement of the Tosefta.

Each of these types of composition follows a well-defined form, so that, if we were given only an account in abstract terms of the arrangement of subject and predicate or a simple account of the selection of citation language (e.g., "as it is said" or "our rabbis have taught"), we could readily predict the purpose of the composition or composite. So formal traits accompany the purpose of the commentary compositions and permit differentiation of one type from another.

The first two of these four procedures remain wholly within the narrow frame of the Mishnah passage subject to discussion. Therefore, in the natural order of things, the two Talmuds will respond to the same facts in a given Mishnah passage and commonly will do so in much the same way. The second pair take an essentially independent stance *vis-à-vis* the Mishnah pericope at hand. Part of the rhetorical convention of the Talmuds governs the order in which types of compositions—Mishnah text criticism, exegesis, scriptural proof texts, and harmonization—are set forth. Ordinarily the order for both Talmuds is the same as given above.

The Bilingual Character of the Talmuds and Its Taxonomic Implications

Both Talmuds utilize both Hebrew and Aramaic. Documents that utilize two or more languages but are addressed to a single audience convey information not only through what is said but also through the language in which a message is set forth. In the Talmuds what is said in Hebrew is represented as authoritative and formulates a normative thought or rule. What is said in Aramaic is analytical and commonly signals an argument and formulates a process of inquiry and criticism. That is how language serves a taxonomic purpose: Hebrew is the language of the result, Aramaic of the way by which the result is achieved; Hebrew is the formulation of the decision, Aramaic of the work of deliberation. Each language serves to classify what is said in that language, and we always know where we stand in a given process of thought and the exposition of thought, by reference to the language that is used at that particular place in the sustained discourse to which we are witness. That fixed rule, utilizing language for the purpose of classifying what is said in that language, characterizes only the Talmuds. All other documents treated in Scripture as canonical, except Daniel, Ezra, and Nehemiah, are monolingual, ordinarily in Hebrew, so that Aramaic occurrences are generally brief allusions to something deemed external to what the author wishes to say in his own behalf, for example, a citation of everyday speech, invariably assumed to be in Aramaic.

The occurrence of Hebrew, the language of quotation, in the Talmuds will commonly signal one of three facts, which, through the very choice of language, our author wishes to tell us: (1) a passage is from the Hebrew Scriptures; (2) a passage is from the Mishnah or the Tosefta (or from a corpus of sayings out of which the Tosefta as we have it was selected; for our purposes that is a distinction that makes no difference); (3) or, most important, a statement is authoritative and forms a normative formulation, a rule to be generalized and obeyed even when not from the Mishnah or Scripture, but from a named or anonymous authority of the time of the document itself.

How the Mishnah Is Read by the Talmuds

The Mishnah is read by the Talmuds as a composite of discrete and essentially autonomous rules, a set of atoms, not an integrated molecule, so to speak. The Mishnah as a whole and complete statement of a viewpoint no longer exists. Its propositions are reduced to details. But what is offered by the Talmuds instead? The answer is a statement that, on occasion, recasts details in generalizations encompassing a wide variety of other details across the gaps between one tractate and another. This immensely creative and imaginative approach to the Mishnah vastly expands the range of discourse. But the consequence is to deny to the Mishnah both its own mode of speech and its distinctive and coherent message.

The Mishnah rarely finds it necessary to adduce proof texts from the written Torah in support of its statements. The Talmuds, by contrast, find it appropriate whenever possible to cite scriptural proof texts for the propositions of the Mishnah. Proof texts for Mishnaic rules are required, and are supplied in substantial numbers. The Mishnah now is systematically represented as not standing free and separate from Scripture, but dependent upon it. The authority of the Mishnah's laws, then, is reinforced. But the autonomy of the Mishnah as a whole is severely compromised. Just as the Mishnah is represented in the Talmuds as a set of rules rather than as a philosophical essay, so it is presented, rule by rule, as a secondary and derivative development of Scripture. It would be difficult to imagine a more decisive effort to reformulate the Torah than is accomplished by the Talmuds.

The question has now to be asked, When do the Talmuds speak for themselves and not for the Mishnah? Further, what sorts of units of discourse contain what is "Talmudic" in the two Talmuds? These two questions produce the same answers for both Talmuds, allowing us to characterize their topical or propositional programs.

(1) THEORETICAL QUESTIONS OF LAW NOT ASSOCIATED WITH A PARTICULAR PASSAGE OF THE MISHNAH. In the first of the two Talmuds there is some tendency—and in the second, a very marked tendency—to move beyond the legal boundaries set by the Mishnah's rules themselves. More general inquiries are taken up. These of course remain

within the framework of the topic of one tractate or another, although there are some larger modes of thought characteristic of more than a single tractate.

(2) EXEGESIS OF SCRIPTURE SEPARATE FROM THE MISHNAH. It is under this rubric that we find the most important instances in which the Talmuds present materials essentially independent of the Mishnah.

(3) HISTORICAL STATEMENTS. The Talmuds contain a fair number of statements that something happened, or narratives about how something happened. While many of these are replete with biblical quotations, in general they do not provide exegesis of Scripture, which serves merely as illustration or reference point.

(4) STORIES ABOUT AND RULES FOR SAGES AND DISCIPLES, SEPARATE FROM DISCUSSION OF A PASSAGE OF THE MISHNAH. The Mishnah contains a tiny number of tales about rabbis. These serve principally as precedents for or illustrations of rules. The Talmuds by contrast contain a sizable number of stories about sages and their relationships to other people.

When the Talmuds present us with ideas or expressions of a world related to but fundamentally separate from that of the Mishnah—that is, when the Talmuds wish to say something other than what the Mishnah says and means—they will take up one of two modes of discourse. Either we find exegesis of biblical passages, with the value system of the rabbis read into the scriptural tales, or we are told stories about holy men and paradigmatic events, once again through tales told in such a way that a didactic and paraenetic purpose is served. It follows that the two Talmuds are composites of three kinds of materials: (1) exegeses of the Mishnah (and other materials classified as authoritative, that is, Tannaite); (2) exegeses of Scripture; and (3) accounts of the men who provide both.

Both Talmuds, then, constitute elaborate reworkings of the two antecedent documents: the Mishnah, lacking much reference to Scripture, and Scripture itself. The Talmuds bring the two together into a synthesis of their compilers' own making, both in reading Scripture into the Mishnah, and in reading Scripture alongside of, and separate from, the Mishnah.

A simple and brief illustration derives from both Talmuds' reading of a brief passage of Mishnah tractate *Makkot*. The unity of purpose—Mishnah commentary—and the identity of proposition—the unity of the Torah, its perfection—should not obscure the simple fact that the two Talmuds do not intersect except at the Mishnah and at Scripture. The Talmuds bear each its own message, but both ask the same questions. Mishnah and Tosefta passages in both Talmuds are in boldface, with Bavli's use of Aramaic in italics, and Hebrew in regular type. We begin with the Yerushalmi:

YERUSHALMI TO MISHNAH *MAKKOT* 1:8

[A] He whose trial ended and who fled and was brought back before the same court—

[B] they do not reverse the judgment concerning him [and retry him].

[C] In any situation in which two Gerim [proselytes] up and say, "We testify concerning Mr. So-and-so that his trial ended in the court of such-and-such, with Mr. So-and-so and Mr. So-and-so as the witnesses against him,"

[D] lo, this one is put to death.

[E] [Trial before] a Sanhedrin applies both in the Land and abroad.

[F] A Sanhedrin which imposes the death penalty once in seven years is called murderous.

[G] R. Eleazar b. Azariah says, "Once in seventy years."

[H] R. Tarfon and R. Aqiba say, "If we were on a Sanhedrin, no one would ever be put to death."

[I] Rabban Simeon b. Gamaliel says, "So they would multiply the number of murderers in Israel."

[I.A] [Trial before a] Sanhedrin applies both in the Land and abroad [M. 1:8E],

[B] as it is written, "And these things shall be for a statute and ordinance to you throughout your generations in all your dwellings" (Num. 35:29).

[C] And why does Scripture say, "You shall appoint judges and officers in all your towns [which the Lord your God gives you]" (Deut. 16:18) in the towns of the Land of Israel.

[D] The meaning is that in the towns of Israel they set up judges in every town, but abroad they do so only by districts.

[E] It was taught: R. Dosetai b. R. Yannai says, "It is a religious requirement for each tribe to judge its own tribe, as it is said, 'You shall appoint *judges* and officers in all your towns which the Lord your God gives you, according to your tribes'" (Deut. 16:18).

[II.A] Rabban Simeon b. Gamaliel taught, "Those declared liable to the death penalty who fled from the Land abroad—they put them to death forthwith [upon recapture].

[B] "If they fled from abroad to the Land, they do not put them to death forthwith, but they undertake a trial *de novo.*"

The Yerushalmi wants the scriptural proof for the Mishnah's allegation. The Mishnah has set forth a variety of rules. The framers of the Yerushalmi's composition therefore go in search of the scriptural foundations for those rules. The task, then, is to harmonize the implications at hand. Since the proof text, I.B, yields results contrary to the assumed implications of C, D must indicate otherwise. Unit II is an independent saying, generally relevant to M. 1:8E. It is a simple paraphrase and clarification.

The Bavli does the same thing, but makes its own points. The comparison is based on the shared program; the contrast derives from the different results.

BAVLI TO MISHNAH *MAKKOT* 1:10

A. He whose trial ended and who fled and was brought back before the same court—

B. they do not reverse the judgment concerning him [and retry him].

C. In any situation in which two get up and say, "We testify concerning Mr. So-and-so that his trial ended in the court of such-and-such, with Mr. So-and-so and Mr. So-and-so as the witnesses against him,"

D. lo, this one is put to death.

E. [Trial before] a sanhedrin applies both in the land and abroad.

F. A sanhedrin which imposes the death penalty once in seven years is called murderous.

G. R. Eleazar b. Azariah says, "Once in seventy years."

H. R. Tarfon and R. Aqiba say, "If we were on a sanhedrin, no one would ever be put to death."

I. Rabban Simeon b. Gamaliel says, "So they would multiply the number of murderers in Israel."

I.1   A. He whose trial ended and who fled and was brought back before the same court — they do not reverse the judgment concerning him [and retry him]:

B. Before that court in particular the judgment is not reversed, but it may be reversed before some other court! *But then it is taught further on:* In any situation in which two get up and say, "We testify concerning Mr. So-and-so that his trial ended in the court of such-and-such, with Mr. So-and-so and Mr. So-and-so as the witnesses against him," lo, this one is put to death!

C. Said Abbayye, "This is no contradiction. The one statement refers to a court in the land of Israel, the other, to a court abroad."

D. *For it has been taught on Tannaite authority:*

E. R. Judah b. Dosetai says in the name of R. Simeon b. Shatah, "If one fled from the land to abroad, they do not reverse the verdict pertaining to him. If he fled from abroad to the land, they do reverse the verdict concerning him, because of the higher priority enjoyed by the land of Israel" [T. San. 3:11A-B].

II.1   A. [Trial before] a sanhedrin applies both in the land and abroad:

B. *What is the source of this rule?*

C. *It is in line with that which our rabbis have taught on Tannaite authority:*

D. "And these things shall be for a statute of judgment to you throughout your generations in all your dwellings" (Num. 35:29)—

E. we learn from that statement that the sanhedrin operates both in the land and abroad.

F. If that is so, then why does Scripture state, "Judges and offices you shall make for yourself in all your gates that the Lord God gives you tribe by tribe" (Deut. 16:18) [meaning only in the tribal land, in the land of Israel]?

39

G. "In your own gates you set up courts in every district and every town, but outside of the land of Israel you set up courts in every district but not in every town."

III.1 A. **A sanhedrin which imposes the death penalty once in seven years is called murderous. R. Eleazar b. Azariah says, "Once in seventy years:"**

B. *The question was raised: does the statement,* **A sanhedrin which imposes the death penalty once in seven years is called murderous** *mean that even one death sentence was enough to mark the sanhedrin as murderous, or is this merely a description of how things are?*

C. *The question stands.*

IV.1 A. **R. Tarfon and R. Aqiba say, "If we were on a sanhedrin, no one would ever be put to death." Rabban Simeon b. Gamaliel says, "So they would multiply the number of murderers in Israel:"**

B. *So what would they actually do?*

C. R. Yohanan and R. Eleazar both say, "Did you see whether or not the victim was already dying from something, or was he whole when he was killed?" [Such a question would provide grounds for dismissing the charge of murder, if the witnesses could not answer properly.]

D. *Said R. Ashi, "If they said that he was whole, then, 'Maybe the sword only cut an internal lesion?'"*

E. *And in the case of a charge of consanguineous sexual relations, what would they actually do?*

F. *Both Abbayye and Raba said, "'Did you see the probe in the kohl-flask [actually engaged in sexual relations]?"*

G. *And as to rabbis, what would suffice for conviction?*

H. *The answer accords with Samuel, for* said Samuel, "In the case of a charge of adultery, if the couple appeared to be committing adultery [that would be sufficient evidence]."

Standard Mishnah exegesis in both Talmuds is represented by this brief passage from Bavli *Makkot*. The Yerushalmi presents numerous exercises that follow the same program. We start, I, with a challenge to the implications of the stated rule, I.B, yielding a dissonance that is ironed out by a suitable distinction. We proceed, II, to a scriptural source for the passage at hand. Item III raises a theoretical question meant to clarify the sense of the language before us. Entry IV reverts to the systematic glossing of the language and sense of the Mishnah. There is no kind of comment in this passage that the Yerushalmi does not provide as well; each of these types of inquiry is standard for both Talmuds.

Comparing the Two Talmuds' Reading of the Same Mishnah Paragraph

If we compare the way in which the two Talmuds read the same Mishnah paragraph, we discern consistent differences between them.

The principal difference between the Talmuds is the same difference that distinguishes jurisprudence from philosophy. The Yerushalmi talks in details, the Bavli in large truths; the Yerushalmi tells us what the Mishnah says, the Bavli what it means. The Bavli demonstrates how the Mishnah's laws form law, the way in which its rules attest to the onto-logical unity of truth. The Bavli thinks more deeply about deep things, and, in the end, its authors also think about things different from those that occupy the writers of the Yerushalmi. How do the Talmuds compare? The example yields these generalizations: (1) the first Talmud analyzes evidence, the second investigates premises; (2) the first remains wholly within the limits of its case, the second vastly transcends the bounds of the case altogether; and (3) the first wants to know the rule, the second asks about the principle and its implications for other cases.

The Talmud of the Land of Israel

So much for the two Talmuds viewed as species of a common genus. What about the Yerushalmi on its own? The Yerushalmi is best described as a systematic commentary on tractates of the Mishnah, a commentary shaped within a cogent program and answering a systematic set of questions. Nearly every discourse—perhaps 90 percent of the whole—of the Yerushalmi[5] addresses one main point: the meaning of the Mishnah. For the Yerushalmi,[6] the life of Israel reaches the level of analysis within the integument of the Mishnah. That is to say, the Mishnah is about life, while the Yerushalmi is about the Mishnah. Accordingly, the traits of the Mishnah defined the problematic of both intellect and politics confronting the heirs of the Mishnah, the disciples of the final generation of the Mishnah's redaction and formulation. They for their part set the patterns that followed, treating the Mishnah as Torah, proposing to receive and realize its revelation. But the question is, How can people make a statement of their own when their focus is upon statements of others who came before them?

The Yerushalmi speaks about the Mishnah in essentially a single voice, about fundamentally few things. Its mode of speech as much as of thought is uniform throughout. Diverse topics produce only slight differentiation in modes of analysis. The same sorts of questions phrased in the same rhet-oric—a moving or dialectical argument composed of questions and answers—turn out to pertain equally well to every passage of the Mishnah, and the Yerushalmi generally takes up a program of inquiry that is not very complex or diverse. The Yerushalmi also utilizes a single, rather limited repertoire of exegetical initiatives and rhetorical choices for what-ever discourse about the Mishnah the framers of the Yerushalmi propose to undertake. Accordingly, as is clear, the Yerushalmi presents us with both a uniformity of discourse and a monotony of tone. The Yerushalmi speaks in a single voice. That voice by definition is collective, not greatly differentiated by traits of individuals. (Individuals in the Yerushalmi, unlike in the Mishnah, do not speak uniformly, but the differences are not marked.) Let me spell this out, because its consequences for the history of the ideas contained within the Yerushalmi will prove definitive.

The Yerushalmi speaks in a single voice, uniformly, consistently, and predictably. The voice is the voice of a book, the voice of an author, the voice we hear when we read: one voice. The message is one deriving from a community, the collectivity of sages or textual community for whom and to whom the book speaks. The document seems, in the main, to intend to provide notes, an abbreviated script that anyone may use to reconstruct and reenact formal discussions of problems: about this, one says that. Curt and often arcane, these notes can be translated only with immense bodies of inserted explanation. All of this script of information is public and undifferentiated, not individual and idiosyncratic. We must assume people took for granted that, out of the signs of speech, it would be possible for anyone to reconstruct speech, doing so in accurate and fully conventional ways. So the literary traits of the document presuppose a uniform code of communication: a single voice.

The Talmud of Babylonia

We come to the single most important document in Rabbinic literature, the Talmud of Babylonia or Bavli.[7] The Bavli has served as the constitution and bylaws of Judaism.[8] It portrayed the way of life and it set forth the worldview of Judaism. As a matter of fact, the Talmud from the time of its closure in circa 600 CE, just before the Muslim conquest of the Middle East, North Africa, and much of southern and western Europe, until the nineteenth century, defined the social order for nearly the whole of its "Israel." The success of the Bavli derives from its union of Halakhic and Aggadic exposition, the Mishnah and Scripture, for large composites serve the latter, and not only the former, as in the case of the Yerushalmi. But the Bavli's intellectual acumen vastly exceeds the Yerushalmi's as well.

This Talmud is distinguished in three matters. First, the Bavli shows how practical reason does its work to make diverse issues and actions conform to a single principle. Second, the Bavli shows how applied logic discerns the regular and the orderly in the confusion and disorder of everyday conflict. Third, the Bavli portrays the right way of thinking about problems that may be worked out in many different analytical modes. Where are we to find massive displays of applied logic and practical reasoning in the analysis of the minutiae of the workaday world, showing in the everyday the intimations of regularity, order, and compelling purpose that together point to the governance of a reasonable Creator of an orderly and sensible creation, including nature and the social order alike? In the Bavli, but not in many other writings.

The Bavli in its thirty-seven tractates is entirely uniform, and the stylistic preferences exhibited on any given page characterize every other page of the document. When people everywhere, whatever the subject or problem, speak in the same way, and even say the same thing about many things, they certainly attract attention to the distinctive traits of expression that they deem correct throughout. What we find on one page we find on every other page: the same rhetoric, the same logic, and the same law underlying laws. When, therefore, we examine a single page or a single chapter, we see the entirety of the writing. Given its massive dimensions, then, we are on firm ground in asking about that textual community that has in such a uniform way communicated its message through its method.

Both Talmuds do appeal to some sources in common: Scripture, the Mishnah, episodic passages that we find also in the Tosefta, and a few sayings attributed to authorities who flourished after the closure of the Mishnah—for example, earlier masters in the Talmudic process that yielded the Talmuds of each country (Yohanan and Simeon ben Laqish for the Land of Israel, Rab and Samuel for Babylonia). But the common usage of received sayings rarely permits us to predict the direction and purpose of the compositions of the two Talmuds; each will go its own way, guided by its own concerns, pursuing its own interests. For the framers of the Bavli drew upon their distinctive local sources for compositions and composites, and the framers of the Yerushalmi drew upon their equivalently distinctive local sources for compositions and composites.

As a matter of fact, the framers of the compositions (especially those of the second Talmud) do precisely what they wish with such shared sayings or stories, and they did not respond to or build upon compositions or, still less, composites shared with the earlier Talmud. The compositions and composites that comprise the Bavli occasionally use imported parts, that is, sayings from the other Talmud, but in any event they are taken apart and then "remanufactured" for the Bavli. "The one whole Torah of Moses, our rabbi"—whether in written form in Scripture, oral form in the Mishnah, or as related sayings classified as Tannaite or of Mishnaic standing and authority—therefore divides by place. The Rabbinic traditions are bound by place. The rabbis' re-presentation of the Torah is profoundly localized and particularized by the Talmud of Babylonia.

Both Talmuds say the same thing in very much the same way, but the second Talmud radically differs from the first. That is so because first, as noted, all of its compositions and composites were prepared locally and not imported from the Holy Land, and second, its hermeneutics of the Mishnah is original. The two Talmuds routinely treat the same Mishnah but only very rarely intersect other than at a given Mishnah paragraph or Tosefta selection. Ordinarily, each Talmud pursues its own interests when reading a passage shared with the other.

Was There a Q?

In this context readers familiar with New Testament Gospels research will wonder whether a common source—a "Q"—was drawn upon by writers of compositions that occur in the respective Talmuds, asking, Do the Bavli and Yerushalmi draw on (a) "Q"? At some points they do draw on available materials, ordinarily sayings floating hither and yon. It is very common that these finished materials occur also in the Tosefta. So in theory there could have been a "Q." But if there was, analysis of the shared sayings proves that it was not like a "Q" of the size and importance of the one that is attested by Matthew and Mark and used by Luke.

Was There a Shared Exegetical Protocol?

If there was no shared corpus of sayings, then does a topical protocol define both Talmuds' Mishnah exegesis—that is, a protocol of topics or problems associated with a given Mishnah pericope but not articulated therein? Such a protocol would have told the exegetes of that pericope, or the compilers of compositions deemed pertinent to that pericope, what subject they should treat (over and above the subject of the pericope), or what problem they should investigate (over and above the problem explicit in the pericope). If such a protocol was in play, then when discussing a given Mishnah paragraph compilers of both Talmuds could have introduced the same themes, not mentioned in the Mishnah (whether in the paragraph at hand or in some other paragraph) but held in common to belong to the clarification of that Mishnah paragraph.

Here again an analogy may clarify for New Testament students what is at stake here. It is clear that for the authors of the four canonical Gospels, as well as all of the extra-canonical ones, a shared protocol, not spelled out, dictated the subjects that should be treated and the order in which they should occur. That is to say, if we propose to talk about Jesus Christ, his life and teachings, we follow an established program. We are going to discuss, for example, the Passion, and moreover the Passion is going to appear at the end of the narrative. A biographical narrative will intrude throughout. That protocol governs in all four Gospels without regard to the character of the Passion Narrative, on the one hand, or the program of sayings and stories to be utilized in the articulation of the various Gospels, respectively, on the other: this is a fine example of a blatant topical (narrative) protocol.

In fact, as our snippet from Yerushalmi and Bavli *Makkot* has shown us, no substantial shared exegetical protocol or tradition, either in fully spelled out statements in so many words, or in the gist of ideas, or in topical conventions, or in intellectual characteristics, governed the two Talmuds' reading of the same Mishnah paragraph. The Bavli presents an utterly autonomous statement, speaking in its own behalf and in its own way about its own interests. The shared traits are formally imposed and extrinsic: documents cited by one set of writers are cited by another. The differentiating characteristics are intrinsic and substantive, and concern what is to be done with the shared formal statements taken from prior writings. The framers of the Bavli in no way found guidance in the processes by which the Yerushalmi's compositions and composites took shape, either in the dim past of the document, or, it goes without saying, in the results of those processes as well. The Talmuds differ not only generally, but in detail—not in how they make their statements or in what they say but, at a more profound level, in their very generative layers, in the intellectual morphology characteristic of each.

What Marks the Bavli as Unique?

What characterizes the Bavli and not the Yerushalmi is the search for the unitary foundations of the diverse laws through an inquiry into the premises of discrete rules, the comparison and contrast of those premises, the statement of the emergent principles, and the comparison and contrast of those principles with the ones that derive from other cases and their premises. This is a process, an inquiry, without end into the law behind the laws. What the Yerushalmi ignores but the Bavli urgently seeks, beyond its presentation of the positions at hand, is to draw attention to the premises of those positions, the reasoning behind them, the evidence that supports them, the argument that transforms evidence into demonstration, and even the authority of the premises among those who settle questions by expressing opinions, those who can hold the combination of principles or premises that underpin a given position.

When we observe that one Talmud—the Bavli—is longer than the other, or one Talmud gives a fuller account than the other, we realize that such an observation is trivial. The real difference between the Talmuds emerges from a different trait: the Bavli's completely different theory of what it wishes to investigate. And that difference derives from the reason that the framers of the Bavli's compositions and composites did the work to begin with. The outlines of the intellectual character of the work flow from the purpose of the project, not the reverse; thence, the modes of thought and the specifics of analytical initiative are all secondary to intellectual morphology. So first comes the motivation for thought, then the morphology of thought, and then the media of thought, in that order.

That explains why the difference between the Yerushalmi and the Bavli is the difference between jurisprudence and philosophy: the one is a work of exegesis in search of clarity of rules and, at its best, in quest of the jurisprudential system, whereas the other is an exercise of sustained critical and dialectical argument and analysis in quest of philosophical truth. To state matters simply, the Yerushalmi presents and explains the laws—the rule for this, the rule for that; "law" bears the conventional meaning of jurisprudence. The Bavli presents the law in the philosophical sense of the abstract issues, the matters of theory, the principles at play far beneath the surface of detailed discussion—the law behind the laws. And that, we see, is not really "law" in any ordinary sense of jurisprudence; it is law in a deeply philosophical sense: the rules that govern the way things are, that define what is proportionate and orderly and properly composed.

What is interesting therefore is that even when the facts are the same, the issues identical, and the arguments matched, the Bavli's authorship manages to lay matters out in a very distinctive way. And that way yields as a sustained, somewhat intricate argument (requiring us to keep in the balance both names and positions of authorities and also the objective issues and facts) what the Yerushalmi's method of representation gives us as a rather simple sequence of arguments. The Bavli's presentation is one of thrust and parry, challenge and response, assertion and counterassertion, theoretical possibility and its exposure to practical facts ("if I had to rely...I might have supposed..."); and, of course, the authorities of the Bavli (not only the framers) are even prepared to rewrite the received Tannaite formulation. That initiative can come only from someone totally in command of the abstractions and able to say that the details have to be this way; so the rule of mind requires, and so it shall be.

The Yerushalmi's message is that the Mishnah yields clear and present rules; its medium is the patient exegesis of Mishnah passages, the provision and analysis of facts required in the understanding of the Mishnah. That medium conveys its message about not the Mishnah alone, but about the laws. The Bavli, for its part, conveys its message in a coherent and persistent manner through its ever-recurring medium of analysis and thought. We miss the point of the message if we misconstrue the medium: what is important is not the dialectical argument, and a mere reportage of questions and answers, thrust and parry, proposal and counterproposal— that does not accurately convey the unique medium of the Bavli, not at all. Dialectical arguments occur, if not commonly, in other Rabbinic writings.

When we ask for authority behind an unstated rule and find out whether the same authority is consistent as to principle in other cases, when we show that authorities are consistent with positions taken elsewhere—here above all we stand in the very heart of the Bavli's message, but only if we know what is at stake in the medium of inquiry.

What is unique about the Bavli's hermeneutics? The medium for the expression of the Bavli's statement was dictated by the form and assignment of the document. Since a talmud generically defined was a commentary in form, hermeneutics served as the mode of expression for whatever, within or beyond the commentary, the framers wished to say. When we understand how the Bavli's own statement is made—its principles for the reading of the received writing—then we can identify the hermeneutics. What makes the second Talmud unique is contained in the ways in which its hermeneutics differed from that of the first. By showing people how to think, then, in the context of the revealed Torah, the Bavli's framers maintained that one can also guide them concerning what to think: by means of right reasoning formed into right attitudes, right thoughts lead to right deeds. In the "how" of thought, the "what" found form and substance.

The Bavli's discourse forms a closed system in which people say the same thing about everything. To state in a single phrase the governing hermeneutic of the Talmud: the task of interpretation is to uncover the integrity of the truth that God has manifested in the one and unique revelation, the Torah (oral and written). By "integrity" is meant not merely the result of facile harmonization but the rigorous demonstration that the Torah at its foundations makes a single statement, whole, complete, cogent, coherent, harmonious, unified, and beyond all division. The message of the first document of the oral Torah, the Mishnah, was the hierarchical unity of all being in the One on high. The right medium for that message is the Bavli on account of the character of its hermeneutics, best summarized as its quest for abstraction. Since the Mishnah's authorship undertook precisely the same inquiry, how the Mishnah and the Bavli deal with the problem of showing the integrity of truth reveals the center and soul of the Rabbinic literature, as the two dominant documents of Judaism set matters forth.

The Mishnah's version of the integrity of truth focuses upon the unity of all being in hierarchical ontology. A single metaproposition encompasses the multitude of the Mishnah's propositions, which is, all classes of things stand in a hierarchical relationship to one another, and in that encompassing hierarchy there is a place for everything. The theological proposition that is implicit but never spelled out, of course, is that one God occupies the pinnacle of the hierarchy of all being. To that one God all things turn upward, ascending from complexity to simplicity; from that one God, all things flow downward, descending from singularity to multiplicity. Showing that all things can be ordered, and that all orders can be set into relationship with one another, transforms method into message. The message of hierarchical classification is that many things really form a single thing, the many species a single genus, the many genera an encompassing and well-crafted, cogent whole. Every time we speciate, we affirm that position. Each successful formation of relationships among species, for example, making them into a genus, or identifying the hierarchy of the species, proves the point again. Not only that, but when we can show that many things are really one, or that one thing yields many (the reverse and confirmation of the former), we state in a fresh way a single immutable truth concerning the unity of all being in an orderly composition of all things within a single taxon. Exegesis always is repetitive—and a sound exegesis of the systemic exegesis must then be equally so, everywhere explaining the same thing in the same way. To state with emphasis the one large argument—the metaproposition—that the Mishnah's authorship sets forth in countless small ways: *the very artifacts that appear multiple in fact form classes of things, and, moreover, these classes themselves are subject to a reasoned ordering by appeal to this-worldly characteristics signified by properties and indicative traits.*

Thus, for example, monotheism is to be demonstrated in the Bavli's philosophy by appeal to those very same data that for paganism prove the opposite. The way to one God, ground of being and ontological unity of the world, lies through rational reflection on themselves and on the world, which yields a living unity encompassing the whole. That claim, conducted in an argument covering overwhelming detail in the Mishnah, emerges quite directly. The whole composition of thought is set forth, in the correct intellectual manner, through the patient classification of things by appeal to the traits that they share, with comparison and contrast among points of difference then yielding the governing rule for a given classification. And the goal is through proper classification of things to demonstrate the hierarchical order of being, culminating in the proposition that all things derive from, and join within (in secular language) one thing or (in the language of philosophy of religion) the One, or (in the language of Judaism) God.

How does the Bavli join in the work of forming a monotheist canon? Matching the Mishnah's ontology of the hierarchical unity of all being is the Bavli's principle that many principles express a single one, many laws embody one governing law, which is the law behind the laws. The Mishnah establishes a world in stasis with lists of like things, subject to like rules. The Bavli portrays a world in motion: lists of like things form series, but series too conform to rules. The Mishnah sets forth lists, the Bavli establishes a series. Demonstrating in conclusion and in message that the truth is one, whole, comprehensive, cogent, coherent, and harmonious, and showing that fact of intellect—these sustained points of insistence on the character of mind and the result of thought form the goal of the Bavli's framers. The Bavli's paramount intellectual trait is its quest through abstraction for the unity of the law, the integrity of truth. The Bavli's quest for unity leads to the inquiry into the named authorities behind an unassigned rule, showing that a variety of figures can concur—meaning, names that stand for a variety of distinct principles can form a single proposition of integrity. That same quest insists on the fair and balanced representation of conflicting principles behind discrete laws, not to serve the cause of academic harmony but to set forth how, at their foundations, the complicated and diverse laws may be explained by appeal to a few simple principles; the conflict of principles then is less consequential than the demonstration that diverse cases may be reduced to only a few principles.

The Bavli's version of the integrity of truth aims to show in countless cases the cogency of (jurisprudential) laws in (philosophical) law. And it is through the right hermeneutics that that is demonstrated, and the message is conveyed in a rational manner. Having shown that diverse topics of the Mishnah are so represented as to make a single set of cogent points about hierarchical classification, we now turn directly to the problem of the Bavli: can the claim that it too says one thing about many things be made of the Mishnah's greatest single commentary? The answer lies in rhetoric: do the figures represented in the Bavli talk in the same way about many subjects? The answer is that they do.

The Bavli's Theology Expressed through Hermeneutics

We have already observed how the two Talmuds equally engage in a process of dismantling the Mishnah into selected paragraphs or even lone sentences, these to be read in their own fresh context. Now we realize that the Mishnah's deconstruction forms only one phase of the larger systematic definition of that of which the Torah's oral part consists. And that consists of sentences, at most paragraphs, but not whole chapters, and certainly not whole "books." It follows that the first rule of reading was to read sentences on their own, but also in relationship to other sentences; people do not pay attention to which book a saying derives from but homogenize everything. Five hermeneutical rules yielding theological facts govern throughout the Bavli, all of them serving to express the hermeneutics that convey the theological principles defined by the Talmud of Babylonia, which became the summa of Judaism.

(1) *Defining the Torah and the context for meaning.* The Torah consists of freestanding statements and sentences, sometimes formed into paragraphs, more often not; and we are to read these sentences both on their own—for what they say—and also in the context of the entirety of the

Torah, oral and written. Therefore the task is to set side by side and show the compatibility of discrete sentences; entire documents mean nothing, the Torah being a unity. The entirety of the Torah defines the context of meaning. All sentences of the Torah, equally, jointly, and severally, form the facts out of which meaning is to be constructed.

(2) *Specifying the rules of making sense of the Torah.* Several premises govern in our reading of the sentences of the Torah, and these dictate the rules of reading. The first is that the Torah is perfect and flawless. The second is that the wording of the Torah yields meaning. The third is that the Torah contains, and can contain, nothing contradictory, incoherent, or otherwise contrary to common sense. The fourth is that the Torah can contain no statement that is redundant, banal, silly, or stupid. The fifth is that our sages of blessed memory, when they state teachings of the Torah, stand for these same traits of language and intellect: sound purpose, sound reasoning, and sound result, in neat sentences. The task of the reader (in secular language) or the master of the Torah (in theological language; in context the two are one and the same) then is to identify the problems of the Torah, whether written or oral, and to solve those problems. Knowing what will raise a difficulty, we also know how to resolve it.

(3) *Identifying the correct medium of discourse.* Since our principal affirmation is that the Torah is perfect, and the primary challenge to that affirmation derives from the named classifications of imperfection, the proper mode of analytical speech is argument. That is because if we seek flaws, we come in a combative spirit seeking proof and conflict, not truth and consequence. Only by challenging the Torah sentence by sentence, at every plausible point of imperfection, are we going to show in the infinity of detailed cases the governing fact of perfection. We discover right thinking by finding the flaws in wrong thinking, the logical out of the failings of illogic. Only by the sustained confrontation of opposed views and interpretations will truth result.

(4) *The harmony of what is subject to dispute, the unity and integrity of truth.* Finding what is rational and coherent: the final principle of hermeneutics is to uncover the rationality of dispute. Once our commitment is to the sustained conflict of intellect, it must follow that our goal can only be the demonstration of three propositions, everywhere meant to govern. This is spelled out below.

(5) *Knowing God through the theology expressed in hermeneutics.* In a protracted quest for the unity of the truth, in the detailed demonstration that beneath the laws is law, with a few wholly coherent principles inherent in the many diverse rules and their cases—in that sustained quest, which defines the premise and the goal of all Talmudic discourse, Israel meets God, and it is in mind, in intellect, where that meeting takes place. That is what is at stake in Rabbinic literature, from beginning to end.

Disputes

The integrity of truth above all is repeatedly shown in the harmony of what is subject to dispute. This is demonstrated by finding what is rational and coherent in disagreement. Throughout the Talmud, in identifying and solving every problem of disharmony and incoherence, our goal can only be the demonstration of three propositions.

(1) Disputes give evidence of rationality, meaning each party has a valid, established principle in mind; no one simply stands by an unexplained opinion without articulated rationality.

(2) Disputes are subject to resolution, showing either that each party invokes a valid principle or that to begin with there was no dispute at all, and each was talking about different things.

(3) Truth wins out every time we show not the resolution of dispute but the rationality of the law.

The first proposition therefore proves to be the most important. If we can demonstrate that reasonable sages can differ about equally valid propositions—regarding, for instance, which principle governs in a particular case in which two distinct and otherwise harmonious principles pertain—then schism affords evidence not of imperfection but of profound coherence. The principles are affirmed, their application subjected to conflict. So too, if disputes worked out in extended, moving arguments, covering much ground, can be brought to resolution, as is frequently the case in either a declared decision or an agreement to disagree, then the perfection of the Torah once more comes to detailed articulation in the wonder of dialectics.

The single prevalent means of demonstrating the integrity of the truth is supplied by the ubiquitous effort to show the rationality of disputes. For the Mishnah, and therefore the Tosefta, the corpus of Tannaite statements, the very conduct and character of the Rabbinic sages in conveying their component of the Torah, put forth not so much rules as conflicting opinions on rules in a vast array of disputes. What do we gain by establishing that disputes are rational? When, first of all, we can show that disputes concern the application of principles, or which of two or more principles govern in a particular case, we show that, while details are subject to dispute, principles are affirmed and prevail. So the unity of truth is underscored. Second, if we find two or more sages in dispute about a given principle, one party affirming, the other party denying the same, then our task is to show that each side has a valid reason in mind. Then the principle may be subject to dispute, but for solid reason; then the law is reasonable, even if the conclusions are conflicted. That too demonstrates that the law is orderly and never capricious.

The theology that comes to expression maintains the proposition of the

51

integrity of the Torah's laws. Disputes, which are ubiquitous in the Mishnah and the Talmud and form the raw materials of the writers of compositions and framers of composites, underscore the law's rationality—and therefore, in the nature of intellect, its unity. One way or the other, therefore, the stakes for the analysis of the reasoned basis for disagreement are high. The laws yield a law, governing principles for the social order are few and coherent, and, in the here and now of Israel's life, God's rule prevails because it should, because God has revealed in the Torah the rules of life, and those rules yield a society we can understand and trust. All of this is expressed in concrete cases.

Rabbinic Exegesis of Scripture's Law
Exodus: *Mekhilta Attributed to Rabbi Ishmael*

In addition to the Mishnah, Tosefta, Yerushalmi, and Bavli, there are four other Rabbinic documents devoted to the exposition of the Halakhah. These present the Halakhah in relationship to Scripture and not as a free-standing topical exposition such as the Mishnah and its continuators set forth. They cover Exodus, Leviticus, Numbers, and Deuteronomy.

Mekhilta[9] *Attributed to Rabbi Ishmael*[10] seen in the aggregate presents a composite of three kinds of materials concerning the book of Exodus.[11] The first is a set of *ad hoc* and episodic exegeses of some passages of Scripture. The second is a group of propositional and argumentative essays in exegetical form, in which theological principles are set forth and demonstrated. The third consists of topical articles, some of them sustained, many of them well crafted, about important subjects of Rabbinic Judaism. The entire document forms a sustained address on the book of Exodus, covering Ex. 12:1–23:19; Ex. 31:12-13; and Ex. 35:1-3. It comprises nine tractates: *Pisha* (Ex. 12:1–13:16), *Beshallah* (Ex. 13:17–14:31), *Shirata* (Ex. 15:1-21), *Vayassa* (Ex. 15:22–17:7), *Amalek* (Ex. 17:8–18:27), *Bahodesh* (Ex. 19:1–20:26), *Neziqin* (Ex. 21:1–22:23), *Kaspa* (Ex. 22:24–23:19), and *Shabbata* (Ex. 31:12-17 and 35:1-3). There are eighty-two sections, subdivided into paragraphs. The division of the book of Exodus has no bearing on the lections read in the synagogue as we now know them. The document is variously dated; circa 250 CE[12] is presently favored by many scholars, but rejected by others.

In *Mekhilta Attributed to Rabbi Ishmael* we deal with a compilation of teachings, not a sustained argument: a systematic presentation of conventions, not a focused argument in behalf of distinct and urgent propositions, such as we find in *Sifra* and in *Sifré* to Deuteronomy. The document comprises the first scriptural encyclopedia of Judaism. A scriptural encyclopedia joins together expositions of topics, disquisitions on propositions, in general precipitated by the themes of scriptural narrative or the dictates of biblical law, and collects and arranges in accord with Scripture's order and program the exegeses—paraphrases or brief explanations—of clauses of biblical verses. The nine authorships of *Mekhilta Attributed to Rabbi Ishmael* treat as a given—that is to say, a corpus of facts or, more aptly, a body of tradition—what the other authorships or compilers of Midrash compositions set forth as components of a system that requires defense and demands apologetic exposition. For *Mekhilta*'s authorship, the facts comprise a corpus of information to which people require ready access. By setting forth an important component of information, that is, the data of revealed truths of Rabbinic Judaism, that authorship provides such access. What was needed, then, was an encyclopedia of things one should know on themes dictated by Scripture, resulting in the sequence of topics and propositions of the *Mekhilta*, in the order demanded by Scripture.

A model for long centuries to come, *Mekhilta Attributed to Rabbi Ishmael* attracted many imitators and continuators. The conception of collecting information and holding it together upon the frame of Scripture attracted many, so that a vast literature of Midrash compilation much like the *Mekhilta* came into being in succeeding periods. Not one but dozens, and ultimately hundreds, of Midrash compilations, interesting, traditional, and, of course, pointless and merely informative, would fill the shelves of the library that emerged in medieval and modern times. Accordingly, *Mekhilta Attributed to Rabbi Ishmael* stood at the beginning of centuries of work carried on in the pattern set by that authorship. There would be only one Bavli, but many, many Midrash compilations: *Mekhiltas, Yalquts,* Midrash this and Midrash that, and, in due course, a secondary development would call into being commentaries to Scripture (as to the Bavli) as well.

The nine tractates of *Mekhilta Attributed to Rabbi Ishmael* prove discrete. We have to take account of a document behind which, even at the end product, stand nine authorships, not one single authorship whose hand is evident all the way through. For in formal and logical traits, and all the more so in their topical program, the nine tractates are scarcely cogent when seen whole and complete. They make no one point over and over again. They undertake no sustained methodical analysis that joins bits and pieces of exegesis into a large-scale composition bearing meaning. They do not pursue a single range of problems in such a way as to demonstrate in many ways a single coherent position.

While the authorship of *Mekhilta Attributed to Rabbi Ishmael* sets forth propositions, overall these do not serve to organize or impose coherency upon the document as a whole. That is why it is an encyclopedia, cogent in the pieces, but not overall. Only one tractate of the document, *Neziqin,* clearly does exhibit fundamental coherency, since in the main it follows a single program of exegesis, aimed at establishing a set of uniform conceptual results. These, briefly stated, point to the conclusions that (1) cases may be generalized into rules; (2) Scripture does not repeat itself even when it covers the same legal subjects more than once; and (3) the categories that make sense of reality derive from Scripture's classification of things, not from the traits of things viewed independently of Scripture. The other eight tractates into which the document is divided present a variety of conclusions.

The main points that this Midrash compilation makes in its several parts may be conveniently divided into three classifications: (1) generalizations about the character of Scripture, (2) rules for correct conduct, and (3) theological teachings, with special reference to the relationship between Israel and God and the implications of that relationship for the fate of Israel among the nations. The first two are in volume and intellectual dimensions not imposing, but the third is enormous and important, bearing the weight of the burden of our document.

Traits of Scripture. The order in which Scripture sets forth two or more propositions does not necessarily indicate the priority assigned to those items. Scripture itself will dictate priority. Scripture uses euphemistic language. Scripture is not bound by temporal considerations, for example, of sequence.

The Moral Life in Israel. When one party pays respect to another, they speak in harmony. With the measure with which one metes out to others is one's own reward meted out. Welcoming a fellow is like welcoming the face of the Presence of God. Do not favor either rich or poor in judging a case.

Theological Convictions. These add up to a great collection of the basic theses of the theology of Rabbinic Judaism. Let me simply state the items as they come.

Through doing religious duties Israel was redeemed, and preparation of the rite well in advance was the religious duty to which the redemption of Israel would serve as reward. What God says he will do, he does. Wherever Scripture indicates that God has said something, we can find in some other passage precisely where and what he had said. The upshot, of course, is that by carefully reading Scripture, we are able to identify the rules that govern history and salvation. The vindication of Moses' demands turns the demands into prophecies of precisely what would come about. This is further underlined by the careful delineation of the degradation and humiliation of Pharaoh, portrayed as one running about. And then comes the striking contrast between the reverence in which Israelites hold the rule of God and the humiliation of the Egyptian ruler. People get what is coming to them. Divine punishment is inexorable, and so too is divine reward. When God exacts punishment of the nations, his name is made great in the world. Merit is what saved Israel at the sea. The issue to be pursued is, what sort of merit, deriving from what actions or persons? The acts of healing of the Holy One, blessed be he, are not like the acts of healing of mortals. The redemption at the sea prefigures the redemption at the end of time. Faith in God is what saves Israel.

God punishes the arrogant person by exacting a penalty precisely from that about which such a person takes pride. With that in which the nations of the world take pride before him he exacts punishment from them. Numerous cases in a long line of instances, based upon historical facts provided by Scripture, serve to demonstrate that proposition. Israel is unique among the nations. Mortals have the power to praise and glorify God. God takes many forms. The Lord is master of all media of war. The Lord needs none of those media. The Lord is a man of war, but the Lord is in no way comparable to a man of war, making war in a supernatural way, specifically by retaining, even while making war, the attributes of mercy and humanity. God is just, and God's justice ensures that the worthy are rewarded and the unworthy are penalized. God responds to human actions and attitudes. Those who oppose Israel are as though they opposed God. God is unique and God's salvation at the sea will be repeated at the end of time.

Israel gained great merit because it alone was willing to accept the Ten Commandments. The Israelites deserve praise for accepting the Torah. The "other gods" are not really gods at all. They are called "other" for various theological reasons. Suffering is precious and will not be rejected. One must not act in regard to God the way the outsiders treat their gods. They honor their gods in good times, not in bad, but Israel, exemplified by Job, honors God in bad times as much as in good. These fundamental principles of faith hardly exhaust the allusions to, or representations of, theological and normative statements in *Mekhilta Attributed to Rabbi Ishmael*. They represent only those convictions that are spelled out in massive detail and argued with great force, the points of emphasis within a vast fabric of faith.

While familiar, these propositions form a miscellany. The characterization of the propositional message of our authorship(s) strongly suggests that we are dealing with a repertoire of normative dogmas of Rabbinic Judaism. Nothing in the representation just now set forth points toward controversy or can be shown to contradict convictions contained within other documents.

Compared to other Midrash compilations, *Mekhilta Attributed to Rabbi Ishmael* therefore is abnormal in two aspects. First, it is animated by no paramount questions and does not lay out compelling and sharply etched responses to them. Second, it is not predominantly a propositional writing at all. So in its topical and propositional character, this document differs from others of its classification. If the others bear singular messages, *Mekhilta Attributed to Rabbi Ishmael* speaks in eternal verities that, in the context of controversy, enjoy the authority of accepted commonplaces, or, less cordially classified, mere banalities—theological truths, but routine and broadly acknowledged ones. If the others employ as their paramount mode of discourse propositional compositions, this compilation is first of all exegetical and miscellaneous, and only in moderate measure propositional at all. Other compilations prove points and bear a weighty message; this one does not.

Leviticus: *Sifra*

Sifra,[13] a compilation of Midrash exegeses on the book of Leviticus,[14] forms a massive and systematic statement concerning the definition of the Mishnah in relationship to Scripture.[15] Unlike the other Midrash compilations that concern the Pentateuch, the two *Sifrés* and *Mekhilta Attributed to Rabbi Ishmael*, the document is programmatically coherent from beginning to end in its sustained treatment of the issues defined by the Mishnah. For the heirs of the Mishnah, the relationship of the Mishnah to Scripture—in mythic language, of the oral to the written part of the Torah—required definition. The authorship of *Sifra* composed the one document to accompany tractate *Abot* in addressing the issue head-on. It succeeded in accomplishing through reason, not merely a chain of tradition, the union of the two Torahs: Scripture, or the written Torah, and the Mishnah, or the oral Torah.

This was achieved not merely formally by provision of proof texts from Scripture for statements of the Mishnah—as in the two Talmuds—but through a profound analysis of the Torah's interior structure of thought. It was by means of the critique of practical logic and the rehabilitation of the probative logic of hierarchical classification (accomplished through the form of *Listenwissenschaft*) in particular that the authorship of *Sifra* accomplished this remarkable feat of intellect. That authorship achieved the (re)union of the two Torahs into a single cogent statement within the framework of the written Torah by penetrating into the deep composition of logic that underlay the creation of the world in its correct components, rightly classified, and in its right order, as portrayed by the Torah.

This was done in two ways. Specifically it involved, first of all, systematically demolishing the logic that sustains an autonomous Mishnah. That logic appeals to the intrinsic traits of things to accomplish classification and hierarchization. Secondly, it was done by demonstrating that the identification of the correct classification of things depended not upon the traits of things viewed in the abstract but upon the classification of things by

Scripture in particular. The framers of *Sifra* recast the two parts of the Torah into a single coherent statement through unitary and cogent discourse. So in choosing, as to structure, a book of the Pentateuch, and, as to form, the exegetical form involving paraphrase and amplification of a phrase of a base text of Scripture, the authorship of *Sifra* made its entire statement *in nuce*. Then by composing a document that for very long stretches simply cannot have been put together without the Mishnah and at the same time subjecting the generative logical principles of the Mishnah to devastating critique, that same authorship took up its position. The destruction of the Mishnah as an autonomous and freestanding statement based upon its own logic is followed by the reconstruction of large tracts of the Mishnah as a statement wholly within, and in accord with, the logic and program of the written Torah in Leviticus. That is what defines *Sifra*, the one genuinely cogent and sustained statement among the four Midrash compilations that present exegetical discourse on the Pentateuch.

The dominant approach to uniting the two Torahs, oral and written, into a single cogent statement involved reading the written Torah into the oral. In form, as we noted in the two Talmuds, this was done through inserting into the Mishnah (that is, the oral Torah) a long sequence of proof texts. The other solution required reading the oral Torah into the written one by inserting into the written Torah citations and allusions to the oral one, and also by demonstrating on both philosophical and theological grounds the utter subordination and dependency of the oral Torah, the Mishnah, to the written Torah, while at the same time defending and vindicating that same oral Torah. *Sifra*, followed unsystematically to be sure by the two *Sifrés*, did just that. *Sifra*'s authorship attempted to set forth the dual Torah as a single cogent statement by reading the Mishnah into Scripture not merely for proposition but for expression of proposition. On the surface that decision represented a literary, not merely a theological, judgment. But within the deep structure of thought, it was far more than a mere matter of how to select and organize propositions.

That judgment upon the Mishnah forms part of the polemic of *Sifra*'s authorship—but only part of it. *Sifra*'s authorship conducts a sustained polemic against the failure of the Mishnah to cite Scripture very much or to link its ideas systematically to Scripture through the medium of formal demonstration by exegesis. *Sifra*'s rhetorical exegesis follows a standard redactional form. Scripture will be cited. Then a statement will be made about its meaning, or a statement of law correlative to that Scripture will be given. That statement sometimes cites the Mishnah, often verbatim. Finally, the authorship of *Sifra* invariably states, "Now is that not (merely) logical?" And the point of that statement will be, Can this position not be gained through the working of mere logic, based upon facts supplied (to be sure) by Scripture?

The polemical power of *Sifra* lies in its repetitive demonstration that the stated position, the citation of a Mishnah pericope, is not only not the product of logic, but is, and only can be, the product of exegesis of Scripture. That is only part of the matter, as I shall explain, but that component of the larger judgment of *Sifra*'s authorship does make the point that the Mishnah is subordinated to Scripture and validated only through Scripture. In that regard the authorship of *Sifra* stands with the position of the authorships of the other successor writings, even though *Sifra*'s writers carried to a much more profound level of thought the critique of the Mishnah. They did so by rethinking the logical foundations of the entire Torah.

The framers of the Mishnah effect their taxonomy through the traits of things. The authorship of *Sifra* insists that the source of classification is Scripture. *Sifra*'s authorship time and again demonstrates that classification cannot be carried out without Scripture's data, and, it must follow, hierarchical arguments based on extra-scriptural taxa always fail.

Sifra's authorship rejects the principles of the logic of hierarchical classification *as these are worked out by the framers of the Mishnah*. Theirs is a critique of classifying things without scriptural warrant. The critique applies to the way in which a shared logic is worked out by the other authorship. For it is not the principle that like things follow the same rule and unlike things the opposite rule that is at stake. Nor is the principle of hierarchical classification embodied in the argument *a fortiori* at issue. What our authorship disputes is that we can classify things on our own by appeal to the traits or indicative characteristics, that is, utterly without reference to Scripture.

The argument is simple. On our own, we cannot classify species into genera. Everything is different from everything else in some way. But Scripture tells us what things are like what other things for what purposes, hence Scripture imposes on things the definitive classifications, not traits we discern in the things themselves. When we see the nature of the critique, we shall have a clear picture of what is at stake when we examine, in some detail, precisely how the Mishnah's logic works.

In *Sifra* no one denies the principle of hierarchical classification such as we saw in operation in Mishnah *Sanhedrin* 2:1ff. That principle is an established fact, a self-evident trait of mind. The argument of *Sifra*'s authorship is that, by themselves, things do not possess traits that permit us finally to classify species into a common genus. There always are traits distinctive to a classification. Accordingly, it is the argument of *Sifra*'s authorship that without the revelation of the Torah we are not able to effect any classification at all—we are left, that is to say, only with species, not genus, only with cases, not rules. The thrust of *Sifra*'s authorship's attack on the Mishnah's taxonomic logic is readily discerned. Time and again, we can easily demonstrate, things have so many and such diverse and contradictory indicative traits that, comparing one thing to something else, we can always distinguish one species from another. Even though we find something in common, we also can discern some other trait characteristic of one thing but not the other.

Consequently, we also can show that the hierarchical logic on which we rely, the argument *a fortiori* or *qol vehomer*, will not serve. For if on the basis of one set of traits that yield a given classification we place into hierarchical order two or more items on the basis of a different set of traits, we have either a different classification altogether or, much more commonly, simply a different hierarchy. So the attack on the way in which the Mishnah's authorship has done its work appeals not merely to the limitations of classification solely on the basis of the traits of things. The more telling argument addresses what is, to *Listenwissenschaft*, the source of power and compelling proof: hierarchization. That is why, throughout, we must designate the Mishnah's mode of *Listenwissenschaft* a logic of hierarchical classification. Things are not merely like or unlike, therefore following one rule or its opposite. Things also are weightier or less weighty, and that particular point of likeness or difference generates the logical force of *Listenwissenschaft*.

Sifra's authorship repeatedly demonstrates the formation of classifications based on monothetic taxonomy. What that means is this: traits that are not only common to both items but that are shared throughout both of the items subject to comparison and contrast simply will not serve. These shared traits are supposed to prove that the items that are compared are alike, and therefore should be subjected to the same rule. But the allegation of comparability proves flawed. The proposition maintains that the two items are alike because they share one trait in common (thus: "monothetic taxonomy"). But I shall show that they also exhibit traits that are different for the respective items. Then we have both likeness and difference.

Then, the argument proceeds, at every point at which someone alleges uniform, that is to say, monothetic likeness, *Sifra*'s authorship will demonstrate difference. Then how to proceed? Appeal to some shared traits as a basis for classification: this is not like that, and that is not like this, but the indicative trait that both exhibit is such and so—that is to say, proceed by polythetic taxonomy. The self-evident problem in accepting differences among things and insisting, nonetheless, on their monomorphic character for purposes of comparison and contrast cannot be set aside. Who sets the limitations? That is, if I can adduce as evidence for a shared classification of things only a few traits among many characteristic of each thing, then what stops me from treating all things alike? Polythetic taxonomy opens the way to an unlimited exercise in finding what diverse things have in common and imposing, for that reason, one rule on everything. Then the very working of *Listenwissenschaft* as a tool of analysis, differentiation, comparison, contrast, and the descriptive determination of rules yields the opposite of what is desired. Chaos, not order—a mass of exceptions with no rules, a world of examples, each subject to its own regulation, instead of a world of order and proportion, composition, and stability—will result.

Sifra's authorship affirms taxonomic logic when applied to the right categories. It systematically demonstrates the affirmative case that *Listenwissenschaft* is a self-evidently valid mode of demonstrating the truth of propositions. But *the* source of the correct classification of things is Scripture and only Scripture. Without Scripture's intervention into the taxonomy of the world, we should have no knowledge at all of which things fall into which classifications and therefore are governed by which rules. How then do we appeal to Scripture to designate the operative classifications? *Sifra* is a simple example of the alternative mode of classification, one that does not appeal to the traits of things but to the utilization of names by Scripture. What we see is how by naming things in one way rather than in another, Scripture orders all things, classifying and, in the nature of things, also hierarchizing them.

Three forms dictate the entire rhetorical repertoire of this document. The first, the dialectical form, is the demonstration that if we wish to classify things, we must follow the taxa dictated by Scripture rather than relying solely upon the traits of the things we wish to classify. The second, the citation form, invokes the citation of passages of the Mishnah or the Tosefta in the setting of Scripture. The third is the commentary form, in which a phrase of Scripture is followed by an amplificatory clause of some sort. The forms of the document admirably expressed the polemical purpose of the authorship at hand. What they wished to prove was that a taxonomy resting on the traits of things without reference to Scripture's classifications cannot serve. They further wished to restate the oral Torah in the setting of the written Torah. And finally they wished to accomplish the whole by rewriting the written Torah. The dialectical form accomplishes the first purpose, the citation form the second, and the commentary form the third.

The simple commentary form is familiar in *Mekhilta Attributed to Rabbi Ishmael*, in which a verse or an element of a verse is cited, and then a very few words explain the meaning of that verse. Second come the complex forms, in which a simple exegesis is augmented in some important way, commonly by questions and answers, so that we have more than simply a verse and a brief exposition of its elements or of its meaning as a whole. The authorship of *Sifra* time and again wishes to show that prior documents, the Mishnah or Tosefta, cited verbatim, require the support of exegesis of Scripture for important propositions, which are not presented in the Mishnah and the Tosefta on the foundation of exegetical proof at all.

In the main, moreover, the authorship of *Sifra* tends not to attribute its materials to specific authorities, and most of the pericopae containing attributions are shared with Mishnah and Tosefta. As we should expect, just as in *Mekhilta Attributed to Rabbi Ishmael*, *Sifra* contains a fair number of pericopae that do not make use of the forms common in the exegesis of specific scriptural verses and mostly do not pretend to explain the meaning of verses, but rather resort to forms typical of the Mishnah and Tosefta. When *Sifra* uses forms other than those in which its exegeses are routinely phrased, it commonly, though not always, draws upon materials also found in the Mishnah and Tosefta. It is uncommon for *Sifra* to make use of non-exegetical forms for materials peculiar to its compilation. To state matters simply, *Sifra* quotes the Mishnah or Tosefta, but its own materials follow its own distinctive exegetical forms.

Every example of a complex form, that is, a passage in which we have more than a cited verse and a brief exposition of its meaning, may be called "dialectical," the mode of moving or developing an idea through questions and answers, sometimes implicit, but commonly explicit. What "moves" is the argument, the flow of thought, from problem to problem. The dialectics of *Sifra* differs in form and purpose from that of the Talmuds. Here the movement is generated by the raising of contrary questions and theses. There are several subdivisions of the dialectical exegesis, so distinctive as to be treated by themselves. But all exhibit a flow of logical argument unfolding in questions and answers, characteristic, in the later literature, of the Talmud. One important subdivision of the stated form consists of those items, somewhat few in number but all rather large in size and articulation, intended to prove that logic alone is insufficient, and that only through revealed law will a reliable view of what is required be attained. The polemic in these items is pointed and obvious; logic by itself never wins the argument. It is always shown that a proof text from Scripture is required.

For its topical program the authorship of *Sifra* takes the book of Leviticus. For propositions *Sifra*'s authorship presents episodic and ad hoc sentences. If we ask how these sentences form propositions other than amplifications of points made in the book of Leviticus itself, and how we may restate those propositions in a coherent way, nothing sustained and coherent emerges. *Sifra* does not constitute a propositional document transcending its precipitating text. But, as we have now seen in detail, that in no way implies that the document's authorship merely collected and arranged this and that about the book of Leviticus. For three reasons we must conclude that *Sifra* does not set forth propositions in the way in which the Rabbah compilations and *Sifré* to Deuteronomy do (as we shall see in the Rabbah compilations in chapter 4 and in *Sifré* to Deuteronomy later in this chapter).

61

First, in general there is no topical program distinct from that of Scripture. *Sifra* remains wholly within Scripture's orbit and range of discourse, proposing only to expand and clarify what it found within Scripture. Where the authorship moves beyond Scripture, it is not toward fresh theological or philosophical thought, but rather to a quite different set of issues altogether, concerning Mishnah and Tosefta. When we describe the topical program of the document, the blatant and definitive trait of *Sifra* is simple: the topical program and order derive from Scripture. Just as the Mishnah defines the topical program and order for Tosefta, the Yerushalmi, and the Bavli, so Scripture does for *Sifra*. It follows that *Sifra* takes as its structure the plan and program of the written Torah, in contrast to the decision of the framers or compilers of Tosefta and the two Talmuds.

Second, for sizable passages, the sole point of coherence for the discrete sentences or paragraphs of *Sifra*'s authorship derives from the base verse of Scripture that is subject to commentary. That fact corresponds to the results of form analysis and the description of the logics of cogent discourse. While, as we have noted, the Mishnah holds thought together through propositions of various kinds, with special interest in demonstrating propositions through a well-crafted program of logic of a certain kind, *Sifra*'s authorship appeals to a different logic altogether. It is one that I have set forth as fixed-associative discourse. That is by definition not a propositional logic.

The third fundamental observation draws attention to the paramount position, within this restatement of the written Torah, of the oral Torah. We may say very simply that, in a purely formal and superficial sense, a sizable proportion of *Sifra* consists in the association of completed statements of the oral Torah with the exposition of the written Torah, the whole *re*-presenting as one unified Torah the dual Torah received by Moses at Sinai (speaking within the Torah myth). Even at the very surface we observe a simple fact. Without the Mishnah or the Tosefta, our authorship has virtually nothing to say about one passage after another of the written Torah. Far more often than citing the Mishnah or the Tosefta verbatim, our authorship cites principles of law or theology fundamental to the Mishnah's treatment of a given topic, even when the particular passage of the Mishnah or the Tosefta that sets forth those principles is not cited verbatim.

It follows that the three basic and definitive topical traits of *Sifra* are, first, its total adherence to the topical program of the written Torah for order and plan; second, its very common reliance upon the phrases or verses of the written Torah for the joining into coherent discourse of discrete thoughts, for example, comments on or amplifications of words or phrases; and third, its equally profound dependence upon the oral Torah for its program of thought, the problematic that defines the issues the authorship wishes to explore and resolve.

That brings us to the positive side of the picture. While *Sifra* in its details presents no paramount propositions, as a whole it demonstrates a highly distinctive and vigorously demonstrated proposition. We should drastically misunderstand the document if the miscellaneous character of the parts obscured the powerful statement made by the whole. For while in detail we cannot reconstruct a topical program other than that of Scripture, viewed in its indicative and definitive traits of rhetoric, logic, and implicit proposition *Sifra* does take up a well-composed position on a fundamental issue, namely, the relationship between the written Torah, represented by the book of Leviticus, and the oral Torah, represented by the passages of the Mishnah deemed by the authorship of *Sifra* to be pertinent to the book of Leviticus. As we noted at the outset, *Sifra* joins the two Torahs into a single statement, accomplishing a re-presentation of the written Torah in topic and in program and in the logic of cogent discourse, and within that rewriting of the written Torah a re-presentation of the oral Torah in its paramount problematic and in many of its substantive propositions. Stated simply, the written Torah provides the form, the oral Torah the content. What emerges is not merely a united dual Torah but *the* Torah, stated whole and complete, in context defined by the book of Leviticus.

Numbers: *Sifré*[16] to Numbers

Sifré to Numbers provides a miscellaneous reading of most of the book of Numbers,[17] but examining the implicit propositions of the recurrent forms of the document yields a clear-cut purpose.[18] The document follows no topical program; but it also is unlike *Mekhilta Attributed to Rabbi Ishmael* because of its recurrent effort to prove a few fundamental points. These are general and not limited to a given set of cases or issues, so that the successive compositions that comprise *Sifré* to Numbers yield no propositional program. But the recurrent proofs of discrete propositions that time and again bear one and the same implication do accumulate, and when we see what is implicit in the various explicit exercises we find a clear-cut and rather rich message indeed.

The document as a whole, through its fixed and recurrent formal preferences or literary structures, makes two complementary points. (1) Reason unaided by Scripture produces uncertain propositions. (2) Reason operating within the limits of Scripture produces truth. These two principles are never articulated but left implicit in the systematic reading of most of the book of Numbers, verse by verse. The exegetical forms stand for a single proposition: the human mind joins God's mind when humanity receives and sets forth the Torah. The Torah opens the road into the mind of God, and our minds can lead us on that road because our mind and God's mind are comparable. We share a common rationality. Only when we examine the rhetorical plan and then in search of the topical program reconsider the forms of the document does this propositional program emerge.

As with *Sifra*, therefore, *Sifré* to Numbers follows no topical program distinct from that of Scripture, which is systematically clarified. An interest in the relations between Scripture and the Mishnah and Tosefta, a concern with the dialectics characteristic of *Sifra*—these occur episodically, but scarcely define the character of the document. Its topical program and order derive from Scripture. As with *Sifra*, here too, as we have already noticed, the sole point of coherence for the discrete sentences or paragraphs derives from the base verse of Scripture that is subject to commentary. At the same time, if we examine the incremental message, the cumulative effect of the formal traits of speech and thought revealed in the uniform rhetoric and syntax of the document, we may discern a propositional program that is implicit in the rhetoric and logic of the compilation. What is required here is the articulation of the general consequences of numerous specific exegetical exercises.

One principal point of emphasis we discern in *Sifré* to Numbers takes an equally central role in the propositional, topical program of the other two compilations, *Sifra* and *Sifré* to Deuteronomy. It is the insistence on the principle that logic alone cannot suffice, and that all law must in the end derive from the written part of the Torah. The single sustained proposition of the several writings is that truth derives from Scripture, not from reason unaided by revelation. But a further proposition will attract our attention. By the very labor of explaining the meaning of verses of Scripture, the Rabbinic exegetes laid claim to participation in the work of revelation. And by distinguishing their contribution from the received text of the Torah, they announced their presence within the process of revelation. In these two ways the exegetes who composed *Sifra* and the two *Sifrés* announced not one but two fundamental propositions. The first is that God's revelation in the written Torah takes priority. The second is that man's reason in the exegesis of the written Torah enjoys full and legitimate place in the unfolding of the lessons of Sinai. No one can doubt that our authorship concurs on both principles.

The rhetorical form of both documents underlines the topical program contained in the first of the two propositions. For to underline over and over again the priority of not proposition, and hence reason, but process, and hence the exegesis of Scripture, the best choice is an obvious one. Begin at all points with a verse of Scripture and demonstrate that only by starting with the word choices and propositions of that verse of Scripture does all further progress of interpretation take place. But the second proposition, that humanity has a place in the process of revealing the

Torah of Sinai, comes to expression in the careful separation of the cited verse of the written Torah from the contribution of the contemporary exegete. In that formal preference too the authorship made a major point and established—if implicitly—a central syllogism: God's will follows the rules of reason; man can investigate the consequences of reason as expressed in God's will; therefore man can join in the labor of exploring God's will in the Torah.

Consequently, the authorships of all three Midrash compilations make their powerful case by their rhetorical program, which relies first and foremost on the citation and gloss of a verse of Scripture, as much as by their proposition and syllogism: only by Scripture does truth gain certainty. The appeal to Scripture, however, comes once the proposition is established, and that appeal then dictates the rhetoric and topic alike. Only when we know what question we bring to Scripture may we devise appropriate formal and programmatic policies for our Midrash exegesis and Midrash compilation alike. A second formal preference in all three documents, in addition to the exegetical form, makes the same point. The second form involves citation of a passage of the Mishnah followed by an extensive discourse on how the verse of Scripture that pertains to the topic of that Mishnah passage must contribute its facts, revealed at Sinai, if we wish to know the truth. Reason alone, which is systematically tested through a sequence of propositions shown to fail, will not serve.

To state matters simply: in the presentation of *Sifré* to Numbers, as in those of *Sifra* and *Sifré* to Deuteronomy, Scripture is complete, harmonious, and perfect.[19] Logic not only does not generate truth beyond the limits of Scripture but also plays no important role in the harmonization of difficulties yielded by what appear to be duplications or disharmonies. These forms of internal exegesis then make the same point that the extrinsic ones do.

Concerning the single most profuse category of exegesis, (1) a verse of Scripture or a clause, followed by (2) a brief statement of the meaning at hand, I see in our document or in its companions no unifying polemic in favor of, or against, a given proposition. The most common form also proves to be the least pointed: X bears this meaning, Y bears that meaning, or, as we have seen, citation of verse X, followed by [what this means is. . .]. Whether simple or elaborate, the upshot is the same. What can be at issue when no polemic expressed in the formal traits of syntax and logic finds its way to the surface? What do I do when I merely clarify a phrase? Or to frame the question more logically: What premises must validate my *intervention*, that is, my willingness to undertake to explain the meaning of a verse of Scripture? These justify the labor of intrinsic exegesis as we have seen its results here:

(1) My independent judgment bears weight and produces meaning. I—that is, my mind—therefore may join in the process.

(2) God's revelation to Moses at Sinai requires my intervention. I have the role, and the right, to say what that revelation means.

(3) What validates my entry into the process of revelation is the correspondence between the logic of my mind and the logic of the document.

Only if I think in accord with the logic of the revealed Torah can my thought processes join issue in clarifying what is at hand: the unfolding of God's will in the Torah. To state matters more accessibly: If the Torah does not make statements in accord with a syntax and a grammar that I know, I cannot so understand the Torah as to explain its meaning. But if I can join in the discourse of the Torah, it is because I speak the same language of thought, the same syntax and grammar at the deepest levels of my intellect.

(4) Then to state matters affirmatively and finally: Since a shared logic of syntax and grammar joins my mind to the mind of God as revealed in the Torah, I can say what a sentence of the Torah means. So I too can amplify, clarify, expand, revise, or rework—that is to say, create a commentary. So the work of commenting upon the written Torah bears profound consequence for the revelation of the Torah, the sage becoming partner with God in the giving of the Torah. In that conclusion we find ourselves repeating in the context of *Sifré* to Numbers the main point that *Sifra* yields in the description of Rabbinic literature as a whole.

Deuteronomy: *Sifré* to Deuteronomy

Out of cases and examples, sages in *Sifré* to Deuteronomy[20] seek generalizations and governing principles. Since in the book of Deuteronomy Moses explicitly sets forth a vision of Israel's future history, sages in *Sifré* to Deuteronomy examined that vision to uncover the rules that explain what happens to Israel.[21] That issue drew attention from cases to rules, with the result that, in the book of Deuteronomy, they set forth a systematic account of Israel's future history, the key to Israel's recovery of command of its destiny. Like *Sifra*, *Sifré* to Deuteronomy pursues a diverse topical program in order to demonstrate a few fundamental propositions. The survey of the topical and propositional program of *Sifré* to Deuteronomy dictates what is truly particular to that authorship: its systematic mode of methodical analysis, in which it does two things. First, the document's compilers take the details of cases and carefully reframe them into rules pertaining to all cases. The authorship therefore asks those questions of susceptibility to generalization ("generalizability") that first-class philosophical minds raise. And it answers those questions by showing what details restrict the prevailing law to the conditions of the case, and what details exemplify the encompassing traits of the law overall. These are the two possibilities. The law is either limited to the case and to all cases that replicate this one, or the law derives from the principles exemplified, in detail, in the case at hand. Essentially, as a matter of both logic and topical program, our authorship has reread the legal portions of the book of Deuteronomy and turned Scripture into what we now know is the orderly and encompassing code supplied by the Mishnah. To state matters simply, this authorship "mishna-izes" Scripture. We find in *Sifré* to Numbers no parallel to this dominant and systematic program of *Sifré* to Deuteronomy.

But in other aspects the document presents no surprises. In the two *Sifrés* and *Sifra* we find a recurrent motif, intense here, episodic there, of how the written component of the Torah—that is, revelation in written form—serves as the sole source of final truth. Logic or reason untested against Scripture produces flawed or unreliable results. The Torah proves paramount. Reason on its own is subordinate. For their search for the social rules of Israel's society, the priority of the covenant as a reliable account of the workings of reality, and the prevailing laws of Israel's history decreed by the terms of the covenant, their fundamental claim is the same. There are rules and regularities, but reason alone will not show us what they are. A systematic and reasoned reading of the Torah—the written Torah—joined to a sifting of the cases of the Torah in search of the regularities and points of law and order—this is what will tell the prevailing rule. A rule of the Mishnah and its account of the here and now of everyday life rests upon the Torah, not upon (mere) logic. A rule of Israel's history, past, present, and future, likewise derives from a search for regularities and points of order identified not by logic alone, but by logic addressed to the Torah. So these modes of gaining truth apply equally to Mishnah and Scripture. There is logic, applied reason and practical wisdom, such as sages exhibit; there is the corpus of facts supplied by Scripture, read as sages read it. These two together form God's statement upon the world today.

The topical program of the document intersects at its fundamental propositions with programs of other authorships—beginning with those of Scripture itself. The writers and compilers and compositors of Deuteronomy would have found entirely familiar such notions as the conditional character of Israel's possession of the land of Israel, the centrality of the covenant in Israel's relationship with God and with the other nations of the world, the decisive role of the covenant in determining Israel's own destiny, and the covenantal responsibilities and standing of Israel's leadership—surely a considerable motif in the very structure of Deuteronomy, particularly its beginning and end. The reader may well wonder how we may treat as a distinctive authorship a group of writers who simply go over ground familiar in the received literature. In some important ways the authorship of *Sifré* to Deuteronomy makes a statement that is very much its own. Four principal topics encompass the document's propositions, of which the first three correspond to the three relationships into which Israel entered: with heaven, on earth, and within. These yield systematic statements that concern the relationships between Israel and God, with special reference to the covenant, the Torah, and the land; Israel and the nations, with interest in Israel's history, past, present, and future, and how that cyclic is to be known; and Israel on its own terms, with focus upon Israel's distinctive leadership. The fourth rubric encompasses not specific *ad hoc* propositions that form aggregates of proofs of large truths, but rather prevailing modes of thought demonstrating the inner structure of intellect—in this document yielding the formation, out of the cases of Scripture, of encompassing rules.

1. ISRAEL AND GOD: THE IMPLICATIONS OF THE COVENANT. The basic proposition, spelled out in detail, is that Israel stands in a special relationship with God, and that relationship is defined by the contract, or covenant, that God made with Israel. The covenant comes to particular expression in this document, in two matters: first, the land, and second, the Torah. Each marks Israel as different from all other nations, on the one side, and as selected by God, on the other. In these propositions, sages situate Israel in the realm of heaven, finding on earth the stigmata of covenanted election and the concomitant requirement of loyalty and obedience to the covenant.

First comes the definition of those traits of God that our authorship finds pertinent. God sits in judgment upon the world, and his judgment is true and righteous. God punishes faithlessness. But God's fundamental and definitive trait is mercy. The way of God is to be merciful and gracious. The basic relationship of Israel to God is one of God's grace for Israel. God's loyalty to Israel endures, even when Israel sins. When Israel forgets God, God is pained. Israel's leaders, whatever their excellence, plead with God only for grace, not for their own merit. Correct attitudes in prayer derive from the need for grace, Israel having slight merit on its own account. Israel should follow only God, carrying out religious deeds as the covenant requires, in accord with the instructions of prophets. Israel should show mercy to others, in the model of God's merciful character.

Second, the contract or covenant produces the result that God has acquired Israel, which God created. The reason is that only Israel accepted the Torah, among all the nations, and that is why God made the covenant with Israel in particular. Why is the covenant made only with Israel? The Gentiles did not accept the Torah, Israel did, and that has made all the difference. Israel recognized God forthwith; the very peace of the world and of nature depends upon God's giving the Torah to Israel. That is why Israel is the sole nation worthy of dwelling in the palace of God and that is the basis for the covenant, too. The covenant secures for

Israel an enduring relationship of grace with God. The covenant cannot be revoked and endures forever. The covenant, the terms of which are specified in the Torah, has two aspects: if you do well, you will bear a blessing, and if not, you will bear a curse.

That is the singular mark of the covenant between God and Israel. The liberation from Egypt sufficed to impose upon Israel God's claim for their obedience. An important sign of the covenant is the possession of the land. Part of the covenant is the recognition of merit of the ancestors. In judging the descendants of the patriarchs and matriarchs, God promised, in making the covenant, recognition of the meritorious deeds of the ancestors. The conquest of the land and inheriting it are marks of the covenant, which Israel will find easy because of God's favor. The inheritance of the land is a mark of merit, inherited from the ancestors. The land is higher than all others and more choice. All religious duties are important, those that seem trivial as much as those held to be weightier.

God always loves Israel. That is why Israel should carry out the religious duties of the Torah with full assent. All religious duties are equally precious. Israel must be wholehearted in its relationship with God. If it is, then its share is with God, and if not, then it will not be favored by God. But Israel may hate God. The right attitude toward God is love, and Israel should love God with a whole heart. The reason that Israel rebels against God is prosperity. Then people become arrogant and believe that their prosperity derives from their own efforts. But that is not so, and God punishes people who rebel to show them that they depend upon God. When Israel practices idolatry, God punishes them, for example, through exile, through famine, through drought, and the like. Whether or not Israel knows or likes the fact, Israel has no choice but to accept God's will and fulfill the covenant.

The heaven and the earth respond to the condition of Israel and therefore carry out the stipulations of the covenant. If Israel does not carry out religious duties concerning heaven, then heaven bears witness against them, a witness that centers on the land of Israel in particular. Possession of the land is conditional, not absolute. It begins with grace, not merit. It is defined by the stipulation that Israel observe the covenant, in which case Israel will retain the land. If Israel violates the covenant, Israel will lose the land. When Israel inherits the land, in obedience to the covenant and as an act of grace bestowed by God, it will build the Temple, where Israel's sins will find atonement. The conquest of the land itself is subject to stipulations, just as possession of the land, as an act of God's grace, is marked by religious obligations. If Israel rebels or rejects the Torah, it will lose the land, just as the Canaanites in their idolatry did.

The land is not the only, or the most important, mark of the covenant. It is the fact that Israel has the Torah, which shows that Israel stands in a

special relationship to God. The Torah is the source of life for Israel. It belongs to everyone, not only the aristocracy. Children should start studying the Torah at the earliest age possible. The study of the Torah is part of the fulfillment of the covenant. Even the most arid details of the Torah contain lessons, and if one studies the Torah, the reward comes both in this world and in the world to come.

The possession of the Torah imposes a particular requirement involving an action. The most important task of every male Israelite is to study the Torah, which involves memorizing, and not forgetting, each lesson. This must go on every day and all the time. Study of the Torah should be one's main obligation, prior to all others. The correct motive is not for the sake of gain, but for the love of God and the desire for knowledge of God's will. People must direct heart, eyes, and ears to teachings of the Torah. Study of the Torah transforms human relationships, so that strangers become the children of the master of the Torah whom they serve as disciples. However unimportant the teaching or the teacher, all is done as if on the authority of Moses at Sinai. When a person departs from the Torah, that person becomes an idolater. Study of the Torah prevents idolatry.

2. ISRAEL AND THE NATIONS: THE MEANING OF HISTORY. The covenant, through the Torah of Sinai, governs not only the ongoing life of Israel but also the state of human affairs universally. The history of Israel forms a single continuous cycle, in that what happened in the beginning prefigures what will happen at the end of time. Events of Genesis are reenacted both in middle-history, between the beginning and the end, and also at the end of times. So the traits of the tribal founders dictated the history of their families to both the here and now and also the eschatological age. Moses was shown the whole of Israel's history, past, present, and future. The times of the patriarchs are reenacted in the messianic day, which shows how Israel's history runs in cycles, so that events of ancient times prefigure events now. The prophets, beginning with Moses, describe those cycles. What happens bears close ties to what is going to happen. The prophetic promises were also realized in Temple times, and will be realized at the end of time.

The periods in the history of Israel, marked by the exodus and wandering, the inheritance of the land, and the building of the Temple and its destruction, are all part of a divine plan. In this age Rome rules, but in the age to come, marked by the study of the Torah and the offering of sacrifices in the Temple cult, Israel will be in charge. That is the fundamental pattern and meaning of history. The Holy Spirit makes possible actions that bear consequences only much later in time. The prefiguring of history forms the dominant motif in Israel's contemporary life, and the reenacting of what has already been forms a constant. Israel therefore should believe, if not in what is coming, then in what has already been. The very

names of places in the land attest to the continuity of Israel's history, which follows rules that do not change. The main point is that while Israel will be punished in the worst possible way, Israel will not be wiped out.

But the cyclical character of Israel's history should not mislead. Events follow a pattern, but knowledge of that pattern, which is provided by the Torah, permits Israel both to understand and also to affect its own destiny. Specifically, Israel controls its own destiny through its conduct with God. Israel's history is the working out of the effects of Israel's conduct, moderated by the merit of the ancestors. Abraham effected a change in God's relationship to the world. But merit, which makes history, is attained by one's own deeds as well. The effect of merit, in the nation's standing among the other nations, is simple. When Israel enjoys merit, it gives testimony against itself, but when not, then the most despised nation testifies against it.

But God is with Israel in time of trouble. When Israel sins, it suffers. When it repents and is forgiven, it is redeemed. For example, Israel's wandering in the wilderness took place because of the failure of Israel to attain merit. Sin is what causes the wandering in the wilderness. People rebel because they are prosperous. The merit of the ancestors works in history to Israel's benefit. What Israel does not merit on its own, at a given time, the merit of the ancestors may secure in any event. The best way to deal with Israel's powerlessness is through Torah study; the vigor of engagement with Torah study compensates for weakness.

It goes without saying that Israel's history follows a set time; in other words, at the fulfillment of a set period of time, an awaited event will take place. The prophets prophesy concerning the coming of the day of the Lord. Accordingly, nothing is haphazard, and all things happen in accordance with a plan. That plan encompasses this world, the time of the Messiah, and the world to come, in that order. God will personally exact vengeance at the end of time. God also will raise the dead. Israel has overcome difficult times and can continue to do so. The task ahead is easier than the tasks already accomplished. Israel's punishment occurs only once, while the punishment coming upon the nations is unremitting. Peace is worthwhile and everyone needs it. Israel's history ends in the world to come or in the days of the Messiah. The righteous inherit the Garden of Eden. The righteous in the age to come will be joyful.

God acts in history and does so publicly, in full light of day. That is to show the nations who is in charge. The Torah is what distinguishes Israel from the nations. All the nations had every opportunity to understand and accept the Torah, and all declined it; that is why Israel was selected. And that demonstrates the importance of both covenant and the Torah, the medium of the covenant. The nations even had a prophet comparable to Moses: Balaam. The nations have no important role in history except as

God assigns them a role in relationship to Israel's conduct. The nations are estranged from God by idolatry. That is what prevents goodness from coming into the world. The name of God rests upon Israel in greatest measure. Idolaters do not control heaven. The greatest sin an Israelite can commit is idolatry, and those who entice Israel to idolatry are deprived of the ordinary protections of the law. God is violently angry at the nations because of idolatry. As to the nations' relationship with Israel, they are guided by Israel's condition. When Israel is weak, the nations take advantage; when strong, they are sycophantic. God did not apportion love to the nations of the world as he did to Israel.

3. ISRAEL AT HOME: THE COMMUNITY AND ITS GOVERNANCE. A mark of God's favor is that Israel has (or, has had and will have) a government of its own. Part of the covenantal relationship requires Israel to follow leaders whom God has chosen and instructed, such as Moses and the prophets. Accordingly, Israel is to establish a government and follow sound public policy. Its leaders are chosen by God. Israel's leaders, for example, prophets, are God's servants, and that is a mark of the praise that is owing to them. They are to be in the model of Moses, humble, choice, select, well known. Moses was the right one to bestow a blessing, and the people of Israel were the right ones to receive the blessing.

Yet all leaders are mortal, and even Moses died. The saints are leaders ready to give their lives for Israel. The greatest of them enjoy exceptionally long life. But the sins of the people are blamed on their leaders. The leaders depend on the people to keep the Torah, and Moses thanked them in advance for keeping the Torah after he died. The leaders were to be patient, honest, give a full hearing to all sides, and make just decisions in a broad range of matters. To stand before the judge is to stand before God. God makes sure that Israel does not lack for leadership. The basic task of the leader is both to rebuke and also to console the people.

The rulers of Israel are servants of God. The prophets exemplify these leaders, on the model of Moses, and Israel's rulers act only on the instruction of prophets. Their authority rests solely on God's favor and grace. At the instance of God, the leaders of Israel speak, in particular, words of admonition. These are delivered before death, when the whole picture is clear, so that people can draw the necessary conclusions. The words of Deuteronomy, when Moses spoke them, covered the entire history of the community of Israel. The leaders of Israel address admonition to the entire community at once. No one is exempted. But the Israelites can deal with the admonition. They draw the correct conclusions. Repentance overcomes sin, as at the sin of the golden calf. The Israelites were contentious, nitpickers, litigious, and, in general, gave Moses a difficult time. Their descendants should learn not to do so. Israel should remain united and obedient to its leaders. The task of the community is to remain unit-

ed. When the Israelites are of one opinion below, God's name is glorified above.

4. THE LAWS AND LAW: THE STRUCTURE OF INTELLECT. The explicit propositional program of *Sifré* to Deuteronomy is joined by a set of implicit ones. These comprise repeated demonstrations of a point never fully stated. The implicit propositions have to do with the modes of correct analysis and inquiry that pertain to the Torah. There are two implicit propositions that predominate. The first, familiar from other compilations, is that pure reason does not suffice to produce reliable results. Only through linking our conclusions to verses of Scripture may we come to final and fixed conclusions. The implicit proposition, demonstrated many times, may therefore be stated very simply. The Torah (written) is the sole source of reliable information. Reason undisciplined by the Torah yields unreliable results. These items may also occur within the rubrics of the specific propositions that they contain. Some of them moreover overlap with the later catalogue, but if so, are not listed twice.

The second of the two recurrent modes of thought is the more important. Indeed, we shall presently note that it constitutes the one substantial, distinctive statement made by our authorship. It is the demonstration that many things conform to a single structure and pattern. We can show this uniformity of the law by addressing the same questions to disparate cases and, in so doing, composing general laws that transcend cases and form a cogent system. What is striking, then, is the power of a single set of questions to reshape and reorganize diverse data into a single cogent set of questions and answers, all things fitting together into a single, remarkably well-composed structure. Not only that, but when we review the numerous passages at which we find what in the logical repertoire I called methodical-analytical logic, we find a single program. It is an effort to ask whether a case of Scripture imposes a rule that limits or imparts a rule that augments the application of the law at hand.

A systematic reading of Scripture permits us to restrict or to extend the applicability of the detail of a case into a rule that governs many cases. A standard repertoire of questions may be addressed to a variety of topics, to yield the picture of how a great many things make essentially a single statement. This seems to me the single most common topical inquiry in our document. It covers most of the laws of Deut. 12–26. I have not catalogued the laws of history, which generalize from a case and tell us how things always must be; the list of explicit statements of the proposition that the case at hand is subject to either restriction or augmentation, that the law prevailing throughout is limited to the facts at hand or exemplified by those facts, would considerably add to this list. The size, the repetitious quality, the obsessive interest in augmentation and restriction, and generalization and limitation—these traits of logic and their concomitant propositional results form the centerpiece of the whole.

CHAPTER 4

The Rabbinic Canon: Theology (Aggadah)

The Rabbinic sages claim to set forth through systematic reading of Scripture's details the general rules that govern history: to read forward from Scripture to their own day. Theirs is the realization of the scriptural theology: its articulation and concretization as a coherent system. The seven principal documents of the Aggadah, complemented by Aggadic compositions in the Halakhic compilations, particularly in the Bavli, embody the claim of Judaism with respect to Scripture. That is, they state precisely what the written Torah has revealed: the law and theology set forth by God to Moses at Sinai. In the Aggadic compilations they make that claim stick.

The Rabbinic Reading of Genesis:
Genesis Rabbah

Generally thought to have reached closure circa 400–450 CE, sometime after the Talmud of the Land of Israel had been redacted, *Genesis Rabbah*[1] transforms the book of Genesis from a genealogy and family history of Abraham, Isaac, and Jacob, then Joseph, into a book of the laws of history and rules of the salvation of Israel: the deeds of the founders become omens and signs for the later generations.[2] The narratives yield generalizations, which then encompass both the worldview and the way of life of Judaism.

In *Genesis Rabbah*, specifically, the entire narrative of Genesis is so formed as to point toward the sacred history of Israel and the Jewish people: its slavery and redemption; its coming Temple in Jerusalem; and its exile and salvation at the end of time—the whole being a paradigm of exile and return. In the rereading by the authorship[3] of *Genesis Rabbah*, Genesis proclaims the prophetic message that the world's creation commenced a single, straight line of significant events—that is to say, *history*—leading in the end to the salvation of Israel and, through Israel, of all humanity. The single most important proposition of *Genesis Rabbah* is that, in the story of the beginnings of creation, humanity, and Israel, we find the message of the meaning and end of the life of the Jewish people in the here and now of the fifth century CE. The deeds of the founders supply signals for their children about what is going to come in the future. So the biography of Abraham, Isaac, and Jacob also constitutes a protracted account of the history of later Israel. The fundamental proposition, displayed throughout *Genesis Rabbah*, that yields the specific exegeses of many of the verses of the book of Genesis and even of whole stories, is that the beginnings point toward the endings, and the meaning of Israel's past points toward the message that lies in Israel's future. The things that happened to the fathers and mothers of Israel provide a sign for the things that will happen to the children later on. What is at stake in the book of Genesis, therefore, is the discovery, among the facts provided by the written Torah, of the social rules that govern Israel's history.

What made the Rabbinic sages raise questions of history and its meaning? *Genesis Rabbah* in its final form emerges from that momentous century in which the Roman Empire passed from pagan to Christian rule, and in which, in the aftermath of Julian's abortive reversion to paganism circa 360 (which endangered the Christian character of the Roman empire), Christianity adopted that politics of the repression of paganism that rapidly engulfed Judaism as well. Christian theologians in the fourth century, from Eusebius at its beginning to Augustine at its end, raised the same questions of the meaning of the course of human events.

The Judaic theologian-exegetes framed matters as did the Christians, starting from creation. But the issue confronting Israel in the Land of Israel therefore proved immediate: the meaning of the new and ominous turn of history, the implications of Christ's worldly triumph for the otherworldly and supernatural people, Israel, whom God chooses and loves. The message of the exegete-compositors addressed the circumstance of historical crisis and generated remarkable renewal, a rebirth of intellect in the encounter with Scripture, now in quest of the rules, not of sanctification—these had already been found—but of salvation. So the book of Genesis, which portrays how all things had begun, would testify to the message and the method of the end: the coming salvation of patient, hopeful, enduring Israel.

That message—that history heads toward Israel's salvation—the sages derived from the book of Genesis. Therefore in their reading of Scripture a given story will bear a deeper truth about what it means to be Israel, on the one hand, and what in the end of days will happen to Israel, on the other. True, their reading makes no explicit reference to what, if anything, had changed in the age of Constantine. But we do find repeated references to the four kingdoms of Babylonia, Media, Greece, Rome. Then, time and again it is alleged, beyond the fourth will come Israel, fifth and last. So the sages' message, in their theology of history, was that the present anguish prefigured the coming vindication of God's people.

It follows that the sages read Genesis as the history of the world with emphasis on Israel. So the lives portrayed, the domestic quarrels and petty conflicts with the neighbors, all served to yield insight into what was to be. That is how the deeds of the patriarchs taught lessons on how the children were to act, and, it further followed, the lives of the patriarchs signaled the history of Israel. Israel constituted one extended family, and the metaphor of the family, serving the nation as it did, imparted to the stories of Genesis the character of a family record. History as genealogy conveyed the message of salvation. These propositions really laid down the same judgment, one for the individual and the family, the other for the community and the nation, since there was no differentiating one from the other. Every detail of the narrative therefore served to prefigure what was to be, and Israel found itself, time and again, in the revealed facts of the history of the creation of the world, the decline of humanity down to the time of Noah, and finally, its ascent through Abraham, Isaac, and Israel.

Genesis Rabbah undertakes two tasks. First comes the exegesis of clauses of verses, read in sequence, just as we noted in *Sifra* and the *Sifrés* to Numbers and Deuteronomy. Second, a not-quite-fresh but vigorous and now fully exploited exegetical technique makes its first appearance in the Rabbinic canonical writings here, and then in the successor documents. It requires citing what I call "an intersecting verse," one that has nothing to do with the passage subject to exegesis, and the reading of the base verse in light of that intersecting verse. Thus the technique of reading Scripture as a whole involves the introduction, at the beginning of a sustained composition, of a verse other than the one under analysis. That other verse intersects with the verse under discussion.

This formal arrangement of verses predominates from *Genesis Rabbah* forward. The effect of this form—the juxtaposition of two verses, one derived from the document at hand, the other from some other document altogether—is simple yet powerful. On the surface, the intersecting verse expands the frame of reference of the base verse, introducing data otherwise not present. But just beneath the surface lies the implicit premise:

both the intersecting verse and the base verse make the same point, and, in their meeting, each rises out of its narrow framework as a detail or an instance of a rule and testifies to the larger picture, the encompassing rule itself. The intersecting verse/base verse construction therefore yields a proposition that transcends both verses and finds proof in each case, and that powerful way of composing something new forms the centerpiece of the present document and the two that follow.

The reason that this rhetorical program—intersecting verse/base verse—serves so well derives from the program of the document that we discerned at the outset: to demonstrate that there are reliable rules that govern Israel's history. The Rabbinic sages intended, specifically, to discover and validate those fixed and governing rules within the details of the stories of the origins of the family of Abraham, Isaac, and Jacob, which Israel now constitutes. A process of searching for the governing laws of history and society requires not specific cases but general rules, and an inductive process will demand that sages generate rules out of cases. The meeting of rhetoric, logic, and topic takes place here.

Putting together the cases represented by two verses, one deep within the narrative of Genesis, the other far distant from that narrative, the exegetes found it possible to state a case and along with the case to point toward an implicit generalization yielded by the two or more cases at hand. The rhetoric involves the recurrent arrangement of verses, the logic involves the inquiry into the general rule that holds together two cases and makes of them a single statement of an overriding law, and the topic involves the direction of the history of Israel, specifically, its ultimate salvation at the end of time.

The first of the three forms of the document, then, is the recurrent mode of organization, namely, the base verse/intersecting verse construction. In the sort of passage under discussion, (1) a verse of the book of Genesis will be followed by (2) a verse from some other book of the Hebrew Scriptures. The latter (2) will then be subjected to extensive discussion. But in the end the exposition of the intersecting verse will shed some light, in some way, upon (1) the base verse cited at the outset.

The second paramount form, which always follows in sequence as well, is the exegesis of a single verse: a verse of the book of Genesis will be subjected to sustained analysis and amplification, not with reference to some other intersecting verse but now, commonly, with regard to numerous proof texts, or to no proof texts at all.

Finally, the syllogism form—proving a proposition of an other-than-theological character—will cite a variety of verses drawn from a broad range of books of the Hebrew Scriptures, with the verses ordinarily composed in a list of like grammatical and syntactical entries.

A single, simple example shows how the document systematically reads Genesis in light of the contemporary history of Israel. One rule of Israel's history is yielded by the facts at hand. Israel is never left without an appropriate hero or heroine. The relevance of the long discourse becomes clear at the end. Each story in Genesis may forecast the stages in Israel's later history, from beginning to end. A matter of deep concern focused the sages' attention on the sequence of world empires to which, among other nations, Israel was subjugated: Babylonia, Media, Greece, and Rome—Rome above all. What will follow? The Rabbinic sages maintained that beyond the rule of Rome lay the salvation of Israel:

> XLII:IV.1.A. "And it came to pass in the days of Amraphel" (Gen. 14:1):
> 4. A. Another matter: "And it came to pass in the days of Amraphel, king of Shinar" (Gen. 14:1) refers to Babylonia.
> B. "Arioch, king of Ellasar" (Gen. 14:1) refers to Greece.
> C. "Chedorlaomer, king of Elam" (Gen. 14:1) refers to Media.
> D. "And Tidal, king of Goiim [nations]" (Gen. 14:1) refers to the wicked government [Rome], which conscripts troops from all the nations of the world.
> E. Said R. Eleazar bar Abina, "If you see that the nations contend with one another, look for the footsteps of the king-messiah. You may know that that is the case, for lo, in the time of Abraham, because the kings struggled with one another, a position of greatness came to Abraham."

The exposition links the events of the life of Abraham to the history of Israel and even ties the whole to the messianic expectation. I suppose that any list of four kings will provoke inquiry into the relationship of the entries of that list to the four kingdoms among which history, in Israel's experience, is divided. The process of history flows in both directions. Just as what Abraham did prefigured the future history of Israel, so what the later Israelites were to do imposed limitations on Abraham. Time and again events in the lives of the patriarchs prefigure the four monarchies, among which the fourth, last, and most intolerable was Rome.

Genesis is read as if it portrayed the history of Israel and Rome. For that is the single obsession binding the sages of the document at hand to common discourse with the text before them. Why Rome in the form it takes in *Genesis Rabbah*? And why the obsessive character of the sages' disposition of the theme of Rome? Were their picture merely of Rome as tyrant and destroyer of the Temple, we should have no reason to link the text to the problems of the age of redaction and closure. But they present Rome as Israel's brother, counterpart, and nemesis, Rome as the one thing standing in the way of Israel's, and the world's, ultimate salvation. So the stakes are different, and much higher. It is not a political Rome but a Christian and messianic Rome that is at issue: Rome as surrogate for

Israel, Rome as obstacle to Israel. Why? It is because Rome now confronts Israel with a crisis. The program of *Genesis Rabbah* constitutes a response to that crisis. Rome in the fourth century became Christian. The Rabbinic sages respond by facing that fact quite squarely and saying, "Indeed, it is as you say, a kind of Israel, an heir of Abraham as your texts explicitly claim. But we remain the sole legitimate Israel, the bearer of the birthright—we and not you. So you are our brother: Esau, Ishmael, Edom." And the rest follows.

By rereading the story of the beginnings, sages discovered the answer and the secret of the end. Rome claimed to be Israel, and, indeed, sages conceded, Rome shared the patrimony of Israel. That claim took the form of the Christians' appropriation of the Torah as "the Old Testament," so sages acknowledged a simple fact in acceding to the notion that, in some way, Rome too formed part of Israel. But it was the rejected part, the Ishmael, the Esau, not the Isaac, not the Jacob. The advent of Christian Rome precipitated the sustained, polemical, rigorous, and well-argued rereading of beginnings in light of the end. Rome, then, marked the conclusion of human history as Israel had known it. What was beyond? The coming of the true Messiah, the redemption of Israel, the salvation of the world, the end of time. So the issues were not inconsiderable, and when the sages spoke of Esau/Rome, as they did so often, they confronted the life-or-death issue of the day.

The Rabbinic Reading of Leviticus: *Leviticus Rabbah*

When we come to *Leviticus Rabbah*,[4] we find the interest in the exposition of verse after verse has waned, while the proposition comes to the fore as the definitive and dominant organizing motif throughout.[5] With *Genesis Rabbah*, *Sifra*'s and the two *Sifrés*' mode of exegesis of verses and their components, one by one in sequence, comes to its conclusion and a new approach commences. The mixed character of *Genesis Rabbah*, joining propositional to exegetical rhetoric in order to make points of both general intelligibility and also very specific and concrete amplification of detail, marks a transitional moment in the workings of Midrash.

Exactly what did the framers of *Leviticus Rabbah* learn when they opened the book of Leviticus? When they read the rules of sanctification of the priesthood, they heard the message of the salvation of all Israel. Leviticus became the story of how Israel, purified from social sin and sanctified, would be saved. The framers of *Leviticus Rabbah*, which was closed in the mid-fifth century CE, set forth, in the thirty-seven *parashiyyot* or chapters into which their document is divided, thirty-seven well-crafted propositions. They made no pretense at a systematic exegesis of sequences of verses of Scripture. Each of the thirty-seven chapters proves cogent, and all of them spell out their respective statements in an intellectually economical, if rich, manner. Each *parashah* makes its own point, but all of them form a single statement.

The message of *Leviticus Rabbah*—congruent with that of *Genesis Rabbah*—is that the laws of history may be known, and that these laws, so far as Israel is concerned, focus upon the holy life of the community. If Israel then obeys the laws of society aimed at Israel's sanctification, then the foreordained history, resting on the merit of the ancestors, will unfold as Israel hopes. So there is no secret to the meaning of the events of the day, and Israel, for its part, can affect its destiny and effect salvation. The authorship of *Leviticus Rabbah* has thus joined the two great motifs of sanctification and salvation by reading a biblical book, Leviticus, that is devoted to the former in the light of the requirements of the latter. In this way they made their fundamental point, which is that salvation at the end of history depends upon sanctification in the here and now.

To prove these points, the authors of the compositions make lists of facts that bear the same traits and show the working of the rules of history. It follows that the mode of thought brought to bear upon the theme of history remains exactly the same as in the Mishnah: list-making, with data exhibiting similar taxonomic traits drawn together into lists based on common monothetic traits or definitions. These lists, then, through the power of repetition make a single enormous point or prove a social law of history. The catalogues of exemplary heroes and historical events serve a further purpose. They provide a model of how contemporary events are to be absorbed into the biblical paradigm. Since biblical events exemplify recurrent happenings—sin and redemption, forgiveness and atonement—they lose their one-time character. At the same time and in the same way, current events find a place within the ancient, but eternally present, paradigmatic scheme. So no new historical events, other than exemplary episodes in lives of heroes, demand narration because, through what is said about the past, what was happening in the times of the framers of *Leviticus Rabbah* would also come under consideration.

A single example of the list-making syllogism is supplied by the proof of the proposition that God favors the pursued over the pursuer:

LEVITICUS RABBAH XXVII:V
1. A. "God seeks what has been driven away" (Qoh. 3:15).
    B. R. Huna in the name of R. Joseph said, "It is always the case that 'God seeks what has been driven away' [favoring the victim].
    C. "You find when a righteous man pursues a righteous man, 'God seeks what has been driven away.'
    D. "When a wicked man pursues a wicked man, 'God seeks what has been driven away.'

E. "All the more so when a wicked man pursues a righteous man, 'God seeks what has been driven away.'

F. "[The same principle applies] even when you come around to a case in which a righteous man pursues a wicked man, 'God seeks what has been driven away.'"

2. A. R. Yosé b. R. Yudan in the name of R. Yosé b. R. Nehorai says, "It is always the case that the Holy One, blessed be he, demands an accounting for the blood of those who have been pursued from the hand of the pursuer.

B. "Abel was pursued by Cain, and God sought [an accounting for] the pursued: 'And the Lord looked [favorably] upon Abel and his meal offering' [Gen. 4:4].

C. "Noah was pursued by his generation, and God sought [an accounting for] the pursued: 'You and all your household shall come into the ark' [Gen. 7:1]. And it says, 'For this is like the days of Noah to me, as I swore [that the waters of Noah should no more go over the earth]' [Is. 54:9].

D. "Abraham was pursued by Nimrod, 'and God seeks what has been driven away': 'You are the Lord, the God who chose Abram and brought him out of Ur' [Neh. 9:7].

E. "Isaac was pursued by Ishmael, 'and God seeks what has been driven away': 'For through Isaac will seed be called for you' [Gen. 21:12].

F. "Jacob was pursued by Esau, 'and God seeks what has been driven away': 'For the Lord has chosen Jacob, Israel for his prized possession' [Ps. 135:4].

G. "Moses was pursued by Pharaoh, 'and God seeks what has been driven away': 'Had not Moses His chosen stood in the breach before Him' [Ps. 106:23].

H. "David was pursued by Saul, 'and God seeks what has been driven away': 'And he chose David, his servant' [Ps. 78:70].

I. "Israel was pursued by the nations, 'and God seeks what has been driven away': 'And you has the Lord chosen to be a people to him' [Deut. 14:2].

J. "And the rule applies also to the matter of offerings. A bull is pursued by a lion, a sheep is pursued by a wolf, a goat is pursued by a leopard.

K. "Therefore the Holy One, blessed be he, has said, 'Do not make offerings before me from those animals that pursue, but from those that are pursued': 'When a bull, a sheep, or a goat is born'" (Lev. 22:27).

This mode of dealing with biblical history and contemporary events produces two reciprocal effects. The first is the mythicization of biblical stories, their removal from the framework of ongoing, unique patterns of history and sequences of events and their transformation into accounts of things that happen all the time. The second is that contemporary events too lose all of their specificity and enter the paradigmatic framework of established mythic existence. So (1) the Scripture's myth happens every day, and (2) every day produces reenactment of the Scripture's myth.

The focus of *Leviticus Rabbah*'s laws of history is upon the society of Israel, its national fate and moral condition. Indeed, nearly all of the *parashiyyot* of *Leviticus Rabbah* turn out to deal with the national, social condition of Israel, and this in three contexts: (1) Israel's setting in the history of the nations, (2) the sanctified character of the inner life of Israel itself, and (3) the future, salvific history of Israel. So the biblical book that deals with the tabernacle in the wilderness, which sages understood to form the model for the holy Temple later built in Jerusalem, now is shown to address the holy people. That is no paradox, but rather a logical next step in the exploration of sanctification. Leviticus really discusses not the consecration of the cult but the sanctification of the nation—its conformity to God's will laid forth in the Torah and to God's rules. *Leviticus Rabbah* executes the paradox of shifting categories, applying to the nation—not a locative category—and its history the category that in the book subject to commentary pertained to the holy place—a locative category—and its eternal condition. The nation now is like the cult then, the ordinary Israelite now like the priest then. The holy way of life lived now, through acts to which merit accrues, corresponds to the holy rites then. The process of metamorphosis is full, rich, complete. When everything stands for something else, the something else repeatedly turns out to be the nation. This is what our document spells out in exquisite detail, yet never missing the main point.

The message of *Leviticus Rabbah* paradoxically attaches itself to the book of Leviticus, as though that book had come from prophecy and addressed the issue of salvation. But it came from the priesthood and spoke of sanctification. The paradoxical syllogism—the *as-if* reading, the opposite of how things seem—of the composers of *Leviticus Rabbah* therefore reaches simple formulation. In the very setting of sanctification the authors find the promise of salvation. In the topics of the cult and the priesthood they uncover the national and social issues of the moral life and redemptive hope of Israel. The repeated comparison and contrast of priesthood and prophecy, sanctification and salvation, turn out to produce a complement, which comes to most perfect union in the text at hand.

What we have in *Leviticus Rabbah* is the result of the mode of thought not of prophets or historians, but of philosophers and scientists. The framers propose not to lay down, but to discover, rules governing Israel's life. As we find the rules of nature by identifying and classifying facts of natural life, so we find rules of society by identifying and classifying the facts of Israel's social life. In both modes of inquiry we make sense of things by bringing together like specimens and finding out whether they form a species, then bringing together like species and finding out whether they form a genus—in all, classifying data and identifying the rules that make possible the classification. That sort of thinking lies at the deepest level of list-making, which is the work of offering a proposition and facts (for social rules) as much as a genus and its species (for rules of nature). Once discovered, the social rules of Israel's national life yield explicit statements, such as that God hates the arrogant and loves the humble. The logical status of these statements, in context, is as secure and unassailable as the logical status of statements about physics, ethics, or politics, as these emerge in philosophical thought. What differentiates the statements is not their logical status—as sound, scientific philosophy—but only their subject matter, on the one hand, and distinctive rhetoric, on the other.

From Commentary to Propositional Statements

The framers of *Leviticus Rabbah* treat topics, not particular verses. They make generalizations that are freestanding. They express cogent propositions through extended compositions, not episodic ideas. Earlier in *Genesis Rabbah*, things people wished to say were attached to predefined statements based on an existing text, constructed in accord with an organizing logic independent of the systematic expression of a single, well-framed idea. That is to say, the sequence of verses of Genesis and their contents played a massive role in the larger-scale organization of *Genesis Rabbah* and the expression of its propositions. Now the authors of *Leviticus Rabbah* so collected and arranged their materials that an abstract proposition emerges. That proposition is not expressed only or mainly through episodic restatements assigned to an order established by a base text (whether Genesis or Leviticus, or a Mishnah tractate, for that matter). Rather, it emerges through a logic of its own.

What is new is the move from an essentially exegetical mode of logical discourse to a fundamentally philosophical one. It is the shift from discourse framed around an established (hence old) text to syllogistic argument organized around a proposed (hence new) theorem or proposition. What changes, therefore, is the way in which cogent thought takes place, as people moved from discourse contingent on some prior principle of organization to discourse autonomous of a ready-made program inherited from an earlier paradigm. When they read the rules of sanctification of the priesthood, the sages responsible for *Leviticus Rabbah* heard the message of the salvation of all Israel. Leviticus became the story of how Israel, purified from social sin and sanctified, would be saved.

The authors of *Leviticus Rabbah* express their ideas, first, by selecting materials already written for other purposes and using them for their own, second, by composing materials, and third, by arranging both in *parashiyyot* into an order through which propositions may reach expression. This involves both the modes of thought and the topical program, and also the unifying proposition of the document as a whole. To summarize:

(1) The principal mode of thought required one thing to be read in terms of another, one verse in light of a different verse (or topic, theme, symbol, idea), one situation in light of another.
(2) The principal subject of thought is the moral condition of Israel, on the one hand, and the salvation of Israel, on the other.
(3) The single unifying proposition—the syllogism at the document's deepest structure—is that Israel's salvation depends upon its moral condition.

It follows that *Leviticus Rabbah* constitutes not merely diverse thoughts but a single, sustained composition. The authors make their statement through a rich tapestry of unstated propositions that are only illustrated, delineated at the outset, by the statement of some propositions. And these also are illustrated. It is, in a word, a syllogism by example—that is, by repeated appeal to facts—rather than by argument alone. For in context, an example constitutes a fact. The source of many examples or facts is Scripture, the foundation of all reality. Accordingly, in the context of Israelite life and culture, in which Scripture recorded facts, we have a severely logical, because entirely factual, statement of how rightly organized and classified facts sustain a proposition. In context that proposition is presented as rigorously and critically as the social rules of discourse allowed.

The authors of the document's compositions and composites transformed scriptural history from a sequence of one-time events, leading from one place to some other, into an ever-present mythic world. No longer does Scripture speak of only one Moses, one David, one set of happenings of a distinctive and never-to-be-repeated character. Now whatever happens of which the thinkers propose to take account must enter and be absorbed into that established and ubiquitous pattern and structure founded in Scripture. It is not that biblical history repeats itself. Rather, biblical history no longer constitutes history at all—that is, history as a linear, purposeful, continuous story of things that happened once, long ago, and pointed to some one moment in the future. It becomes an account of things that happen every day—hence, an ever-present mythic world. In this way the basic trait of history in the salvific framework, its one-timeness and linearity, is reworked into the generative quality of sanctification, its routine and everyday, ongoing reality. When history enters a paradigm, it forms an exercise within philosophy, the search for the rules and regularities of the world. That is the profound achievement of the document before us.

And that is why, in *Leviticus Rabbah*, Scripture—the book of Leviticus—as a whole does not dictate the order of discourse, let alone its character. In this document the authorship chose in Leviticus itself an isolated verse here, an odd phrase there. These then presented the pretext for propositional discourse commonly quite out of phase with the cited passage. The verses that are quoted ordinarily shift from the meanings they convey to the implications they contain, as they are shown to speak about something, anything, other than what they seem to be saying. So the *as-if* frame of mind brought to Scripture precipitates the renewal of Scripture, requiring one to see everything with fresh eyes. And the result of the new vision was a reimagining of the social world envisioned by the document at hand—I mean the everyday world of Israel in its Land in that same difficult time at which *Genesis Rabbah* was taking shape, sometime in the fifth century CE and the first century after the conversion of Constantine and the beginning of the Christian chapter of Western civilization. For what the sages now proposed was a reconstruction of existence along the lines of the ancient design of Scripture as they read it. What that meant was that, instead of a sequence of one-time and linear events, everything that happened was turned into a repetition of known and already experienced paradigms, hence, once more, a mythic being. The source and core of the myth derive from Scripture—Scripture reread, renewed, and reconstructed along with the society that revered Scripture.

While *Leviticus Rabbah* focuses the discourse of each of its thirty-seven *parashiyyot* on a verse of the book of Leviticus, these verses in no way are sequential, for example, Lev. 1:1, then Lev. 1:2, in the way in which the structure of *Genesis Rabbah* dictates exegesis of the verses of the book of Genesis, read in sequence. *Leviticus Rabbah*'s chapters work out theses on a sequence of themes, for example, the evils of gossip or of drink, the unique character of Moses, and the like. But the respective themes cover a variety of propositions, and a *parashah* ordinarily displays and demonstrates more than a single cogent syllogism.

The single most striking recurrent literary structure of *Leviticus Rabbah* is the base verse/intersecting verse construction, already familiar from *Genesis Rabbah*, and to be repeated in *Pesiqta deRab Kahana*. In such a construction, a base verse drawn from the book of Leviticus is juxtaposed with an intersecting verse drawn from any book other than a Pentateuchal one. Then this intersecting verse is subjected to systematic exegesis. On the surface the exegesis is out of all relationship with the base verse. But in a stunning climax, all of the exegeses of the intersecting verse are shown to relate to the main point the exegete wishes to make about the base verse. What that means is that the composition as a whole is so conceived as to impose meaning and order on all of the parts, original or ready-made, of which the author of the whole has made use.

Another classification of rhetorical pattern, familiar from *Sifra* and *Sifré* to Numbers as well as from *Genesis Rabbah*, derives from the clause-by-clause type of exegesis of the base verse, with slight interest in intersecting verses or in illustrative materials deriving from other books of

Scripture. The base verse in this classification defines the entire frame of discourse, either because of its word choices or because of its main point. Where verses of other passages are quoted, they serve not as the focus of discourse but only as proof texts or illustrative texts. They therefore function in a different way from the verses adduced in discourse in the first two classifications, for in those former cases the intersecting verses form the center of interest. The categories of units of discourse also explain the order of arrangement of types of units of discourse. First will come the base verse/intersecting verse construction; then will come intersecting verse/base verse construction; finally we shall have clause-by-clause exegetical constructions.

In the base verse/intersecting verse exegesis characteristic of *Leviticus Rabbah*, exegetes read one thing in terms of something else. To begin with, they read the base verse in terms of the intersecting verse. They also read the intersecting verse in other terms as well, in a multiple layered construction of analogy and parable. The intersecting verse's elements always turn out to stand for, to signify, to speak of, something other than that to which they openly refer. If water stands for Torah, or the skin disease for evil speech, and one thing refers to some other thing entirely, then the mode of thought at hand is simply explained. One thing symbolizes another, speaks not of itself but of some other thing entirely. It is as if a common object or symbol really represented an uncommon one. Nothing says what it means. All statements carry deeper meaning, which inheres in other statements altogether. The profound sense, then, of the base verse emerges only through restatement within and through the intersecting verse—as if the base verse spoke of things that, on the surface, we do not see at all. Accordingly, if we ask the single prevalent literary construction to testify to the prevailing frame of mind, its message is that things are never what they seem.

The recurrent message of the document may be stated in brief way. God loves Israel and so gave them the Torah, which defines their life and governs their welfare. Israel is alone in its category (*sui generis*), so what is a virtue to Israel is a vice to the nations; what is life-giving to Israel is poison to the Gentiles. True, Israel sins, but God forgives that sin, having punished the nation on account of it. Such a process has yet to come to an end, but it will culminate in Israel's complete regeneration. Meanwhile, Israel's assurance of God's love lies in the many expressions of special concern for even the humblest and most ordinary aspects of the national life: the food the nation eats, the sexual practices by which it procreates. These life-sustaining, life-transmitting activities draw God's special interest as a mark of his general love for Israel. Israel, then, is supposed to adjust its life in conformity with the marks of God's love.

These indications moreover signify also the character of Israel's difficulty, namely, subordination to the nations in general, but to the fourth kingdom, Rome, in particular. Both food laws and skin diseases stand for the nations. There is yet another category of sin, also collective and generative of collective punishment, and that is social. The moral character of Israel's life, the treatment of people by one another, the practice of gossip and small-scale thuggery—these too draw down divine penalty. The nation's fate therefore corresponds to its moral condition. The moral condition, however, emerges not only from the current generation. Israel's richest hope lies in the merit of the ancestors, and thus in the scriptural record of the merits attained by the founders of the nation, those who originally brought it into being and gave it life.

The world to come will right all presently unbalanced relationships. What is good will go forward, what is bad will come to an end. The simple message is that the things people revere, the cult and its majestic course through the year, will go on; Jerusalem and the Temple will come back in all their glory. Israel will be saved through the merit of the ancestors, atonement, study of Torah, and practice of religious duties. The prevalence of the eschatological dimension in the formal structures, with its messianic and other expressions, here finds its counterpart in the repetition of the same few symbols in the expression of doctrine.

The theme of the moral life of Israel produces propositions concerning not only the individual but, more important, the social virtues that the community as a whole must exhibit. First of all, the message to the individual constitutes a revision, for this context, of the address to the nation: humility as against arrogance, obedience as against sin, constant concern not to follow one's natural inclination to do evil or to overcome the natural limitations of the human condition. Israel must accept its fate, and obey and rely on the merits accrued through the ages and God's special love. The individual must conform, in ordinary affairs, to this same paradigm of patience and submission. Great men and women, that is, individual heroes within the established paradigm, conform to that same pattern, exemplifying the national virtues. Among these, Moses stands out; he has no equal. The special position of the humble Moses is complemented by the patriarchs and by David, all of whom knew how to please God and left as an inheritance to Israel the merit they had thereby attained.

If we now ask about further recurring themes or topics, there is one so commonplace that we should have to list the majority of paragraphs of discourse in order to provide a complete list. It is the list of events in Israel's history, meaning, in this context, Israel's history solely in scriptural times, down through the return to Zion. The one-time events of the generation of the flood, Sodom and Gomorrah, the patriarchs and the sojourn in Egypt, the exodus, the revelation of the Torah at Sinai, the golden calf, the Davidic monarchy and the building of the Temple, Sennacherib, Hezekiah, and the destruction of northern Israel, Nebuchadnezzar and the destruction of the Temple in 586 BCE, the life of Israel in Babylonian captivity, Daniel and his associates, Mordecai and Haman—these events occur over and over again. They turn out to serve as paradigms of sin and atonement, steadfastness and divine intervention, and equivalent lessons.

We find, in fact, a fairly standard repertoire of scriptural heroes or villains, on the one hand, and conventional lists of Israel's enemies and their actions and downfall, on the other. The boastful, for instance, include the generation of the flood, Sodom and Gomorrah, Pharaoh, Sisera, Sennacherib, Nebuchadnezzar, and the wicked empire (Rome)—all contrasted to Israel, "despised and humble in this world." The four kingdoms recur again and again, always ending with Rome, with the repeated message that after Rome will come Israel. But Israel has to make this happen through its faith and submission to God's will. Lists of enemies run through the names of Cain, the Sodomites, Pharaoh, Sennacherib, Nebuchadnezzar, Haman.

At the center of the pretense—that is, the *as-if* mentality of *Leviticus Rabbah* and its framers—we find a simple proposition: Israel receives God's special love. Israel's present condition of subordination derives from its own deeds. It follows that God cares, so Israel may look forward to redemption on God's part in response to Israel's own regeneration through repentance. When the exegetes proceeded to open the scroll of Leviticus, they found numerous occasions to state that proposition in concrete terms and specific contexts. The sinner brings on his own sickness. But God heals through that very ailment. The nations of the world govern in succession, but Israel's lack of faith guaranteed their rule and Israel's moment of renewal will end Gentile rule. Israel's leaders— priests, prophets, kings—fall into an entirely different category from those of the nations, as does Israel. In these and other concrete allegations, the same message comes forth. Israel's sorry condition in no way testifies to Israel's true worth—this is the grandest pretense of all. All of the little evasions of the primary sense in favor of some other sense testify to this: the great denial that what is, is what counts. *Leviticus Rabbah* makes that statement with art and imagination. But it is never subtle about saying so.

Salvation and sanctification join together in *Leviticus Rabbah*. The laws of the book of Leviticus, focused as they are on the sanctification of the nation through its cult, in *Leviticus Rabbah* indicate the rules of salvation as well. The message of *Leviticus Rabbah* attaches itself to the book of Leviticus as though that book was prophetic in nature and addressed the issue of the meaning of history and Israel's salvation. But the book of Leviticus came from the priesthood and spoke of sanctification. The paradoxical syllogism—the *as-if* reading, the opposite of how things seem—of the composers of *Leviticus Rabbah* therefore reaches simple formulation. In the very setting of sanctification we find the promise of salvation. In the topics of the cult and the priesthood we uncover the national and social issues of the moral life and redemptive hope of Israel.

The Rabbinic Reading of the Lectionary Cycle: *Pesiqta deRab Kahana*

Carrying forward the approach of *Leviticus Rabbah*, *Pesiqta deRab Kahana*[6] sets forth a compilation of twenty-eight propositional discourses. It[7] is innovative because it appeals for its themes and lections to the liturgical calendar rather than to a Pentateuchal book.[8] *Pesiqta deRab Kahana* abandons the pretense that fixed associative connections derive solely from Scripture. Rather, the document follows the synagogal lections. The text that governs the organization of *Pesiqta deRab Kahana* comprises a liturgical occasion of the synagogue, which is identical to a holy day, and has told our authorship what topic it wishes to take up—and therefore also what verses of Scripture (if any) prove suitable to that topic and its exposition.

Adar-Nisan-Sivan [spring]
> Passover-Pentecost: *Pisqaot* 2-12
> [possible exception: *Pisqa* 6]

Tammuz-Ab-Elul [summer]
> The Ninth of Ab: *Pisqaot* 13-22

Tishré [autumn]
> Tishré 1-22: *Pisqaot* 23-28

The twenty-eight *parashiyyot* of *Pesiqta deRab Kahana* follow the synagogal lections from early spring through fall—in the Western calendar, from late February or early March through late September or early October, approximately half of the solar year, twenty-seven weeks, and somewhat more than half of the lunar year. On the surface, the basic building block is the theme of a given lectionary Sabbath—that is, a Sabbath distinguished by a particular lection—and not the theme dictated by a given passage of Scripture, let alone the exposition of the language or proposition of such a scriptural verse. The topical program of the document may be defined very simply: expositions of themes dictated by special Sabbaths or festivals and their lections.

PISQA	BASE VERSE	TOPIC OR OCCASION
1. *On the day Moses completed* (Num. 7:1)		Torah lection for the Sabbath of Hanukkah
2. *When you take the census* (Ex. 30:12)		Torah lection for the Sabbath of Sheqalim; first of the four Sabbaths prior to the advent of Nisan, in which Passover falls
3. *Remember Amalek* (Deut. 25:17-19)		Torah lection for the Sabbath of Zakhor; second of the four Sabbaths prior to the advent of Nisan, in which Passover falls
4. *Red heifer* (Num. 19:1ff.)		Torah lection for the Sabbath of Parah; third of the four Sabbaths prior to the advent of Nisan, in which Passover falls
5. *This month* (Ex. 12:1-2)		Torah lection for the Sabbath of Hahodesh; fourth of the four Sabbaths prior to the advent of of Nisan, in which Passover falls
6. *My offerings* (Num. 28:1-4)		Torah lection for the New Moon which falls on a weekday
7. *It came to pass at midnight* (Ex. 12:29-32)		Torah lection for the first day of Passover
8. *The first sheaf* (Lev. 23:11)		Torah lection for the second day of Passover on which the first sheaves of barley were harvested and waved as an offering
9. *When a bull or sheep or goat is born* (Lev. 22:26)		Lection for Passover
10. *You shall set aside a tithe* (Deut. 14:22)		Torah lection for Sabbath during Passover in the Land of Israel or for the eighth day of Passover outside of the Land of Israel
11. *When Pharaoh let the people go* (Ex. 13:17-18)		Torah lection for the Seventh Day of Passover
12. *In the third month* (Ex. 19:1ff.)		Torah lection for Pentecost
13. *The words of Jeremiah* (Jer. 1:1-3)		Prophetic lection for the first of three Sabbaths prior to the Ninth of Ab
14. *Hear* (Jer. 2:4-6)		Prophetic lection for the second of three Sabbaths prior to the Ninth of Ab
15. *How lonely sits the city* (Lam. 1:1-2)		Prophetic lection for the third of three Sabbaths prior to the Ninth of Ab

16. *Comfort* (Is. 40:1-2)	Prophetic lection for the first Sabbath following the Ninth of Ab
17. *But Zion said* (Is. 49:14-16)	Prophetic lection for the second Sabbath following the Ninth of Ab
18. *O afflicted one, storm tossed* (Is. 54:11-14)	Prophetic lection for the third Sabbath following the Ninth of Ab
19. *I even I am he who comforts you* (Is. 51:12-15)	Prophetic lection for the fourth Sabbath following the Ninth of Ab
20. *Sing aloud, O barren woman* (Is. 54:1ff.)	Prophetic lection for the fifth Sabbath following the Ninth of Ab
21. *Arise, Shine* (Is. 60:1-3)	Prophetic lection for the sixth Sabbath following the Ninth of Ab
22. *I will greatly rejoice in the Lord* (Is. 61:10-11)	Prophetic lection for the seventh Sabbath following the Ninth of Ab
23. *The New Year*	No base verse indicated. The theme is God's justice and judgment.
24. *Return O Israel to the Lord your God* (Hos. 24:1-3)	Prophetic lection for the Sabbath of Repentance between New Year and Day of Atonement
25. *Selihot*	No base verse indicated. The theme is God's forgiveness.
26. *After the death of the two sons of Aaron* (Lev. 16:1ff.)	Torah lection for the Day of Atonement
27. *And you shall take on the first day* (Lev. 23:39-43)	Torah lection for the first day of the Festival of Tabernacles
28. *On the eighth day* (Num. 29:35-39)	Torah lection for the Eighth Day of Day of Solemn Assembly

This structure clearly wishes to follow the line of holy days. It follows that, unlike *Genesis Rabbah* and *Leviticus Rabbah*, the document focuses upon the life of the synagogue. Its framers set forth propositions in the manner of the authorship of *Leviticus Rabbah*. But these are framed by appeal not only to the rules governing the holy society, as in *Leviticus Rabbah*, but also to the principal events of Israel's history, celebrated in the worship of the synagogue. What we do not find in this Midrash compilation is exposition of Pentateuchal or prophetic passages, verse by verse; the basis chosen by our authorship for organizing and setting forth its propositions is the character and theme of holy days and their special synagogue Torah lections. That is, all of the selected base verses upon which the *parashiyyot* or chapters are built, Pentateuchal or prophetic, are identified with synagogal lections for specified holy days, special Sabbaths or festivals.

Following the model of *Leviticus Rabbah*, *Pesiqta deRab Kahana* consists of twenty-eight syllogisms, each presented in a cogent and systematic way by the twenty-eight *pisqaot*. Each *pisqa* contains an implicit proposition, and that proposition may be stated in a simple way. It emerges from the intersection of an external verse with the base verse that recurs through the *pisqa*, and then is restated by the systematic dissection of the components of the base verse, each of which is shown to say the same thing as all the others.

A *pisqa* in *Pesiqta deRab Kahana* systematically presents a single syllogism, which is expressed through the contrast of an external verse with the base verse—hence, the base verse/intersecting verse form. In this form the implicit syllogism is stated through the intervention of an contrastive verse into the basic proposition established by the base verse. The second type of material proceeds to the systematic exegesis of the components of the base verse on their own, hence through the exegetical form. There is a third form, a syllogistic list, familiar from the Mishnah and prior Midrash compilations as well. The first two forms occur in the same sequence, because the former of the two serves to declare the implicit syllogism, and the latter to locate that implicit syllogism in the base verse itself. The third will then be tacked on at the end. Otherwise it would disrupt the exposition of the implicit syllogism. All of these forms are familiar and require no further explanation.

Theology of *Pesiqta deRab Kahana*

Consider the unfolding message imposed by *Pesiqta deRab Kahana* upon the lectionary cycle and essentially distinct from it. From Hanukkah through Pentecost, Israel in nature's time celebrates its meeting with God in the Temple. Then follow the days of desiccation and death, three weeks of mourning, when Israel's rebellion against God brings about God's abandonment of the Temple. With Israel's rebellion fully requited in the disaster, there succeed the seven Sabbaths of consolation for the penitent, corporate Israel. Then, correspondingly, come the Days of Awe, the individual Israelite's time to recapitulate in his or her own being the main lines of corporate Israel's story of sin, punishment, suffering, atonement, and the rest. The Days of Awe, the New Year and the Day of Atonement, marked by repentance for sin, atonement, and prayer for forgiveness, then correspond to the days from the seventeenth of Tammuz to the ninth of Ab and the weeks following. At the end follows the climactic moment, the Festival par excellence, Tabernacles, with the promise of renewal.

That program, laid out in the lectionary cycle superimposed on the Pentateuchal one, presents the main points of Rabbinic theology in its doctrine that builds on the correspondence of Adam and Israel, Eden and the Land. And this rabbinization of the liturgical experience does not match the way in which the Pentateuchal lections, whether annual or triennial, organize the sacred calendar of synagogue worship. A curious disjuncture imposes itself on the two distinct sequences, (1) the narrative-historical sequence of the Pentateuch, and (2) the pattern of the lunar cycle.

The Pentateuchal lectionary cycle recapitulates the narrative sequence from Adam to the border of the promised land. By extension through Joshua, Judges, Samuel, and Kings, the narrative (if not the lectionary) cycle ends where it began: loss of Eden, loss of Jerusalem. In contrast, the lectionary program of *Pesiqta deRab Kahana* hardly works through the same narrative in the same sequence at all. There is no beginning, middle, and end, constructed in a teleological sequence out of the narrative history of Israel. The events of the natural year, signified in the movement of the lunar months correlated with the solar seasons, and built around the first full moon after the vernal and autumnal equinoxes in particular, do match certain moments in Israel's life. But these are not in the temporal order so paramount in the lectionary narrative from Genesis through Numbers plus Deuteronomy. They follow their own order and sequence. The occasions of nature matched by moments in Israel's pattern of conduct and its consequence thus are removed from the narrative framework, for example, of Genesis through Kings. Events are no longer unique, linear, sequential—in other words, teleological. They now are formed into moments of an exemplary character, out of time altogether, out of phase with the Pentateuchal narrative setting. Thought is no longer teleological but rather paradigmatic.

No wonder, then, that *Pesiqta deRab Kahana* starts where it does, with the rededication of the Temple signified by Hanukkah. In the repertoire of events gathered in the document, that is the only logical starting point; the alternative, the end point, is impossible. That is then followed by the leap to the four Sabbaths preparatory to Passover, with the rest in sequence! With the preparations for the celebration of Israel's beginning in the Exodus and at Sinai marking the starting point, the rest of the natural year lays itself out against the main lines of the liturgical year. There is then this cycle:

(1) the preparation of the Temple, its dedication, and purification;

(2) the beginnings at Passover-Pentecost;

(3) the catastrophe of Tammuz-Ab, the season of death, then the consolation quick to follow; and at the end,

(4) the recapitulation of the same cycle in Elul and Tishré—sin, punishment, atonement, consolation, and renewal, as the life cycle of nature and the rhythm of Israelite existence each correspond to and signify the reliability and renewal of the other.

Two Cycles of Time Joined

In their present sequence and only in that sequence, the purposeful ordering of the document's theological propositions emerge. And these represent a decision by the authorship of the document. They bring into relationship two cycles of time: historical-narrative and natural-paradigmatic.

The historical-narrative cycle built on teleology recapitulates the cycle of synagogue lections of the Pentateuch, the one that sets into sequence the events of humanity's history from creation, through the fall, past the flood, to the formation of Israel as a family and its reformation as a kingdom of priests and a holy people. It is the story of Israel's recapitulation of Adam's experience with its calamity but, in the case of Israel when repentant, also has the promise of a different ending.

The natural-paradigmatic cycle, highlighted among the Rabbinic Midrash compilations only here, is the cycle of the seasons, as these flow in sequence from the dedication of the Temple through its rites on distinguished occasions defined by the movement of heavenly bodies, the moon correlated with the solar seasons. This is nature's logic, heaven's logic—a different mode of organizing time altogether, one in which the paradigm of Israel's existence is recast. Israel's history is transformed from a linear sequence of one-time historical events into a pattern of recurrent moments in nature. These heavenly occasions capture points of intersection between Israel and God corresponding to the unfolding of the seasons—and thus may be described as "natural-paradigmatic."

The details of each cycle correspond. And why not? For both cycles focus upon the same entity, Israel in relationship to God. But the established lectionary cycle from Genesis through Deuteronomy tells a story, and the supererogatory lectionary cycle of particular Sabbaths and special occasions celebrates events in the heavens and their corresponding moments in Israel's eternal existence. The narrative-teleological cycle conveys its messages through the story that it tells. In the natural-paradigmatic cycle these messages are abstracted from that story and set forth as propositions of a general character.

The upshot may be simply stated. In bypassing the Pentateuchal cycle altogether, the authorship of *Pesiqta deRab Kahana* has adopted an intellectual structure of its own. It is one that is different from the unfolding of Israel's life in time through a sequence of one-time, particular events: for example, the day this happened, the time that remarkable, unique event took place. Sequence is everything, story nothing. The sequence invokes that logic to which I have already made reference: the logic of Israel's moral, covenanted existence, its life with God.

Pesiqta deRab Kahana builds upon its own cosmic sense of world order.

It makes its own judgment on the meaning of the cyclical sequence of the movement of the heavenly bodies. It defines in its own way the encounter of Israel and God, in earth and in heaven, always in correspondence. This is, then, a different way of framing Israel's and God's relationship from the established one that begins with Genesis and concludes with Deuteronomy, the familiar comparison of Adam and Israel, Eden and the Land.

The Theology of Astral Israel and the Reading of Scripture in *Pesiqta deRab Kahana*

The theology of astral Israel bears consequences for the reading of Scripture. Now the times and the seasons embody heaven's account of Israel on earth. Scripture is not the only voice of God; nature's time and sequence speak for him as well. And, it follows, if Scripture is no longer the sole supernatural medium, then Israel in time no longer follows a simple, linear sequence: this happened, then that; Israel did this, with that result. Rather we have a perspective on matters formed from heaven's view: this season corresponds to Israel's conduct in that circumstance, this event in the heavens correlates with that activity of Israel on earth.

The account bears a cyclicality that the Pentateuchal narrative does not possess. Thus the document viewed as a whole imposes upon the cycle of narrative—the story of Israel in time—that other cycle, the cycle of nature. One may characterize the resulting cycle as a competing, or at least as a correlative, mode of recapitulating Israel's record from its beginnings until now. Annually Israel dedicates the Temple, prepares it for the pilgrims, celebrates the advent of freedom, and receives the Torah. Annually Israel rebels against the Torah and sins, and is punished through the loss of the Temple. Annually Israel atones and repents, and God consoles and forgives. And annually Israelites recapitulate that same cycle of sin and atonement, consolation and forgiveness, so that year by year, the rains follow the festival Tabernacles in a renewal of nature's—and Israel's—cycle.

What has happened to the scriptural story, which is linear, sequential, and historical, not cyclical, episodic, and exemplary? *Pesiqta deRab Kahana* takes over and reshapes *the results* of Israel's continuous narrative from creation to destruction and the hope of restoration and incorporates the linear into the paradigmatic structure. The narrative tells of Adam's loss of Eden, then—with Genesis through Kings in hand—Israel's loss of the Land. The consequences to be drawn from that story—sin leads to punishment, but repentance leads to restoration and renewal—define the paradigm discerned in the very movement of the moon and the solar seasons by *Pesiqta deRab Kahana*. At issue, then, is how to break the cycle signified by the natural year. Israel has the power, at any time, in any year, to disrupt that cycle and inaugurate the end of history and nature as then known. So when I say that *Pesiqta deRab Kahana* has folded the results of Israel's narrative into a pattern yielded by the very givens of the natural world and its times and seasons, I refer to the recapitulation, in reference to the natural year, of the consequences to be drawn from the comparison of Israel and Adam, the Land and Eden, that the scriptural account, read continuously, has yielded.

Then the continuous, linear, one-directional narrative is folded into the cycle of nature's time, marked by seasons and events in heaven with their counterpart. That is the celebration of nature at the altar of the Temple through offerings that signify particular events in the unfolding of the natural year. These, further, are correlated with paradigmatic moments in Israel's year. So the story of the Temple on earth recapitulates in Israel's setting the story of the passage of the seasons. But that is with this proviso. The seasons follow the course that they do because they signal the unfolding existence of Israel, with special reference to its Temple altar, where God and Israel meet. Because Israel repeats its conduct, nature recapitulates its cycles. But there will come a new heaven and a new earth, when Israel completes the work badly begun by Adam.

The Rabbinic Reading of Lamentations:
Lamentations Rabbah

The book of Lamentations, attributed to Jeremiah in the aftermath of the destruction of the first Temple in 586 BCE, is read in light of the destruction of the second Temple in 70 CE and the failure of the war against Rome led by Bar Kokhba in 132–135 CE to reverse the results of the destruction of 70. At issue in the book of Lamentations and in its Rabbinic amplification is whether Israel has been abandoned and rejected by God.

The theme of *Lamentations Rabbati*[9] is Israel's relationship with God, and its message concerning that theme is that the stipulative covenant still and always governs that relationship.[10] Therefore everything that happens to Israel makes sense and bears meaning; and Israel is not helpless before its fate but controls its own destiny. This is the one message of our compilation, and it is the only message that is repeated throughout; everything else is secondary and derivative of the fundamental proposition that the destruction of the Temple in Jerusalem in 70 CE—as much as in 586 BCE—proves the enduring validity of the covenant, its rules and its promise of redemption.

Lamentations Rabbah's is a covenantal theology in which Israel and God have mutually and reciprocally agreed to bind themselves to a common Torah. The rules of the relationship are such that an infraction triggers its penalty; but obedience to the Torah likewise brings its reward—in the context envisaged by our compilers, the reward of redemption. The compilation sets forth a single message, which is reworked in only a few ways: Israel suffers because of sin, but God will respond to Israel's atonement, on the one hand, and loyalty to the covenant in the Torah, on the other. And when Israel has attained the merit that accrues through the Torah, God will redeem Israel. That is the simple, rock-hard, and repeated message of this rather protracted reading of the book of Lamentations. Still, *Lamentations Rabbah* proves nearly as much a commentary in the narrowest sense—verse-by-verse amplification, paraphrase, and exposition—as it is a compilation in the working definition of this inquiry.

What holds the document together and gives it, if not coherence, then at least flow and movement are the successive passages of (mere) exposition. All the more stunning, therefore, is the fact that, when all has been set forth and completed, its simple message is that God's unique relationship with Israel, which is unique among the nations, works itself out even now, in a time of despair and disappointment. Israel's resentment of its present condition, recapitulating the calamity of the destruction of the Temple, finds its resolution and remission in the redemption that will follow Israel's regeneration through the Torah—that is the program, that is the proposition, and in this compilation, there is no other.

A reprise of the propositions as they unfold shows the theological program and coherence of the document. Israel's relationship with God is treated with special reference to the covenant, the Torah, and the land. Because of the sins of the Israelites, they have gone into exile with the destruction of the Temple. The founders of the family, Abraham, Isaac, and Jacob, also went into exile. Now Israelites cannot be accused of lacking in religious duties, attention to teachings of the Torah and of prophecy, carrying out the requirements of righteousness (philanthropy) and good deeds, and the like. The people are at fault for their own condition (I:i.1-7). Torah study defines the condition of Israel, for example, "If you have seen [the inhabitants of] towns uprooted from their places in the land of Israel, know that it is because they did not pay the salary of scribes and teachers" (II:i).

So long as Judah and Benjamin—meaning, in this context, the surviving people, after the northern tribes were taken away by the Assyrians— were in the land, God could take comfort at the loss of the ten tribes; once they went into exile, God began to mourn (II:ii). Israel (now meaning not the northern tribes, but the remaining Jews) survived Pharaoh and Sennacherib, but not God's punishment (III:i). After the disaster in Jeremiah's time, Israel emerged from Eden—but could come back (IV:i). God did not play favorites among the tribes; when any of them sinned, he punished them through exile (VI:i). Israel was punished because of the ravaging of the words of Torah and prophecy, righteous men, religious duties, and good deeds (VII:i). The land of Israel, the Torah, and the Temple are ravaged, to the shame of Israel (Jer. 9:19-21) (VIII:i). If the Israelites practiced idolatry, still more did the pagans; God was neglected by the people, so God responded to the people's actions (X:i). If Israel had achieved merit (using the theological language at hand), then Israel would have enjoyed everything, but since the Israelites did not have the merit, they enjoyed nothing (XI:i).

The Israelites (throughout referring to the surviving Jews, after the northern tribes were taken into exile) did not trust God, so they suffered disaster ((XIII.i). The Israelites scorned God and brought dishonor upon God among the nations (XV:i). While God was generous with the Israelites in the wilderness, under severe conditions, he was harsh with them in civilization, under pleasant conditions, because they sinned and angered him (XVI:i). With merit one drinks good water in Jerusalem; without, bad water in the exile of Babylonia. With merit one sings songs and psalms in Jerusalem; without, dirges and lamentations in Babylonia. At stake is peoples' merit, not God's grace (XIX:i). The contrast is drawn between redemption and disaster, the giving of the Torah and the destruction of the Temple (XX:i). When the Israelites went into exile among the nations of the world, not one of them could produce a word of Torah from his mouth; God punished Israel for its sins (XXI:i). Idolatry was the cause (XXII:i). The destruction of the Temple was possible only because God had already abandoned it (XXIV:ii). When the Temple was destroyed, God was answerable to the patriarchs for what he had done (XXIV:ii). The Presence of God departed from the Temple by stages (XXV:i).

The Holy One punishes Israel only after bringing testimony against them (XXVII:i). The road that led from the salvation of Hezekiah is the one that brought Israel to the disaster brought about by Nebuchadnezzar. Then the Israelite kings believed, but the pagan king did not believe; and God gave the Israelite kings a reward for their faith, through Hezekiah, and to the pagan king, without his believing and without obeying, were handed over Jerusalem and its Temple (XXX:i). Before the Israelites went into exile, the Holy One, blessed be he, called them wicked. But when they had gone into exile, he began to sing their praises (XXXI:i). The Israelites were sent into exile only after they had defied the Unique One of the world, the Ten Commandments, circumcision, which had been given to the twentieth generation (Abraham), and the Pentateuch (XXXV:ii, iii). When the Temple was destroyed and Israel went into exile, God mourned in the manner that mortals do (XXXV:iv). The prophetic critique of Israel is mitigated by mercy. Israel stands in an ambiguous relationship with God, both divorced and not divorced (XXXV:vi, vii).

Before God penalizes, he has already prepared the healing for the penalty. As for all the harsh prophecies that Jeremiah issued against the Israelites, Isaiah first of all anticipated each and pronounced healing for it (XXXVI:ii). The Israelites err for weeping frivolously, "but in the end there will be a real weeping for good cause" (XXXVI:iv, v). The ten tribes went into exile, but the Presence of God did not go into exile. Judah and Benjamin went into exile, but the Presence of God did not go into exile. But when the children went into exile, then the Presence of God went into exile (XXXIX:iii). The great men of Israel turned their faces away when they saw people sinning, and God did the same to them (XL:ii). When the Israelites carry out the will of the Holy One, they add strength to the strength of heaven, and when they do not, they weaken the power of the One above (XL:ii). The exile and the redemption will match (XL:ii). In her affliction, Jerusalem remembered her rebellion against God (XLI:i).

When the Gentile nations sin, there is no sequel in punishment, but when the Israelites sin, they also are punished (XLII:i). God considered carefully how to bring the evil upon Israel (XLVIII:i). God suffers with Israel and for Israel (L:i), a minor theme in a massive compilation of stories. By observing their religious duties the Israelites became distinguished before God (LIII:i). With everything with which the Israelites sinned, they were smitten, and with that same thing they will be comforted. When they sinned with the head, they were smitten at the head, but they were comforted through the head (LVI:i). There is an exact match between Israel's triumph and Israel's downfall. Just as these the people of Jericho were punished through the destruction effected by priest and prophet (the priests and Joshua at Jericho), so the people of Jerusalem in the time of the Babylonian conquest were subject to priest and prophet (Jeremiah). Just as those who were punished were penalized through the ram's horn and shouting, so Israel will be saved through ram's horn and shouting (LVII:ii).

God's relationship to Israel was complicated by the relationship to Jacob, thus: "Isn't it the fact that the Israelites are angering me only because of the icon of Jacob that is engraved on my throne? Here, take it, it's thrown in your face!" (LVII:ii). God is engaged with Israel's disaster (LIX:ii). The Israelites did not fully explore the limits of the measure of justice, so the measure of justice did not go to extremes against them (LX:i; LXI:i). God's decree against Jerusalem comes from of old (LXIV:i). God forewarned Israel and showed Israel favor, but it did no good (LXIX:i). God did to Israel precisely what he had threatened long ago (LXXIII:i). But God does not rejoice in punishing Israel. The argument between God and Israel is framed in this way. The Community of Israel says that they are the only ones who accepted God; God says, I rejected everybody else for you (LXXIX:ii). Israel accepted its suffering as atonement and asked that the suffering expiate the sin (LXXV:i).

God suffers along with Israel, Israel's loyalty will be recognized and appreciated by God, and, in the meantime, the Israelites will find in the Torah the comfort that they require. The nations will be repaid for their actions toward Israel in the interval. Even though the Holy One, blessed be he, is angry with his servants, the righteous, in this world, in the world to come he has mercy on them (LXXXVI:i). God is good to those that deserve it (LXXXVII:i). God mourns for Israel the way human mourners mourn (LXXXVIII:i). God will never abandon Israel (LXXXIX:i). The Holy Spirit brings about redemption (XCV:i). It is better to be punished by God than favored by a Gentile king, thus: "Better was the removing of the ring by Pharaoh [for the sealing of decrees to oppress the Israelites] than the forty years during which Moses prophesied concerning them, because it was through this [oppression] that the redemption came about, while through that [prophesying] the redemption did not come about" (CXXII:i).

The upshot here is that persecution in the end is good for Israel because it produces repentance more rapidly than prophecy ever did, with the result that the redemption is that much nearer. The enemy will also be punished for its sins, and further, God's punishment is appropriate and well placed. People get what they deserve, both Israel and others. God should protect Israel and not leave them among the nations, but that is not what he has done (CXXIII:i). God blames each generation for its own fate, and the ancestors claim that the only reason the Israelites endure is because of the merit of the ancestors (CXXIX:i). The redemption of the past tells us about the redemption in the future (CXXX:i). "The earlier generations, because they smelled the stench of only part of the tribulations inflicted by the idolatrous kingdoms, became impatient. But we, who dwell in the midst of the four kingdoms, how much the more [are we impatient]!" (CXXXI:i).

God's redemption is certain, so people who are suffering should be glad, since that is a guarantee of coming redemption; thus: "For if those who outrage him he treats in such a way, those who do his will all the more so!" So if the words of the prophet Uriah are carried out, the words of the prophet Zechariah will be carried out, while if the words of the prophet Uriah prove false, then the words of the prophet Zechariah will not be true either. "I was laughing with pleasure because the words of Uriah have been carried out, and that means that the words of Zechariah in the future will be carried out" (CXL:i). The Temple will be restored, and Israel will regain its place as God's throne and consort. (CXLI:i). Punishment and rejection will be followed by forgiveness and reconciliation (CXLII:i). The Jews can accomplish part of the task on their own, even though they throw themselves wholly on God's mercy. The desired age is either like that of Adam, or like that of Moses and Solomon, or like that of Noah and Abel; all three possibilities link the coming redemption to a time of perfection, Eden, or to the age prior to idolatry, or to the time of Moses and Solomon, the builders of the Tabernacle and the Temple, respectively (CXLIII:i). If there is rejection, then there is no hope, but if there is anger, there is hope, because someone who is angry may in the end be appeased. Whenever there is an allusion to divine anger, that too is a mark of hope (CXLIV:i).

Israel's relationship with the nations is treated with interest in Israel's history, past, present, and future, and how that cyclical is to be known. But there is no theory of "the other" or the outsider here. The nations are the enemy; the compilers find nothing of merit to report about them. Israel's difference from the other, for which God is responsible, accounts for the dislike that the nations express toward Israel; Israel's present condition as minority, different and despised on account of the difference, is God's fault and choice. Israel was besieged not only by the Babylonians but also by the Ammonites and Moabites (IX:i), and God will punish them too. The public ridicule of Jews' religious rites contrasts with the Jews' own perception of their condition. The exposition of Ps. 69:13 in terms of Gentiles' ridicule of Jews' practices—the Jews' poverty, their Sabbath and Seventh Year observance—is followed by a re-exposition of the Jews' practices, now with respect to the ninth of Ab (XVII:i). Even though the nations of the world go into exile, their exile is not really an exile at all. But as for Israel, their exile really is an exile. The nations of the world, who eat the bread and drink the wine of others, do not really experience exile. But the Israelites, who do not eat the bread and drink the wine of others, really do experience exile (XXXVII:i).

The Ammonites and Moabites joined with the enemy and behaved very spitefully (XLIV:i). When the Israelites fled from the destruction of Jerusalem, the nations of the world sent word to every place to which they fled and shut them out (LV:i). But this was to be blamed on God: "If we had intermarried with them, they would have accepted us" (LXIX:i). There are ten references to the "might" of Israel; when the Israelites sinned, these forms of might were taken away from them and given to the nations of the world. The nations of the world ridicule the Jews for their religious observances (LXXXIII:i). These propositions simply expose, in their own framework, the same proposition as the ones concerning God's relationship to Israel and Israel's relationship to God. The relationship between Israel and the nations forms a subset of the relationship of Israel and God; nothing in the former relationship happens on its own, but all things express in this mundane context the rules and effects of the rules that govern in the transcendent one. All we learn about Israel and the nations is that the covenant endures, bearing its own inevitable sanctions and consequences.

Our authorship has little interest in Israel outside its relationship with either God or the nations. Israel on its own forms a subordinated and trivial theme; whatever messages we do find take on meaning only in the initial framework, that defined by Israel's relationship with God. Israel is never on its own. The bitterness of the ninth of Ab is contrasted with the bit-

101

ter herbs with which the first redemption is celebrated (XVIII:i). The same contrast is drawn between the giving of the Torah and the destruction of the Temple (XX:i). If Israel had found rest among the nations, she would not have returned to the holy land (XXXVII:ii). The glory of Israel lay in its relationship to God, in the sanhedrin, in the disciples of sages, in the priestly watches, in the children (XL:i). Israel first suffers, then rejoices; her unfortunate condition marks the fact that Israel stands at the center of things (LIX:iii). Israel has declined through the generations, thus: "In olden times, when people held the sanhedrin in awe, naughty words were never included in songs. But when the sanhedrin was abolished, naughty words were inserted in songs. In olden times, when troubles came upon Israel, they stopped rejoicing on that account. Now that both have come to an end [no more singing, no more banquet halls], 'The joy of our hearts has ceased; our dancing has been turned to mourning'" (CXXXVII:i). None of this presents surprises. The covenantal theology of Scripture is simply realized in the events of contemporary history. The Rabbinic reading of Scripture moves forward from Scripture, not backward from today to Scripture.

The Rabbinic Reading of Song of Songs:
Song of Songs Rabbah

The Song of Songs (in the Christian Bible, "the Song of Solomon," both titles referring to the opening line, "The Song of Songs, which is Solomon's") finds a place in the Torah because the collection of love songs in fact speaks about the relationship between God and Israel. The intent of the compilers of *Song of Songs Rabbah*[11] is to justify that reading.[12] What this means is that Midrash exegesis turns to everyday experience—the love of husband and wife—for a metaphor of God's love for Israel and Israel's love for God. Thus, when Solomon's song says, "O that you would kiss me with the kisses of your mouth! For your love is better than wine" (Song 1:2), sages of blessed memory think of how God kissed Israel. Reading the Song of Songs as a metaphor, the Judaic sages state in a systematic and orderly way their entire structure and system.

If the Bavli joined the Mishnah to Scripture in its formation of the structure of the dual Torah as one, so too, *Song of Songs Rabbah* joined metaphor to theology, symbol to structure, in setting forth that same whole. Standing in the same period, its authorship accomplished in its way that same summa that the authorship of the Bavli set forth. But the writers deal with not intellect but sentiment, not proposition but attitude and emotion. For the Bavli rules over the mind and tells what to think and do, while *Song of Songs Rabbah* tells how to feel, especially how to make the heart at one with God.

The naturalization of the Song of Songs into the Torah met with opposition. Mishnah tractate *Yadayim* 3:5 defines the setting in which sages took up the Song of Songs. The issue was which documents are to be regarded as holy among the canon of ancient Israel. The specific problem focuses upon Qohelet ("Ecclesiastes") and the Song of Songs. The terms of the issue derive from the matter of uncleanness. For our purpose, it suffices to know that if a document is holy, then it is held to be unclean— meaning, if one touches the document, he has to undergo a process of purification before he can eat food in a certain status of sanctification (the details are unimportant here) or, when the Temple stood, go to the Temple. What that means in practice is that people will be quite cautious about handling such documents, which then will be regarded as subject to special protection. So when sages declare that a parchment or hide on which certain words are written imparts uncleanness to the hands, they mean to say that those words, and the object on which they are written, must be handled reverently and thoughtfully.

MISHNAH *YADAYIM* 3:5

All sacred scriptures impart uncleanness to hands. The Song of Songs and Qohelet impart uncleanness to hands.

R. Judah says, "The Song of Songs imparts uncleanness to hands, but as to Qohelet there is dispute."

R. Yosé says, "Qohelet does not impart uncleanness to hands, but as to Song of Songs there is dispute."

Rabbi Simeon says, "Qohelet is among the lenient rulings of the House of Shammai and strict rulings of the House of Hillel."

Said R. Simeon b. Azzai, "I have a tradition from the testimony of the seventy-two elders, on the day on which they seated R. Eleazar b. Azariah in the session, that the Song of Songs and Qohelet do impart uncleanness to hands."

Said R. Aqiba, "Heaven forbid! No Israelite man ever disputed concerning Song of Songs that it imparts uncleanness to hands. For the entire age is not so worthy as the day on which the Song of Songs was given to Israel. For all the scriptures are holy, but the Song of Songs is holiest of all. And if they disputed, they disputed only concerning Qohelet."

Said R. Yohanan b. Joshua the son of R. Aqiba's father-in-law, according to the words of Ben Azzai, "Indeed did they dispute, and indeed did they come to a decision."

Clearly, this Mishnah passage, from circa 200 CE, records a point at which the status of the Song of Songs is in doubt. By the time of the compilation of *Song of Songs Rabbah*, that question had been settled. Everybody took for granted that the document was holy for the reason given.

The sages who compiled *Song of Songs Rabbah* read the Song of Songs as a sequence of statements of passionate love between God and Israel, the holy people. How they convey the intensity of Israel's love of God forms the point of special interest in this document. For it is not in propositions that they choose to speak, but in the medium of symbols. The Rabbinic sages use language as a repertoire of opaque symbols in the form of words. They set forth sequences of words that connote meanings, elicit emotions, stand for events, and form the verbal equivalent of pictures or music or dance or poetry. Through the repertoire of these verbal symbols and their arrangement and rearrangement, the message the authors wish to convey emerges—not in so many words, but through words nonetheless. The Rabbinic sages chose for their compilation a very brief list of items among many possible candidates. They therefore determined to appeal to a highly restricted list of implicit meanings, calling upon some very few events or persons, and repeatedly identifying these as the expressions of God's profound affection for Israel and Israel's deep love for God. The message of the document comes not so much from stories of what happened or did not happen, assertions of truth or denials of error, but rather from the repetitious rehearsal of sets of symbols.

In reading the love songs of the Song of Songs as the story of the love affair of God and Israel, sages identify implicit meanings that are always few and invariably self-evident. No serious effort goes into demonstrating the fact that God speaks, or Israel speaks; the point of departure is the message and meaning the One or the other means to convey. To take one instance, time and again we shall be told that a certain expression of love in the poetry of the Song of Songs is God's speaking to Israel about (1) the Sea, (2) Sinai, and (3) the world to come; or (1) the first redemption, the one from Egypt; (2) the second redemption, the one from Babylonia; and (3) the third redemption, the one at the end of days.

The repertoire of symbols covers Temple and schoolhouse, personal piety and public worship, and other matched pairs and sequences of coherent matters, all of them seen as embedded within the poetry. Here is Scripture's poetry read as metaphor. So Israel's holy life is metaphorized through the poetry of love and beloved, Lover and Israel. Long lists of alternative meanings or interpretations end up saying just one thing, but in different ways. The implicit meanings prove very few indeed. When in *Song of Songs Rabbah* we have a sequence of items alleged to form a taxon, that is, a set of things that share a common taxic indicator, what we have is a list. The list presents diverse matters that all together share, and therefore also set forth, a single fact or rule or phenomenon. That is why we can list them, in all their distinctive character and specificity, in a common catalogue of "other things" that pertain all together to one thing.

What do the compilers say through their readings of the metaphor of— to take one interesting example—the nut-tree for Israel? First, Israel prospers when it gives scarce resources for the study of the Torah or for carrying out religious duties; second, Israel sins but atones, and Torah is the medium of atonement; third, Israel is identified through carrying out its religious duties, for example, circumcision; fourth, Israel's leaders had best watch their step; fifth, Israel may not be well balanced but will be in glory in the coming age; sixth, Israel has plenty of room for outsiders but cannot afford to lose a single member. What we have is a repertoire of fundamentals dealing with Torah and Torah study, the moral life and atonement, Israel and its holy way of life, Israel and its coming salvation.

The verbal symbols are not shaped into a theological system made up of well-joined propositions and harmonious positions, as we saw in *Lamentations Rabbah*. Nor do we find propositions that are demonstrated syllogistically through comparison and contrast. The point is just the opposite; it is to show that many different things really do belong on the same list. That yields not a proposition that the list syllogistically demonstrates. The list invites our exegesis; the connections among these items require exegesis. What this adds up to, then, is not an argument for proposition, hence comparison and contrast and rule-making of a philosophical order, but rather a theological structure comprising well-defined attitudes. Here is a representative passage of the Midrash compilation. It shows how a sequence of "theological things"—events, religious imperatives, theological doctrines—are joined together in a common list, making a single point.

SONG OF SONGS RABBAH TO SONG 1:5

V:i.1   A. "I am very dark, but comely, [O daughters of Jerusalem, like the tents of Kedar, like the curtains of Solomon]" (Song 1:5):

     B. "I am dark" in my deeds.

     C. "But comely" in the deeds of my forebears.

2.   A. "I am very dark, but comely:"

     B. Said the Community of Israel, "'I am dark' in my view, 'but comely' before my Creator."

     C. For it is written, "Are you not as the children of the Ethiopians to Me, O children of Israel, says the Lord" (Amos 9:7):

     D. "as the children of the Ethiopians"—in your sight.

     E. But "to Me, O children of Israel, says the Lord."

3.   A. Another interpretation of the verse, "I am very dark:" in Egypt.

     B. "but comely:" in Egypt.

     C. "I am very dark" in Egypt: "But they rebelled against me and would not hearken to me" (Ez. 20:8).

     D. "but comely" in Egypt: with the blood of the Passover offering and circumcision, "And when I passed by you and saw you wallowing in your blood, I said to you, In your blood live" (Ez. 16:6)—in the blood of the Passover. [This verse is recited at the rite of circumcision.]

     E. "I said to you, In your blood live" (Ez. 16:6)—in the blood of the circumcision.

4. A. Another interpretation of the verse, "I am very dark:" at the sea, "They were rebellious at the sea, even the Red Sea" (Ps. 106:7).

B. "but comely:" at the sea, "This is my God and I will be comely for him" (Ex. 15:2).

5. A. "I am very dark:" at Marah, "And the people murmured against Moses, saying, 'What shall we drink'" (Ex. 15:24).

B. "but comely:" at Marah, "And he cried to the Lord and the Lord showed him a tree, and he cast it into the waters and the waters were made sweet" (Ex. 15:25).

6. A. "I am very dark:" at Rephidim, "And the name of the place was called Massah and Meribah" (Ex. 17:7).

B. "but comely:" at Rephidim, "And Moses built an altar and called it by the name 'the Lord is my banner'" (Ex. 17:15).

7. A. "I am very dark:" at Horeb, "And they made a calf at Horeb" (Ps. 106:19).

B. "but comely:" at Horeb, "And they said, 'All that the Lord has spoken we will do and obey'" (Ex. 24:7).

8. A. "I am very dark:" in the wilderness, "How often did they rebel against him in the wilderness" (Ps. 78:40).

B. "but comely:" in the wilderness at the setting up of the tabernacle, "And on the day that the tabernacle was set up" (Num. 9:15).

9. A. "I am very dark:" in the deed of the spies, "And they spread an evil report of the land" (Num. 13:32).

B. "but comely:" in the deed of Joshua and Caleb, "Save for Caleb, the son of Jephunneh the Kenizzite" (Num. 32:12).

10. A. "I am very dark:" at Shittim, "And Israel abode at Shittim and the people began to commit harlotry with the daughters of Moab" (Num. 25:1).

B. "but comely:" at Shittim, "Then arose Phinehas and wrought judgment" (Ps. 106:30).

11. A. "I am very dark:" through Achan, "But the children of Israel committed a trespass concerning the devoted thing" (Josh. 7:1).

B. "but comely:" through Joshua, "And Joshua said to Achan, 'My son, give I pray you glory'" (Josh. 7:19).

12. A. "I am very dark:" through the kings of Israel.

B. "but comely:" through the kings of Judah.

C. If with my dark ones that I had, it was such that "I am comely," all the more so with my prophets.

The contrast of dark and comely yields a variety of applications; in all of them the same situation that is the one also is the other, and the rest follows in a wonderfully well-crafted composition. What is the repertoire of items? Dark in deeds but comely in ancestry; dark in my view but comely before God; dark when rebellious, comely when obedient, a point made at numbers 3 for Egypt, 4 for the sea, 5 for Marah, 6 for Massah and Meribah, 7 for Horeb, 8 for the wilderness, 9 for the spies in the Land, 10 for Shittim, 11 for Achan/Joshua and the conquest of the Land, and 12 for

Israel and Judah. We therefore have worked through the repertoire of events that contained the mixture of rebellion and obedience; the theological substrate of this catalogue is hardly difficult to articulate.

The Rabbinic Reading of Ruth:
Ruth Rabbah

Like the other Midrash compilations of its class, *Ruth Rabbah*[13] makes one paramount point through numerous exegetical details.[14] *Ruth Rabbah* has only one message, expressed in a variety of components but single and cogent. It concerns the outsider who becomes the principal, the Messiah out of Moab, and this miracle is accomplished through mastery of the Torah. The main points of the document are these:

(1) Israel's fate depends upon its proper conduct toward its leaders.

(2) The leaders must not be arrogant.

(3) The admission of the outsider depends upon the rules of the Torah. These differentiate among outsiders. Those who know the rules are able to apply them accurately and mercifully.

(4) The proselyte is accepted because the Torah makes it possible to do so, and the condition of acceptance is complete and total submission to the Torah. Boaz taught Ruth the rules of the Torah, and she obeyed them carefully.

(5) Those proselytes who are accepted are respected by God and are completely equal to all other Israelites. Those who marry them are masters of the Torah, and their descendants are masters of the Torah, typified by David. Boaz in his day and David in his day were the same in this regard.

(6) What the proselyte therefore accomplishes is to take shelter under the wings of God's presence, and the proselyte who does so stands in the royal line of David, Solomon, and the Messiah. Over and over again, we see, the point is made that Ruth the Moabitess, perceived by the ignorant as an outsider, enjoyed complete equality with all other Israelites because she had accepted the yoke of the Torah, married a great sage, and through her descendants produced the Messiah-sage, David.

Scripture has provided everything but the main thing: the Moabite Messiah. But sages impose upon the whole their distinctive message, which is the priority of the Torah, the extraordinary power of the Torah to join the opposites—Messiah, utter outsider—into a single figure, and to accomplish this union of opposites through a woman. The femininity of Ruth seems to me to be as critical to the whole as the Moabite origin: the two modes of the (from the Israelite perspective) abnormal—outsider as against Israelite, woman as against man—therefore are invoked, and both for the same purpose, to show how, through the Torah, all things become one. That is the message of the document, and, seen whole, the principal message, to which all other messages prove peripheral.

The authorship decided to compose a document concerning the book of Ruth in order to make a single point. Everything else was subordinated to that definitive intention. Once the work got underway, the task was not one of exposition so much as repetition, not unpacking and exploring a complex conception, but restating the point, on the one hand, and eliciting or evoking the proper attitude that was congruent with that point, on the other. The decision, viewed after the fact, was to make one statement in an enormous number of ways. It is that the Torah dictates Israel's fate, and if you want to know what that fate will be, study the Torah, and if you want to control that fate, follow the model of the Messiah-sage. As usual, therefore, what we find is a recasting of the Deuteronomic-prophetic theology.

Three categories contain the topical and propositional messages of the document, as follows:

Israel and God. Israel's relationship with God encompasses the matter of the covenant, the Torah, and the Land of Israel, all of which bring to concrete and material expression the nature and standing of that relationship. This is a topic treated only casually by our compilers. They make a perfectly standard point, which is that Israel suffers because of sin (I:i). The famine in the time of the judges was because of Israel's rebellion: "My children are rebellious. But as to exterminating them, that is not possible, and to bring them back to Egypt is not possible, and to trade them for some other nation is something I cannot do. But this shall I do for them: lo, I shall torment them with suffering and afflict them with famine in the days when the judges judge" (III:i). This was because they became overconfident (III:ii).

Sometimes God saves Israel on account of its merit, sometimes for his own name's sake (X:i). God's punishment of Israel is always proportionate and appropriate, so LXXIV:i:

> Just as in the beginning, Israel gave praise for the redemption: "This is my God and I will glorify him" (Ex. 15:2), now it is for the substitution [of false gods for God]: "Thus they exchanged their glory for the likeness of an ox that eats grass" (Ps. 106:20). You have nothing so repulsive and disgusting and strange as an ox when it is eating grass. In the beginning they would effect acquisition through the removal of the sandal, as it is said, "Now this was the custom in former times in Israel concerning redeeming and exchanging: to confirm a transaction, the one drew off his sandal and gave it to the other, and this was the manner of attesting in Israel." But now it is by means of the rite of cutting off.

None of this forms a centerpiece of interest, and all of it complements the principal points of the writing.

Israel and the Nations. Israel's relationship with the nations is treated with interest in Israel's history, past, present, and future, and how that cyclical pattern is to be known. But this topic is not addressed at all in *Ruth Rabbah.* Only one nation figures in a consequential way, and that is Moab. Under these circumstances we can hardly generalize and say that Moab stands for everybody outside of Israel. That is precisely the opposite of the fact. Moab stands for a problem within Israel, the Messiah from the periphery; and the solution to the problem lies within Israel and not in its relationships with the other nations.

Israel on Its Own. Israel on its own concerns the holy nation's understanding of itself: who is Israel, and who is not? Within the same rubric we find consideration of Israel's capacity to naturalize the outsider, so to define itself as to extend its own limits, and other questions of self-definition. And finally, when Israel considers itself, a principal concern is the nature of leadership, for the leader stands for and embodies the people. Therein lies the paradox of the base document and the Midrash compilation alike: how can the leader most desired, the Messiah, come from the excluded people and not from the holy people?

And more to the point (for ours is not an accusatory document), how is the excluded included? And in what way do peripheral figures find their way to the center? Phrased in this way, the question yields the obvious answer: through the Torah as embodied by the sage, anyone can become part of Israel, and any Israelite can find his way to the center. Even more—since it is through Ruth that the Moabite becomes the Israelite, and since (for sages) the mother's status dictates the child's—we may go so far as to say that it is through the Torah that the woman may become a man (at least, in theory). But in stating matters in this way, I have gone beyond my representation of the topical and propositional program. Let us review it from the beginning to the end.

The sin of Israel, which caused the famine, was that it was judging its own judges. "He further said to the Israelites, 'So God says to Israel, "I have given a share of glory to the judges and I have called them gods, and the Israelites nonetheless humiliate them. Woe to a generation that judges its judges"'" (I:i). The Israelites were slothful in burying Joshua, and that showed disrespect to their leader (II:i). They were slothful about repentance in the time of the judges, and that is what caused the famine; excess of commitment to one's own affairs leads to sin. The Israelites did not honor the prophets (III:iii). The old have to bear with the young, and the young with the old, or Israel will go into exile (IV:i). The generation that judges its leadership ("judges") will be penalized (V:i). Disdain for the authority of the Torah is penalized (V:i). Elimelech was punished because he broke the peoples' heart; everyone depended upon him, and he proved undependable (V:iii); so bad leadership will destroy Israel. Why was Elimelech punished? Because he broke the Israelites' heart. When the years of drought came, his maid went out into the marketplace with her basket in her hand. So the people of the town said, "Is this the one on whom we depended, that he can provide for the whole town with ten years of food? Lo, his maid is standing in the marketplace with her basket in her hand!" So Elimelech was one of the great men of the town and one of those who sustained the generation. But when the years of famine came, he said, "Now all the Israelites are going to come knocking on my door, each with his basket." The leadership of a community is its glory: "The great man of a town—he is its splendor, he is its glory, he is its praise. When he has turned from there, so too have turned its splendor, glory, and praise" (XI:i.1C).

A distinct but fundamental component of the theory of Israel concerns who Israel is and how one becomes a part of Israel. That theme proves fundamental to our document, so much of which is preoccupied with how Ruth can be the progenitor of the Messiah, deriving as she does not only from Gentile but also from Moabite stock. Israel's history follows rules that are to be learned in Scripture; nothing is random and all things are connected (IV:ii). The fact that the king of Moab honored God explains why God raised up from Moab "a son who will sit on the throne of the Lord" (VIII:i.3). The proselyte is discouraged but then accepted. Thus XVI:i.2B: "People are to turn a proselyte away. But if he is insistent beyond that point, he is accepted. A person should always push away with the left hand while offering encouragement with the right." Orpah, who left Naomi, was rewarded for the little that she did for her, but she was raped when she left her (XVIII:i.1-3). When Orpah went back to her people, she went back to her gods (XIX:i).

Ruth's intention to convert was absolutely firm, and Naomi laid out all the problems for her, but she acceded to every condition (XX:i). Thus she said, "Under all circumstances I intend to convert, but it is better that it be through your action and not through that of another." When Naomi heard her say this, she began laying out for her the laws that govern proselytes. She said to her, "My daughter, it is not the way of Israelite women to go to theaters and circuses put on by idolators." She said to her, "Where you go I will go." She said to her, "My daughter, it is not the way of Israelite women to live in a house that lacks a mezuzah." She said to her, "Where you lodge I will lodge." "Your people shall be my people:" this refers to the penalties and admonitions against sinning. "And your God my God:" this refers to the other religious duties. "For where you go I will go:" to the tent of meeting, Gilgal, Shiloh, Nob, Gibeon, and the eternal house. "And where you lodge I will lodge:" "I shall spend the night concerned about the offerings." "Your people shall be my people:" "so nullifying my

idol." "And your God my God:" "to pay a full recompense for my action."
I find here the centerpiece of the compilation and its principal purpose.
The same message is at XXI:i.1-3.

Proselytes are respected by God, so XXII:i: "And when Naomi saw that
she was determined to go with her, [she said no more]." Said R. Judah b.
R. Simon, "Notice how precious are proselytes before the Omnipresent.
Once she had decided to convert, the Scripture treats her as equivalent to
Naomi." Boaz, for his part, was equally virtuous and free of sins (XXVI:i).
The law provided for the conversion of Ammonite and Moabite women,
but not Ammonite and Moabite men, so the acceptance of Ruth the
Moabite was fully in accord with the law, and anyone who did not know
that fact was an ignoramus (XXVI:i.4, among many passages). An Israelite
hero who came from Ruth and Boaz was David, who was a great master
of the Torah, thus: he was "Skillful in playing, and a mighty man of war,
prudent in affairs, good-looking, and the Lord is with him" (1 Sam. 16:18):
"Skillful in playing:" in Scripture. "And a mighty man of valor:" in
Mishnah. "A man of war:" who knows the give and take of the war of the
Torah. "Prudent in affairs:" in good deeds. "Good-looking:" in Talmud.
"Prudent in affairs:" able to reason deductively. "Good-looking:" enlightened in law. "And the Lord is with him:" the law accords with his opin-
ions.

Ruth truly accepted Judaism upon the instruction, also, of Boaz
(XXXIV:i), thus:

> "Then Boaz said to Ruth, 'Now listen, my daughter, do not go to glean in
> another field:'" This is on the strength of the verse, "You shall have no other
> gods before me" (Ex. 20:3). "Or leave this one:" this is on the strength of the
> verse, "This is my God and I will glorify him" (Ex. 15:2). "But keep close to
> my maidens:" this speaks of the righteous, who are called maidens: "Will
> you play with him as with a bird, or will you bind him for your maidens"
> (Job 40:29 [Hebrew text]).

The glosses invest the statement with a vast tapestry of meaning. Boaz
speaks to Ruth as a Jew by choice, and the entire exchange is now typological. Note also the typological meanings imputed at XXXV:i.1-5. Ruth
had prophetic power (XXXVI:ii). Ruth was rewarded for her sincere conversion by Solomon (XXXVIII:i.1).

Taking shelter under the wings of the Presence of God, which is what
the convert does, is the greatest merit accorded to all who do deeds of
grace, thus:

> So notice the power of the righteous and the power of righteousness are the
> power of those who do deeds of grace. For they take shelter not in the shad-
> ow of the dawn, nor in the shadow of the wings of the earth, not in the

shadow of the wings of the sun, nor in the shadow of the wings of the *hayy-ot*, nor in the shadow of the wings of the cherubim or the seraphim. But under whose wings do they take shelter? "They take shelter under the shadow of the One at whose word the world was created: 'How precious is your loving kindness O God, and the children of men take refuge in the shadow of your wings.'" (Ps. 36:8)

The language that Boaz used with Ruth, "Come here," bore with it deeper reference to six: David, Solomon, the throne as held by the Davidic monarchy, and ultimately, the Messiah, for example, in the following instance:

The fifth interpretation refers to the Messiah: "Come here:" means, to the throne. "And eat some bread:" this is the bread of the throne. "And dip your morsel in vinegar:" this refers to suffering: "But he was wounded because of our transgressions" (Is. 53:5). "So she sat beside the reapers:" for the throne is destined to be taken from him for a time: "For I will gather all nations against Jerusalem to battle and the city shall be taken" (Zech. 14:2). "And he passed to her parched grain:" for he will be restored to the throne: "And he shall smite the land with the rod of his mouth" (Is. 11:4).

R. Berekhiah in the name of R. Levi: "As was the first redeemer, so is the last redeemer: 'Just as the first redeemer was revealed and then hidden from them, so the last redeemer will be revealed to them and then hidden from them'" (XL:i.1ff.).

Boaz instructed Ruth on how to be a proper Israelite woman, so LIII:i:

"Wash yourself:" from the filth of idolatry that is yours. "And anoint yourself:" this refers to the religious deeds and acts of righteousness [that are required of an Israelite]. "And put on your best clothes:" this refers to her Sabbath clothing. So did Naomi encompass Ruth within Israel: "and go down to the threshing floor:" she said to her, "My merit will go down there with you."

Moab, whence Ruth came, was conceived not for the sake of fornication but for the sake of Heaven (LV:i.1B). Boaz, for his part, was a master of the Torah and when he ate and drank, that formed a typology for his study of the Torah (LVI:i). His was a life of grace, Torah study, and marriage for holy purposes. Whoever trusts in God is exalted, and that refers to Ruth and Boaz; God put it in his heart to bless her (LVII:i). David sang psalms to thank God for his great-grandmother, Ruth, so LIX:i.5: "[At midnight I will rise to give thanks to you] because of your righteous judgments" (Ps. 119:62). David speaks:

The acts of judgment that you brought upon the Ammonites and Moabites. And the righteous deeds that you carried out for my great-grandfather and my great-grandmother [Boaz, Ruth, of whom David speaks here]. For had he hastily cursed her but once, where should I have come from? But you put in his heart the will to bless her: "And he said, 'May you be blessed by the Lord.'"

Because of the merit of the six measures that Boaz gave Ruth, six righteous persons came forth from him, each with six virtues: David, Hezekiah, Josiah, Hananiah-Mishael-Azariah (counted as one), Daniel, and the royal Messiah.

God facilitated the union of Ruth and Boaz (LXVIII:i). Boaz's relative was ignorant for not knowing that while a male Moabite was excluded, a female one was acceptable for marriage. The blessing of Boaz was, "May all the children you have come from this righteous woman" (LXXIX:i), and that is precisely the blessing accorded to Isaac and to Elkanah. God made Ruth an ovary, which she had lacked (LXXX:i). Naomi was blessed with messianic blessings (LXXXI:i), thus: "Then the women said to Naomi, 'Blessed be the Lord, who has not left you this day without next of kin; and may his name be renowned in Israel:' Just as 'this day' has dominion in the firmament, so will your descendants rule and govern Israel forever." On account of the blessings of the women, the line of David was not wholly exterminated in the time of Athaliah.

David was ridiculed because he was descended from Ruth, the Moabitess, so LXXXV:i. But many other distinguished families derived from humble origins:

Said David before the Holy One, blessed be he, "How long will they rage against me and say, 'Is his family not invalid [for marriage into Israel]? Is he not descended from Ruth the Moabitess'?" "Commune with your own heart upon your bed:" [David continues,] "You too have you not descended from two sisters? You look at your own origins 'and shut up.'" "So Tamar who married your ancestor Judah — is she not of an invalid family? But she was only a descendant of Shem, son of Noah. So do you come from such impressive genealogy?"

David referred to and defended his Moabite origins, so LXXXIX:i:

Then I said, "Lo, I have come [in the roll of the book it is written of me]" (Ps. 40:8). [David says,] "Then I had to recite a song when I came, for the word 'then' refers to a song, as it is said, 'Then sang Moses'" (Ex. 15:1). "I was covered by the verse, 'An Ammonite and a Moabite shall not come into the assembly of the Lord' (Deut. 23:4), but I have come 'in the roll of the book it is written of me' (Ps. 40:8)." "In the roll:" this refers to the verse, [David continues], "Concerning whom you commanded that they should not enter into your congregation" (Lam. 1:10). "Of the book it is written of me:" "An Ammonite and a Moabite shall not enter into the assembly of the Lord" (Deut. 23:4). "It is not enough that I have come, but in the roll and the book it is written concerning me:" "In the roll:" Perez, Hezron, Ram, Amminadab, Nahshon, Salmon, Boaz, Obed, Jesse, David. "In the book:" "And the Lord said, Arise, anoint him, for this is he" (1 Sam. 16:12).

Just as David's descent from Ruth was questioned, so his descent from Judah via Tamar could be questioned too, and that would compromise the whole tribe of Judah.

The Rabbinic Reading of Esther:
Esther Rabbah I

In *Esther Rabbah* Part One (that is, covering the book of Esther's first two chapters),[15] we find only one message, and it is reworked in only a few ways.[16] It is that the nations are swine, their rulers fools, and Israel is subjugated to them, though it should not be, only because of its own sins. No other explanation serves to account for the paradox and anomaly that prevail. But just as God saved Israel in the past, so the salvation that Israel can attain will recapitulate God's former saving acts. On the stated theme, Israel among the nations, sages set forth a proposition entirely familiar from the books of Deuteronomy through Kings, on the one hand, and much of prophetic literature, on the other.

The proposition is familiar, and so is the theme; but since the book of Esther can hardly be characterized as "Deuteronomic," lacking all interest in the covenant, the land, and issues of atonement (beyond the conventional sackcloth, ashes, and fasting—hardly the fodder for prophetic regeneration and renewal!), the sages' distinctive viewpoint in the document must be deemed an original and interesting contribution of their own. But the message is somewhat more complicated than merely a negative judgment against the nations. If I have to identify one recurrent motif that captures their theology, it is the critical role of Esther and Mordecai, and particularly Mordecai, who, as sage, emerges in the position of a Messiah. And that is a message that is particular to the exposition of the book of Esther's opening chapters.

Esther Rabbah Part One proves nearly as much a commentary in the narrowest sense—verse-by-verse amplification, paraphrase, exposition—as it is a compilation in the working definition of this inquiry. What holds the document together and gives it, if not coherence, then at least flow and movement are the successive passages of (mere) exposition. When all has been set forth and completed, its message is that the Torah (as exemplified by the sage) makes the outsider into an insider, the woman into a heroic leader, just as, in the book of Ruth, we see how the Moabite is turned into an Israelite, and the offspring of the outsider into a Messiah. These paradoxes come about on the condition, the only condition, that the Torah govern. This is a document about one thing, and it makes a single statement, and that statement is coherent, just as is the case with *Ruth Rabbah*, its counterpart and complement. Where we find a woman in the systemic center of a document's statement, there we uncover the document's critical message, that which can account for everything and its opposite, and for the transformation of otherwise fixed values, for example, in this case, the exclusion of women from the center of consideration.

Gender thus defines the focus for both *Esther Rabbah I* and *Ruth Rabbah*, yielding the opposite of what is anticipated. *Ruth Rabbah* has the Messiah born of an outsider; *Esther Rabbah* has salvation come through a woman. Esther and Mordecai, the woman and the Messiah-sage, function in much the same way that Ruth and David, woman and Messiah-sage, work in *Ruth Rabbah*. While the sages of *Ruth Rabbah* face their own, distinctive problem, the way the outsider (the Moabite-Messiah) becomes the insider, *Ruth Rabbah* and *Esther Rabbah* Part One deal with the same fundamental fact: the Messiah-sage dictates the future of Israel because he (never she) realizes the rule of the Torah. In *Esther Rabbah* Part One many things say one thing: the Torah dictates Israel's fate, and if you want to know what that fate will be, study the Torah, and if you want to control that fate, follow the model of the Messiah-sage.

These episodic propositions comprise the document's single message. Bad government comes about because of the sins of the people (VII:i). But that proposition is realized in discourse mainly about bad government by the nations, and, given the base document, that is hardly surprising. God was neglected by the people, so he is left solitary through his own actions, which responded to the people's actions (XVIII:iii). Our compilation concentrates upon this one subject, and all of its important messages present the same proposition in several parts. Israel's life among the nations is a sequence of sorrows, each worse than the preceding: "In the morning, you shall say, 'Would it were evening!' and at evening you shall say, 'Would it were morning!' In the morning, of Babylonia, you shall say, 'Would it were evening!'" But through Torah, Israel can break the cycle:

> Said R. Simeon b. Yohai, "You can acquire rights of ownership of members of the nations of the world, as it says, 'Moreover of the children of the strangers that sojourn among you, of them may you buy' (Lev. 25:45), but they cannot acquire rights of ownership over you. Why not? Because you acquired 'these the words of the covenant.' And the nations? They did not acquire 'these the words of the covenant' ['These are the words of the covenant']" (I:i.4-11).

When Israel is subjugated by the nations, God will not spurn, abhor, or destroy them, or break his covenant with them—either in the age of

Babylonia, Media, the Greeks, and the wicked kingdom, or in that of Vespasian, Trajan, Haman, the Romans (II:i.1). The same is repeated at III:i.1-5.

In comparing the ages through which the Jews had lived—Babylonian, Median, Greek, Roman—the same position recurs. When the righteous achieve great power, there is joy in the world, and when the wicked achieve great power, there is groaning in the world; this is true of Israelite and Gentile kings (IV:i). Gentile kings may do good things or bad things (VI:i). But even the good kings are not without flaws. When a bad king rules, it is because of the sins of the people, those who will not do the will of the creator (VII:i). God worked through whomever he chose. From the beginning of the creation of the world, the Holy One, blessed be he, designated for everyone what was suitable: Ahasuerus the first of those who sell [people at a price], Haman, the first of those who buy [people at a price] (VIII:i). There are decisions made by God that determine the life of nations and individuals. Israel's history follows rules that can be learned in Scripture; nothing is random, all things are connected, and fundamental laws of history dictate the meaning of what happens among the nations (VIII:ii).

Ultimately, God will destroy Israel's enemies (IX:i). God will save Israel when not a shred of merit will be found among the nations of the world (X:i.15). The prosperity of the nations is only for a time; then the nations will be punished and Israel redeemed (XI:i). There will be full recompense, and the contrast between Israel's subjugation and the nations' prosperity will be resolved. The principle of measure for measure governs. Pagan kings propose to do what God himself does not claim to be able to do. They cannot accomplish their goal; if God wanted to, God could do it. But in the age to come, God will accomplish the union of opposites, which in this time pagan kings claim to be able to do but cannot accomplish (XVII:i). Pagan kings rebel against not only God but also their own gods (XVIII:i). But for the slightest gesture of respect for God they are rewarded (XVIII:i).

God is in full control of everyone at all times. The salvation in the time of Ahasuerus was directly linked, detail by detail, to the punishment in the time of Nebuchadnezzar (XVIII:ii). Israel's relationship with one empire is no different from its relationship to the other. The same base verse, Ps. 10:14, accounts for both Rome and Sasanian Iran, the world empires of the day. The relationship of each to Israel is the same. Both of them call into question Israel's faith in the power of God by showing off their own power. Esau/Romulus and Remus pay back God's blessing by building temples of idolatry in Rome. Belshazzar/Vashti/Iran do the same by oppressing Israel. Both intend by their power to prove that they are stronger than God. But, the premise maintains, God will show in the end who is the stronger. The upshot is to underline the irony that derives from the contrast between the empires' power and God's coming display of his power—that and one other thing: the challenge facing God in showing his power over theirs (XVIII:iv).

Israel possesses wise men, but the nations' sages are fools; thus: "'The impious man destroys his neighbor through speech:' this refers to the seven princes of Persia and Media. 'But through their knowledge the righteous are rescued:' this refers to the portion of Issachar" (XXIII:i). We have at XXIII:ii three sets of explanations for the names of various persons mentioned in the text, all of them working with the letters of the respective names and imputing to them other meanings sustained by the same consonants. The passage is worth examining in its entirety, to give the flavor of the reading:

ESTHER RABBAH XXIII:II

1. A. ["the men next to him being Carshena, Shethar, Admatha, Tarshish, Merses, Marsena, and Memucan, the seven princes of Persia and Media, who saw the king's face and sat first in the kingdom:"]
    B. "the men next to him:"
    C. they drew the punishment near to themselves.
2. A. "being Carshena:"
    B. he was in charge of the vetches [*karshinim*].
3. A. "Shethar:"
    B. he was in charge of the wine.
4. A. "Admatha:"
    B. he was in charge of surveying the land [Simon: land measurements].
5. A. "Tarshish:"
    B. he was first in command of the household.
6. A. "Merses:"
    B. he would make chicken hash [Simon: he used to make a hash of (*nenares*) the poultry].
7. A. "Marsena:"
    B. he would beat the flour [with oil].
8. A. "and Memucan:"
    B. he was the one who provided food for all of them, for his wife would prepare for them everything they needed.
9. A. ["Carshena, Shethar, Admatha, Tarshish, Merses, Marsena, and Memucan]:"
    B. Said the ministering angels before the Holy One, blessed be he, "If the counsel of that wicked man [Haman] is carried out, who will offer you offerings?" [So the names of the counselors refer to offerings in the Temple, thus]:
    C. "Carshena:"
    D. "Who will offer you an ox of the first year?" [*par ben shanah*].
10. A. "Shethar:"
    B. "Who will offer you two pigeons?" [*shete torim*].
11. A. "Admatha:"

117

B.   "Who will build you an altar of earth: 'An altar of earth you shall make to me' (Ex. 20:21)?"

12. A.   "Tarshish:"

B.   "Who will wear the priestly garments and minister before you: 'A beryl [*tarshish*] and an onyx and a jasper' (Ex. 28:20)?"

13. A.   "Merses:"

B.   "Who will stir [*memeres*] the blood of the birds that are sacrificed before you?"

14. A.   "Marsena:"

B.   "Who will mix the flour and oil before you?"

15. A.   "and Memucan:"

B.   "Who will set up the altar before you: 'And they set up the altar upon its bases' (Ezra 3:3).

16. A.   Thereupon said the Holy One, blessed be he, to them, "The Israelites are my children, my companions, my nearest, my loving ones, the sons of my beloved, Abraham: 'The seed of Abraham that loved me' (Is. 41:8).

B.   "I will exalt their horn: 'And he has lifted up a horn for his people' (Ps. 148:14)."

17. A.   Another explanation for the verse, "Carshena, [Shethar, Admatha, Tarshish, Merses, Marsena, and Memucan]:"

B.   [As to Carshena,] said the Holy One, blessed be he, "I will scatter vetches before them and clear them out of the world [Simon, p. 58, n. 4: as one feeds an animal before killing it]."

C.   "Shethar:" "I shall make them drink a cup of reeling."

D.   "Admatha, Tarshish:" "I shall treat their blood as free as water."

E.   "Merses, Marsena, and Memucan:" "[Simon, p. 58:] I will stir, twist, and crush [*memares, mesares, mema'ek*] their souls within their bellies."

F.   And where was the doom of all of them made ready?

G.   Said R. Josiah, "It is in line with that which Isaiah, the prophet, said, 'Prepare slaughter for his children for the iniquity of their fathers, that they may not rise up and possess the earth' (Is. 14:21)."

The first set of explanations deals with the tasks each of the princes carried out in the palace, feeding the king. The next deals with the rites of the Temple that each name stands for; here the princes are given a good task, which is to thwart the advice of Haman. But the upshot is to match feeding the wicked (or stupid) king, Ahasuerus, as against tending the King of kings, God. And the third set of explanations then assigns to the seven the punishment that is owing to the wicked government that has endangered the lives of the Jews. So three distinct and yet complementary hermeneutical interests coincide: pagan government and the feeding of pagan kings, divine government and its counterpart, the Temple cult, and finally, God's punishment for the pagan government. While it goes without saying that each set of seven names can stand on its own, it seems clear to me that the compositor has appealed to a single cogent program in order to accomplish what I see as a beautiful piece of sustained and coherent exposition, one that describes a variety of distinct components of a single important proposition. I cannot imagine a finer execution of the exposition of details aimed at registering a major conception.

There is a correspondence between how Israel suffers and how the nations prosper, so XXVIII:I: "With the language with which the throne was taken away from her [Esther's] ancestor, when Samuel said to him, 'And he has given it to a neighbor of yours, who is better than you' (1 Sam. 15:28), with that same language, the throne was given back to him: 'let the king give her royal position to another who is better than she.'" Saul lost the throne because he did not destroy Amalek; Esther got it back because she did. Obedience to divine instructions made the difference. Persian women suffered and were humiliated because they had ridiculed Israelite women (XXXIV:i).

Those who do righteousness at all times are going to be the ones who will carry out God's salvation, thus: "When Haman wanted to exterminate Israel and weighed out ten thousand pieces of silver to those who were to do the work for Ahasuerus, it is written, 'And I will pay ten thousand talents of silver into the hands...'(Est. 3:9), what is then written? 'Now there was a Jew in Susa the capital whose name was Mordecai, son of Jair, son of Shimei, son of Kish, a Benjaminite.'" The point is that they that do righteousness at all times, and are to be remembered when God's salvation is required and it is performed through them. Accordingly, Mordecai in his generation was equivalent to Moses in his generation: "Now the man Moses was very meek" (Num. 12:3). Just as Moses stood in the breach—"Therefore he said that he would destroy them, had not Moses, his chosen one, stood before him in the breach" (Ps. 106:23)—so did Mordecai: "Seeking the good of his people and speaking peace to all his seed" (Est. 10:3). Just as Moses taught Torah to Israel—"Behold, I have taught you statutes and ordinances" (Deut. 4:5)—so Mordecai did: "And he sent letters...with words of peace and truth" (Est. 9:30). Truth refers to Torah: "Buy the truth and do not sell it" (Prov. 23:23).

God always responds to Israel's need. The reason this point is pertinent here is the repeated contrast, also, of Mordecai and Haman. The upshot is that ultimately Israel gets what it has coming, just as the nations do; and when Israel gets its redemption, it is through people such as Moses, Abraham, and Mordecai. The redemptions of Israel in times past then provide the model and paradigm for what is going to happen in the future. None of this has any bearing on the land and nothing invokes the covenant, which is why I see the entire matter in the present context. When God saves Israel, it is always in response to how they have been

119

punished, thus XXXVIII:i.9: R. Berekiah in the name of R. Levi said, "Said the Holy One, blessed be he, to the Israelites, 'You have wept, saying, "We have become orphans and fatherless" (Lam. 5:3). 'By your lives, I shall raise up for you in Media a savior who will have no father and no mother.' Thus: 'for she had neither father nor mother.'" If the mortal king remembers and pays back, how much more so will God (LIV:i).

As to Israel's distinctive leadership and its life within its own boundaries, the nature of our base document, with its concern for its heroes, Mordecai and Esther, secures for this subject a more than negligible place in the propositional program of our compilation. Israel's leadership consistently follows the same norms, and what the ancestors taught, the descendants learn. Thus Esther behaved as had Rachel (LI:i), so:

> "Now Esther had not made known her kindred or her people, as Mordecai had charged her; [for Esther obeyed Mordecai just as when she was brought up by him]:" This teaches that she kept silent like Rachel, her ancestor, who kept silent. All of her great ancestors had kept silent. Rachel kept silent when she saw her wedding band on the hand of her sister but shut up about it. Benjamin, her son, kept silent. You may know that that is so, for the stone that stood for him on the high priest's breastplate was a jasper, indicating that he knew of the sale of Joseph, but he kept silent. [The word for jasper contains letters that stand for] "there is a mouth," [meaning, he could have told], but he kept silent. Saul, from whom she descended: "Concerning the matter of the kingdom he did not tell him" (1 Sam. 10:16). Esther: "Now Esther had not made known her kindred or her people, as Mordecai had charged her."

What happens now therefore has already happened, and Israel knows how to respond and what will come in consequence of its deeds. That is how Scripture guides the reading of the present age.

CHAPTER 5

Rabbinic Literature and the Hebrew Scriptures

How the Halakhah and the Aggadah Cohere in a Systematic Theology of Scripture

The Halakhah realizes in patterns of normative conduct what is implicit in the laws set forth in Scripture (chapter 3). The Aggadah systematizes the narratives of Scripture and transforms them into a theological system (chapter 4). So together, the Halakhic and the Aggadic writings represent a massive exercise in the realization—in a coherent worldview and way of life—of Scripture's laws, narratives, exhortations, and prophecies.

How do the Rabbinic writings recapitulate the theology of Scripture? The Aggadah reconstructs the story of Adam and Eden in the narrative of Israel and the Land, systematically addressing issues of divine justice in the monotheistic framework. These issues encompass sin and atonement, Israel and the nations, and God and humanity created, as God says, "in our image, after our likeness" (Gen. 1:26), which means: God reveals and humanity comprehends. The Halakhah participates in that same story by showing how, in the construction of the godly community, justice shapes world order as the Torah requires. It spells out the norms for that holy community, which now and in the world to come Israel is supposed to embody. And both the Halakhah and the Aggadah work out the implications of Scripture's account of the human condition, from start to finish. That fact highlights how important the Talmud's union of the two media of thought and expression is.[1]

The Aggadah speaks in general terms to the world at large, while the Halakhah uses specific and particular rules to speak to the everyday concerns of ordinary Israelites. The Aggadah recapitulates the story of Israel and its situation among the nations. The Halakhah contemplates Israel in its household, in a timeless realm of unchanging perfection, or aspiring thereto (on the Sabbath and on secular days, respectively, in a condition of purity or aiming thereat). The Aggadah addresses the exteriorities, the Halakhah the interiorities, of Israel in relationship with God. Categorically, the Aggadah faces outward toward humanity in general and correlates—or shows the relationship of—humanity in general and Israel in particular. The Aggadah sets forth the monotheistic theology; the Halakhah explains how to realize that theology in patterns of holy living.

The Aggadic Dimension

A religion of numerous gods finds many solutions to one problem, but a religion of only one God presents one solution to many problems. Life is seldom fair. Rules rarely work. To explain the reason why, polytheists adduce multiple causes of chaos, a god for every anomaly. Diverse gods do various things, so, it stands to reason, ordinarily outcomes conflict. Monotheism by nature explains many things in a single way. One God rules. Life is meant to be fair, and just rules are supposed to describe what is ordinary, all in the name of that one and only God. So in monotheism a simple logic governs, limiting ways of making sense of things. But that logic contains its own dialectics. The tension inherent in the logic of monotheism is simply stated: If one true God has done everything, then, since he is God all-powerful and omniscient, all things are credited to, and blamed on, him. In that case, he can be either good or bad, just or unjust— but not both. Responding to the dialectics of monotheism, the Aggadah systematically reveals the justice of the one and only God of all creation. God is not only God but also good. Appealing to the facts of Scripture, the Written part of the Torah, the sages constructed in the documents of the Oral part of the Torah a coherent theology. This theology adumbrated a cogent structure and logical system.

The working system of the Aggadah finds its dynamic in the struggle between God's plan for creation—to create a perfect world of justice—and man's will. That dialectics embodies in a single paradigm the events contained in the sequences of rebellion, sin, punishment, repentance, and atonement; exile and return; or the disruption of world order and the restoration of world order. The Halakhah manifestly means to form Israel in particular into the embodiment of God's plan for a perfect world of justice. There are four principal parts of the system.

(1) *God formed creation in accordance with a plan, which the Torah reveals.* World order can be shown by the facts of nature and society set forth in that plan to conform to a pattern of reason based upon justice. Those who possess the Torah—Israel—know God and those who do not—the Gentiles—reject him in favor of idols. What happens to each of the two sectors of humanity, respectively, corresponds with their relationship with God. Israel in the present age is subordinate to the nations because God has designated the Gentiles as the medium for penalizing Israel's rebellion, meaning through Israel's subordination and exile to provoke Israel to repent. Private life as much as the public order conforms to the principle that God rules justly in a creation of perfection and stasis.

(2) *The perfection of creation*, realized in the rule of exact justice, is signified by the timelessness of the world of human affairs and their conformity to a few enduring paradigms that transcend change (theology of history). No present, past, or future marks time, but only the recapitulation of those patterns. Perfection is further embodied in the unchanging relationships of the social commonwealth (theology of political economy), which assure that scarce resources, once allocated, remain in stasis. A further indication of perfection lies in the complementarity of the components of creation, on the one hand, and, finally, the correspondence between God and man in God's image (theological anthropology), on the other.

(3) *Israel's condition, public and personal, marks flaws in creation.* What disrupts perfection is the sole power capable of standing on its own against God's power, and that is man's will. What man controls and God cannot coerce is man's capacity to form intention and therefore choose either arrogantly to defy, or humbly to love, God. Because man defies God, the sin that results from man's rebellion flaws creation and disrupts world order (theological theodicy). The paradigm of the rebellion of Adam in Eden governs, with the act of arrogant rebellion leading to exile from Eden thus accounting for the condition of humanity. But, as in the original transaction of alienation and consequent exile, God retains the power to encourage repentance through punishing man's arrogance. In mercy, moreover, God exercises the power to respond to repentance with forgiveness—that is, a change of attitude evoking a corresponding change. Since, commanding his own will, man also has the power to initiate the process of reconciliation with God through repentance, an act of humility, man may restore the perfection of that order that through arrogance he has marred.

(4) *God ultimately will restore the perfection that embodied his plan for creation.* In the work of restoration death, which comes about by reason of sin,

will die, the dead will be raised and judged for their deeds in this life, and most of them, having been justified, will go on to eternal life in the world to come. The paradigm of man restored to Eden is realized in Israel's return to the Land of Israel. In that world or age to come, however, that sector of humanity that through the Torah knows God will encompass all of humanity. Idolaters will perish, and the humanity that comprises Israel at the end will know the one, true God and spend eternity in his light.

This statement of monotheism in mythic form proves remarkably familiar, with its stress on God's justice (to which his mercy is integral), man's correspondence with God in his possession of the power of will, man's sin of rebellion against God, and God's response. If we translate into the narrative of scriptural Israel—from its beginning to the calamity of the destruction of the (first) Temple—the picture of matters that is set forth in both abstract and concrete ways in the Aggadah, we turn out to state the human condition in terms of Israel. We produce a reprise of the history laid out in Genesis through Kings and amplified by the principal prophets. The Israelite set his will against God's word, sinned, and was exiled from Eden. The Israelite's counterpart, Israel formed by the Torah, entered the Land, sinned, and was exiled from the Land.

Each of the four parts of the theology of the Aggadah—(1) the perfectly just character of world order, (2) indications of its perfection, (3) sources of its imperfection, and (4) means for the restoration of world order and the result of the restoration—forms part of an unfolding story that can be told in only one direction and in the dictated order and in no other way.

Adam and Israel

The single narrative logic that encompasses the entire system is captured in the following composition concerning Adam and Israel and their parallel stories. Adam stands for humanity at large, Israel for that portion of humanity formed by acceptance of the Torah of Sinai.

> *GENESIS RABBAH* XIX:IX.1-2
> 2. A. R. Abbahu in the name of R. Yosé bar Haninah: "It is written, 'But they [Israel] are like a man [Adam], they have transgressed the covenant' (Hos. 6:7).
> B. "'They are like a man,' specifically, like the first man. [We shall now compare the story of the first man in Eden with the story of Israel in its land.]

Now the sage identifies God's action in regard to Adam with a counterpart action in regard to Israel, in each case matching verse for verse, beginning with Eden and Adam. Adam is brought to Eden as Israel is brought to the Land, with comparable outcomes:

C. " 'In the case of the first man, I brought him into the garden of Eden, I commanded him, he violated my commandment, I judged him to be sent away and driven out, but I mourned for him, saying "How..." '[which begins the book of Lamentations, hence stands for a lament, but which, as we just saw, also is written with the consonants that also yield, 'Where are you'].

D. " 'I brought him into the garden of Eden,' as it is written, 'And the Lord God took the man and put him into the garden of Eden' (Gen. 2:15).

E. " 'I commanded him,' as it is written, 'And the Lord God command-ed...' (Gen. 2:16).

F. " 'And he violated my commandment,' as it is written, 'Did you eat from the tree concerning which I commanded you' (Gen. 3:11).

G. " 'I judged him to be sent away,' as it is written, 'And the Lord God sent him from the garden of Eden' (Gen. 3:23).

H. " 'And I judged him to be driven out.' 'And he drove out the man' (Gen. 3:24).

I. " 'But I mourned for him, saying, "How...".' 'And he said to him, "Where are you"' (Gen. 3:9), and the word for 'where are you' is written, 'How....' "

Now comes the systematic comparison of Adam and Eden with Israel and the Land of Israel:

J. "'So too in the case of his descendants, [God continues to speak,] I brought them [Israel] into the Land of Israel, I commanded them, they vio-lated my commandment, I judged them to be sent out and driven away but I mourned for them, saying, "How...."'

K. "'I brought them into the Land of Israel.' 'And I brought you into the land of Carmel' (Jer. 2:7).

L. " 'I commanded them.' 'And you, command the children of Israel' (Ex. 27:20). 'Command the children of Israel' (Lev. 24:2).

M. " 'They violated my commandment.' 'And all Israel have violated your Torah' (Dan. 9:11).

N. "'I judged them to be sent out.' 'Send them away, out of my sight and let them go forth' (Jer 15:1).

O. " '... and driven away.' 'From my house I shall drive them' (Hos. 9:15).

P. "'But I mourned for them, saying, "How...."' 'How has the city sat soli-tary, that was full of people' (Lam. 1:1)."

We end with Lamentations, the writing of mourning produced after the destruction of the Temple in Jerusalem in 586 BCE by the Babylonians. Here we end where we began, Israel in exile from the Land, like Adam in exile from Eden. But the Torah is clear that there is a difference, which we shall address in its proper place: Israel can repent.

These persons, Israel and Adam, form not individual and particular one-time characters, but are exemplary categories. Israel is Adam's counterpart. Israel is the other model for the Israelite, the one being without the Torah, the other possessing and possessed by the Torah. Adam's failure defined Israel's task and marked the occasion for the formation of Israel. Israel came into existence in the aftermath of the failure of Creation with the fall of the Adam and his ultimate near extinction; in the restoration that followed the Flood, God identified Abraham to found in the Land, the new Eden, a supernatural social entity to realize his will in creating the world. Called, variously, a family, a community, a nation, and a people, Israel above all embodies God's abode in humanity, his resting place on earth.[2]

The theological system is one that specifically, sets forth the parallel stories of humanity and Israel. Each begins with Eden (the counterpart for Israel being the Land of Israel). The tale of each is marked by sin and punishment (Adam's and Israel's respective acts of rebellion against God, the one through disobedience, the other through violating the Torah). The parallel histories unfold as they describe the penalty of exile for the purpose of bringing about repentance and atonement (Adam from Eden, Israel from the Land). These same stories come together for humanity through Israel, with humanity's restoration to Eden taking place in Israel's return to the Land of Israel and Israel's recovery of eternal life for those who regain Eden/the Land. The dialectics of the tale—the conflict of God's word and man's will—resolve themselves in that narrative, which holds together all of the details of the Aggadic reading of Scripture.

The Rabbinic system therefore takes as its critical problematic the identification of Israel with the Torah and the nations with idolatry. It comes to a climax in showing how the comparable stories intersect and diverge at the grave. Israel enjoys the power of repentance and is destined to the resurrection, judgment, and eternity (the world to come), while the nations (that is, the idolaters to the end) are destined for death.

The Halakhic Dimension

The Halakhic complement embodies the extension of God's design for world order into the inner-facing relationships. Specifically, the Halakhah must respond to issues posed by the monotheism of justice regarding (1) Israel's relationships with God when these relationships do not take place in the intersection of God, Israel, and the nations, but within Israel's own frame of reference, which is to say, the Torah and its laws; (2) Israelites' relationships with one another; and (3) the interior life of the individual Israelite household on its own, with God. If, then, we wish to explore the interiority of Israel in relationship with God, as a shared order, and of Israel's autonomous building block, the household, we are required to take

up the norms of everyday conduct that define Israel and signify its sanctification. These norms prevail through time differentiated only by the giving of the Torah at Sinai, the destruction of the Temple, and the recovery of
eternal life and of Eden/the Land at the end of time. They prevail through
space differentiated only between the Land of Israel and everywhere else.

Norms of conduct, more than norms of conviction, served to convey the
sages' interior statement. The Halakhah presents a systematic, continuous,
and orderly picture. It entails dense and intense writing. Above all, in the
sages' entire corpus it is the sole arena of dialectics. The Halakhah and its
analysis and exposition involve articulated tension and conflict, demanding
lavish expenditure of intellectual energy. And from the closure of the
Talmud to our own day, those who mastered the documents of the Aggadah
themselves insisted upon the priority of the Halakhah, which is clearly signaled as normative, over the Aggadah, which commonly is not treated as
normative in the same way as is the Halakhah. The sages represent as
encompassing and coherent the entirety of the Halakhah itself, detail by
detail. That is why in their magnum opus, the Talmud, they insist upon the
harmony of the parts and the cogency of the whole. Details exemplify the
whole, and the system all together speaks the same message through details.

How Rabbinic Literature Actualizes
Scripture's Story

Rabbinic literature actualizes Scripture's story. The Aggadic documents
(and Aggadic compositions in Halakhic ones) state the problem, the
Halakhic documents set forth the solution.

1. *The Theological Problem.* God created nature as the setting for his
encounter with humanity. Creation was meant as God's Kingdom for the
Israelites' bliss. But with the sin of the Israelite committed in rebellion
against God's will, the loss of Eden, and the advent of death began the
long quest for the regeneration of the Israelite. In the unfolding of generations—ten from Adam to Noah, ten from Noah to Abraham and thence
to Sinai—it was only Israel that presented itself for the encounter. But then
Israel too showed itself to be no different from Adam. For on the other
side of Sinai came the celebration of the golden calf.

2. *The Halakhic Solution.* What to do now? Rebuild God's Kingdom
among that sector of humanity that undertakes to respond to God's self-
manifestation in the Torah and to realize God's dominion and imperatives: the Torah, the commandments. God provided for Israel, the
surrogate of humanity, the commandments as a medium of sanctification
for the reconciliation with God and renewal of Eden, the triumph over the
grave. Freed of sin through offerings that signified obedience to God's

will, by reason of repentance and atonement, and that signified man's acceptance of God's will over his own, which had brought about the fall from Eden, man might meet God, with the two in mutual and reciprocal commitment. Where Israel atoned for sin and presented itself as ready for the meeting, there God and Israel would found their Eden, not a place but an occasion. In overcoming the forces of death and affirming life through purity, Israel brings into being such an occasion. The Halakhah then serves as the medium of sanctification of Israel in the here and now, in preparation for the salvation of Israel and its restoration to Eden.

The Halakhah lays out how Israel's entire social order may be constructed to realize the situation represented by Eden now and to restore Eden then. But this time it would happen through the willing realization of God's rule, both in the present hour and at the end of days. That actualization takes place within Israel. How will it happen? Tutored by the Torah to want by nature what God wants but will not coerce them to want—"the commandments were given only to purify the heart of man"—Israel makes itself able to realize God's will and to form his kingdom within its holy community. Through examining the Halakhah in its native categories or tractates, these propositions are shown to animate the entire Halakhic corpus, which is thus proved to embody a theological system, one that rests firmly upon the foundations of Scripture both as a whole and in detail.

The Halakhah reworks two parallel stories, the story of the creation and fall of Adam and Eve from Eden, and the story of the regeneration of humanity through the Torah's formation of Israel. The two stories then are linked in the encounter of Israel and the nations, represented by the uncleanness of death that, through the disciplines of purity, Israel is to overcome. The tension between them comes to its resolution in the resurrection of Israel from death, those who know God being destined for eternal life. The two stories, adumbrated in the section headings bearing Roman numerals in the outline that follows, represent the native category formations of the Aggadah. I then fold into these the native category formations of the Halakhah. These are given in ordinary type bearing Arabic numerals. Here is how the two bodies of canonical writing join together to make a single coherent statement, theology realized in law, law animated by theology:

I. THE STORY OF MAN AND REBELLION, SIN AND ATONEMENT, EXILE AND RESTORATION
   1. Where and When Is Eden?
   2. Who Owns Eden?
II. THE PARALLEL STORY: ISRAEL AND GOD, SIN AND JUST PUNISHMENT, REPENTANCE AND ATONEMENT, FORGIVENESS AND RESTORATION
   3. Adam and Eve
   4. Sin and Atonement
   5. Intentionality and the Civil Order

III. THE STORY OF ISRAEL AND THE NATIONS, SPECIFICALLY, ISRAEL AND THE TORAH, THE GENTILES LACKING THE TORAH
   6. Enemies of Eden, Tangible and Invisible
   7. The Contest between Death and Life
   8. Overcoming Death
   9. The Kingdom of God

The sages' philosophical reading of Scripture—its Halakhah and its Aggadah alike—leads to the transformation of the Torah's account of humanity's story into the design for Israel's social order: God's kingdom, Eden realized now, and restored at the end. Now let us recapitulate the main findings derived from the specific category formations/tractates that we meet in the Mishnah and the Tosefta:

1. Where and When Is Eden?
   i. *Shebi'it*, the Sabbatical year, the Sabbath for the Land
   ii. *Orlah*, the prohibition of the fruit of a tree in the first three years after it is planted
   iii. *Kila'yim*, the prohibition of mixed seeds in the vineyard
   iv. *Shabbat-Erubin*, the recapitulation of Eden on the Sabbath day, the sanctification of the day through repose

By "Eden" Scripture means that place whole and at rest that God sanctified; "Eden" stands for creation in perfect repose. In the Halakhah Eden stands not for a particular place but for nature in a defined condition, at a particular moment: creation in Sabbath repose, sanctified. Then a place in repose at the climax of creation, at sunset at the start of the seventh day, whole and at rest, embodies and realizes Eden. The Halakhah means to systematize the condition of Eden, to define Eden in its normative traits and also to localize Eden within Israel the people. How so? Eden is the place to the perfection of which God responded in the act of sanctification at the advent of the seventh day. While the Land in the Written Torah's explicit account of matters claims the right to repose on the seventh day and in the seventh year of the septennial cycle, it is also the location of Israel, wherever that may be, at the advent of sunset on the eve of the seventh day of the week of creation that recapitulates Eden.

2. Who Owns Eden?
   i. *Ma'aserot*, tithing
   ii. *Terumot*, priestly rations
   iii. *Hallah*, dough offering
   iv. *Ma'aser Sheni*, second tithe
   v. *Bikkurim*, first fruits
   vi. *Pe'ah*, leaving the corner of the field for the poor
   vii. *Demai*, doubtfully tithed produce

The story expands to within the motif of Eden, the matter of ownership and possession as media for the expression of the relationship between the Israelite and God. God accorded to Adam and Eve possession of nearly everything in Eden, retaining ownership—the right to govern according to his will—for himself. The key to the entire system of interaction between God and Israel through the Land and its gifts emerges in the Halakhah of *Ma'aserot* and its companions, which deal—along the lines of *Shebi'it* and *Erubin*—with the difference between possession and ownership. God owns the world, which he made. But God has accorded to man the right of possession of the earth and its produce. This he did twice, once to the Israelite— Adam and Eve—in Eden, the second time to Israel in the Land of Israel. And to learn the lesson that the Israelite did not master, that possession is not ownership but custody and stewardship, Israel has to acknowledge the claims of the creator to the glory of all creation, which is the Land. This Israel does by giving back God's share of the produce of the Land at the time and in the manner that God defines. The enlandised (defined within the Land) components of the Halakhah therefore form a single, cogent statement of matters.

3. Adam and Eve
    i.   *Qiddushin*, betrothals
    ii.   *Ketubot*, marriage contracts
    iii.   *Nedarim*, vows
    iv.   *Nazir*, the special vow of the Nazirite
    v.   *Sotah*, the ordeal imposed on the wife suspected of adultery
    vi.   *Gittin*, writs of divorce
    vii.   *Yebamot*, levirate marriages

The Halakhah of the family, covering the act of sanctification of a woman by a man (*Qiddushin*), the marriage agreement (*Ketubah*), vows and special vows, the disposition of a charge of unfaithfulness against a woman, and the severance of the marital bond of sanctification through a writ of divorce or death, does not ubiquitously invoke the metaphor of Adam and Eve in Eden. Our task, then, is to identify the principal foci of that Halakhah and to investigate the appropriate context in which it is to be interpreted. How does Eden figure? The connection is made articulate by the (possibly later) liturgical framework in which the Halakhah plays itself out. There, in the liturgy of the marriage canopy, the act of creation of the Israelite is recapitulated, the bride and groom explicitly compared to Adam and Eve. Not only that, but the theme of the Land and Israel intervenes as well—two motifs dominant in the Halakhic theology examined to this point.

4. Sin and Atonement
    i.   *Sheqalim*, the half-sheqel offering to support the public sacrifices

ii.   *Tamid* & *Yoma*, the daily whole offering, the rite of the Day of Atonement
iii.   *Zebahim* & *Menahot*, offerings of meat and cereal
iv.   *Arakhin*, the pledge of valuation
v.   *Bekhorot*, firstlings
vi.   *Me'ilah*, sacrilege
vii.   *Temurah*, substituting a beast for an already consecrated beast

The Halakhah takes account of the tragedy of Eden and provides for a new moral entity and a reformed transaction accorded that entity, one not available to Adam and Eve. For God at Eden made no provision for atonement for sin, but, in the unfolding of the Israelite's story, God grasped the full measure of the Israelite's character and drew the necessary conclusion and acted on it. Endowed with autonomous will, the Israelite has the power to rebel against God's will. Therefore the Halakhah finds urgent the question, How is the Israelite, subject to God's rule, to atone for the sin that, by his rebellious nature, the Israelite is likely to commit? The Torah, to answer that question, formulates the rules that govern the Israelite both (1) when under God's dominion and (2) when in rebellion against God's will. These represent the two aspects of the one story that commences with Eden, leads to the formation of Israel through Abraham, Isaac, and Jacob, God's antidotes to Adam, and climaxes at Sinai. But Israel also is the Israelite, so that story accommodates both Adam's fall and Israel's worship of the golden calf, and, as the denouement, Adam and Eve's exile from Eden and Israel's ultimate exile from the Land. How, then, does God propose to repair the world he has made to take account of the Israelite's character and Israel's own proclivity?

5.   Intentionality and the Civil Order
i.   *Keritot*, sins penalized by extirpation (dying young)
ii.   *Sanhedrin-Makkot*, the court system & criminal justice
iii.   *Baba Qamma-Baba Mesi'a-Baba Batra*, the civil law
iv.   *Horayot*, when the authorities err in the law
v.   *Shebu'ot*, oaths

The Halakhah dictates the character of Israel's civil order—its political institutions and system of criminal justice. It undertakes a labor of differentiation of power, indicating what agency or person has the power to precipitate the working of politics as legitimate violence. When we understand the differentiating force that imparts to politics its activity and dynamism, we grasp the theology that animates the structures of the politics and propels the system. The details of the Halakhah, in particular the sanctions assigned to various infractions, effect the taxonomy of power, which forms an implicit exegesis of the story of Eden, translated into reflection on the power of intentionality.

6. Enemies of Eden, Tangible and Invisible
    i.   Tangible Enemies: *Abodah Zarah*, idolatry
    ii.   Invisible Enemies: Death. *Ohalot*, corpse uncleanness
    iii.   *Nega'im*, the skin-ailment, equivalent to death
    iv.   *Zabim* and *Niddah*, the uncleanness of flux

The enemies of Eden take shape around the grand struggle between life and death, in the here and now (meaning Israel and the Gentiles), and at the end of days (meaning those who will stand in judgment and go onward to the world to come and eternal life, and those who will perish in the grave). Specifically, the world beyond the limits of Israel forms an undifferentiated realm of idolatry and uncleanness. Then how is Israel to negotiate life with the world of Gentiles and their idolatry, with corpses and their contamination? Among the sources of uncleanness, tangible and invisible, we begin with the Gentiles and proceed to corpse and comparable kinds of uncleanness. But the two—Gentiles and corpses—form a single domain. The former bears exactly the same uncleanness as the latter. Gentiles, defined as idolaters, and Israelites, defined as worshipers of the one and only God, part company at death. Israelites die, only to rise from the grave. Gentiles die for eternity. The roads intersect at the grave, each component of humanity taking its own path beyond. Israelites—meaning those possessed of right conviction—will rise from the grave and stand in judgment, but then enter upon eternal life, to which no one else will enjoy access.

7. The Contest between Death and Life
    i.   *Makhshirin*, liquids that render formerly dry produce susceptible to uncleanness
    ii.   *Tohorot*, cases of doubt in matters of uncleanness
    iii.   *Uqsin*, the uncleanness of parts of produce
    iv.   *Kelim*, uncleanness affecting utensils

The sources of change and disruption that threaten the cleanness, and thus the sanctification of the Temple, are the same sources that threaten the norm of cleanness of the household. If the same uncleanness affects the Temple and the table, then the only difference is one of degree, not of kind, as the Halakhah states explicitly. And the rest follows. The web of relationships between sanctification and uncleanness spins itself out into every corner of the Israelite household, where the system makes a difference. And it is the will of the householder that determines the difference that the distinction between clean and unclean is going to make. Everything is relative to the householder's will; he has it in his power to draw the household table into alignment with the altar in the Temple—that is to say, to place the table and the food set thereon into relationship, onto a continuum, with the altar and the Holy Things of the cult. This he can accomplish through an act of will that motivates an attitude of constant watchfulness in the household for those very sources of contamination that Scripture identifies as danger to the Lord's altar in the Jerusalem Temple.

8. Overcoming Death
    i.   *Parah*, preparing purification-water
    ii.   *Miqva'ot*, immersion pools
    iii. *Tebul Yom*, the uncleanness of one who has immersed, which lasts until sunset completes the rite of purification
    iv.   *Yadayim*, the special case of the uncleanness of hands
    v.   *Hagigah*, home and Temple in hierarchical formation

From death and its effect upon food and drink—that is, the uncleanness caused by, and analogous to, death—we turn to the media for the restoration of life. Still water unaffected by human agency restores the natural condition disrupted by uncleanness other than that of the corpse and its analogues, while by contrast purification water systematically subjected to human intervention—constant attention and deliberate action, from start to finish—alone removes corpse uncleanness. We have then to account for the exclusion of man from the one process, and the radical insistence upon his inclusion, in full deliberation, within the other. Uncleanness that comes about by reason of any cause but death and its analogues is removed by Heaven's own dispensation, not by man's intervention: rainfall or sunset suffice. Ordinary purification is done by nature, resulting from natural processes. But as to persons and objects that have contracted uncleanness from death, nature on its own cannot produce the kind of water that bears the power to remove that uncleanness and restore the condition of nature. Only man can. And man can do this only by the highest level of concentration, the most deliberate and focused action. The Israelite's act of will overcomes the uncleanness of death, just as man's act of deliberate rebellion brought about death to begin with. The Israelite restores what man has disrupted. Had the Halakhah wished in its terms and categories to accomplish a reprise of the story of Adam's fall, it could not have made a more eloquent statement than it does in the contrast between the Halakhah of *Miqva'ot* and that of *Parah*.

9. The Kingdom of God
    i.   *Berakhot*, reciting the Shema, the Prayer, and Blessings over food
    ii.   *Hullin*, slaughter of animals for domestic use
    iii. *Megillah*, the celebration of Purim
    iv.   *Rosh Hashanah*, the celebration of the New Year
    v.   *Pesahim*, the celebration of Passover
    vi.   *Sukkah*, the celebration of Tabernacles
    vii. *Mo'ed Qatan*, the intermediate days of a week-long festival

viii.   *Besah*, cooking on festival days

ix.   *Ta'anit*, special fast days

As much as the Israelite by his nature rebels against God, the Israelite tutored by the commandments willingly accepts God's will and therefore his rule. What are the Halakhah's media for the reformation, regeneration, and renewal of the Israelite? The Halakhah here legislates not for Eden but for the kingdom of God. For Sinai's answer to Eden's question transcends the matter of sin and atonement and encompasses the conduct of the ordinary, everyday life lived under God's rule. The normative deals with the normal, so the final solution to God's dilemma with the Israelite—how to accord the Israelite free will but to nurture in the Israelite freely given love for God—lies in the Torah. That way of life in accord with God's rule means to form the *Paideia*, the character-building education that transforms the Israelite by making the Israelite's freely given obedience to God as natural as was the first Israelite's (Adam) contumacious rebellion against God. That is why the Halakhic provision for life in God's kingdom moves from the ordinary day and its duties to the table and its everyday nourishment, then to the meeting with God that is seasonal and temporal, and finally to the climax of the system, confrontation with routine crisis.

This brief précis shows how a few large motifs form of the details of the Halakhah a single coherent system, one that tells a story. Clearly, the Halakhah works from Scripture forward. But, being theologians and systematic thinkers, speaking through symbol and myth but intent on a philosophical reading of religion in quest of a coherent, proportionate, and rigorously argued statement, the sages do not randomly rework this detail or that. Rather, their philosophical reading of Scripture that comes to its climax in the Talmud—its Halakhah and its Aggadah alike—produces a coherent theology. It leads to the transformation of the Torah's account of humanity's story into the detailed design for Israel's social order. The details all find their place within the structure of the whole, and in its workings, the system that sages have constructed animates the whole, the parts working well together to make a simple statement, which is easily set forth. In its actualities Israel embodies—or is meant to embody—God's plan for humanity, not individually, but as a social entity: God's kingdom, Eden realized in both the here and now and restored at the end of days.

The Halakhah brings about the transformation of the here and now, of the particular occasion, into the embodiment, the exemplification, of the abstract ground of being. Involved is the relationship of realms of the sacred: the rules of engagement between and among God, Land, Israel, time, place, and circumstance. Through the fabric of the everyday life of the Land lived out in the household, village, and the holy metropolis,

Jerusalem (the three dimensions of the social order of which the Halakhah takes account), Eden is read not as a historical moment but as situation and occasion. That then precipitates thought about the human condition. But Eden does not impose narrow limits on the amplification of that thought. It is not the only condition.

There is also the situation brought about by the second great theme, besides Eden, that is implicit in the Halakhah. It is God's self-manifestation in the Torah: the occasion for the reform and renewal of humanity through Israel, the counterpart and opposite of the Israelite. The Halakhah therefore begins with Eden but progresses to the realization of God's kingdom within holy Israel's social order, conceiving of Israel both enlandised (defined within the Land) and utopian (located anywhere), as the category of the Halakhah requires.

A third general motif involves Eden once more, this time under God's rule, and it too engages with the Torah's account of Israel at Sinai. It concerns the re-embodiment of Israel, the restoration that comes about not alone in the end of days when the Messiah comes, but in the here and now of the workaday world. It is there that the Israelite formed by the discipline of the Torah learns both to atone for, and to overcome, his natural propensity willfully to rebel against God. Within the social order of an enlandised Israel moral persons construct a godly society. That reading of the Written Torah and translation of its law into the canons of ordinary life speaks in the acutely present tense to portray for the Israelite a worthy future well within the Israelite's own capacities to realize: "the commandments were given only to purify the heart of the Israelite," and "All-Merciful wants the heart," as the Talmud frames matters.

CHAPTER 6

Rabbinic Literature and the Christian Scriptures

Because they share a common Scripture, the writings of early Christianity and of Rabbinic Judaism intersect. They form an ideal arena for the comparative study of religions: they are enough alike to validate comparison, but different enough to yield interesting contrasts. Each represents a choice that Scripture affords and each gives perspective to the other.

What conclusions do people draw, however, from the intersection of teachings? Take, for example, one attributed to Jesus and to Hillel. Citing Lev. 19:18, Jesus said as the Golden Rule, "You will love your neighbor as yourself." Citing the same verse, Hillel said, "What is hateful to yourself do not do to your neighbor; that is the entire Torah; all the rest is commentary; now go forth and learn." From the intersection of these two responses to Lev. 19:18, scholars have set forth such conclusions as, "Jesus' formulation was superior because...," or "Hillel's was superior because...," or "Jesus was not original, because Hillel said it first...," or "Jesus was nothing more than a rabbi, like any other," and so on—comparative study in the service of religious polemics. But reciprocity prevails. Rabbinic literature may contribute to the study of the Christian Scriptures a keen perspective upon the choices the competing system embodies. And Christian writings offer a counterpart illumination of Rabbinic Judaism. When, for instance, in discussing *Genesis Rabbah* we referred to Eusebius and Augustine, we asked Christianity to testify to issues faced by the fourth and fifth century Rabbinic sages.

But there are problems. Comparing and contrasting sayings and stories

136

that first reached documentary closure in the third or fifth or seventh centuries with those of the letters of Paul and of the Gospels requires us to treat as first-century writings what manifestly belong to much later centuries. That formidable objection can be overcome in one of two ways.

First, we undertake the act of faith that affirms all attributions as valid. In that case, why not give up the so-called critical quest for the historical Jesus—meaning, what he really said among the sayings attributed to him—and believe it all?

Or, second, we may redefine our quest altogether, asking for data of another-than-synchronic character to provide a perspective of a different kind from the narrowly historical one. Work that yields little of value in the synchronic setting produces much of interest in the diachronic one.

Specifically, if we seek to characterize an entire religious system and structure—Rabbinic Judaism that records its Oral Torah in the score of documents from the Mishnah through the Talmud of Babylonia, or the Christianity that reaches written form in the Gospels, the letters of Paul, and the Church Fathers—diachronic work vastly helps. For characterizing wholes—the whole of one structure and system—gains nuance and detail when brought into juxtaposition with comparable wholes.

But how would such diachronic comparison of whole systems work? The basic premise of systemic description, analysis, and interpretation enters in here. The premise of systemic study of religions maintains that details contain within themselves and recapitulate the system as a whole, so that from the parts we can reconstruct much of the entirety of the structure, much as anthropologists and paleontologists do in dealing with details of culture or of mammals, respectively. That premise flows from the very notion of a system—an entire structure that imparts proportion and cogency to details and that holds the whole together in a single cogent statement.

Comparing Gospels and Rabbinic Writings: An Aggadic Instance

For a single concrete case I have chosen a parable that occurs in the Synoptic Gospels and in the Talmud of Babylonia; in the Gospels it is attributed to Jesus, and in the Talmud to Yohanan ben Zakkai, who is assumed to have lived in the first century. Early on, people recognized that the parable set forth in Yohanan's name looks something like the one set forth in Jesus', and they therefore asked Yohanan to clarify the sense and meaning of Jesus. But later, most people conceded that a parable attributed to a first-century authority in a seventh-century compilation cannot be taken at face value to record what really was said and done on that day in the first century to which reference is made.

Diachronic reading of religious systems leads us past the impasse. But we learn then about the Christian system of the Gospels and the Judaic system of the Talmud of Babylonia. The shape and structure of Christianity and of Judaism then come under study and into perspective. Narrowly historical questions give way to broad and encompassing ones concerning the religious order. The parable allows for the comparison and contrast of religions.

What we shall see is how finding what Christian and Judaic canonical documents share permits a process of comparison as well as contrast. Likeness takes priority. When we see how matters are alike, we perceive the differences as well, and having established a solid basis for comparison, contrast proves illuminating. The parable concerns a king who gave a feast, but did not specify the time. Some people responded to the invitation wisely, some foolishly. Some were ready when the time came, some were not. The parable in that form contains no determinate message and does not hint at its own interpretation. That is all that the Judaic and Christian versions of the parable have in common: the king who gave a banquet but did not specify the time. Everything else, as we shall see, is particular to the two religious traditions that utilized the parable, each for its own message. The contrast then permits us to show where each differs from the other, what each really wishes to say—no small point of clarification when it comes to the description and analysis of religions.

Let us consider, first, how the naked components of the parable are clothed in the formulation attributed to Jesus:

> And again Jesus spoke to them in parables, saying, "The kingdom of heaven may be compared to a king who gave a marriage feast for his son, and [1] sent his servants to call those who were invited to the marriage feast; but they would not come. Again [2] he sent other servants, saying, 'Tell those who are invited, Behold, I have made ready my dinner, my oxen and my fat calves are killed, and everything is ready; come to the marriage feast.' But they made light of it and went off, one to his farm, another to his business, while the rest seized his servants, treated them shamefully, and killed them. The king was angry, and he sent his troops and destroyed those murderers and burned their city. Then he said to his servants, 'The wedding is ready, but those invited were not worthy. [3] Go therefore to the thoroughfares, and invite to the marriage feast as many as you find.' And those servants went out into the streets and gathered all whom they found, both bad and good; so the wedding hall was filled with guests.
>
> "But when the king came in to look at the guests, he saw there a man who had no wedding garment; and he said to him, 'Friend, how did you get in here without a wedding garment?' And he was speechless. Then the king said to the attendants, 'Bind him hand and foot, and cast him into the outer

darkness; there men will weep and gnash their teeth.' For many are called, but few are chosen."

Matthew 22:1-14 (NRSV; cf. Luke 14:15-24)

As Jesus shapes the parable, it tells a rather protracted and complicated story. That is because, read as a unitary formulation, the story of the king's feast is told thrice, and each version makes its own point. First, the king has issued invitations, but no one will come. This is made deliberate and blameworthy: people reject the invitation, and they do so violently. The wedding is ready, but those invited were not worthy. Then the king issues new invitations. People now come as they are. They have no choice, having been summoned without notice or opportunity to get ready. Those who are unready are punished: they should have been ready.

Then is tacked on a new moral: many are called but few are chosen. But no version of the parable of the king's fiasco matches that moral. The first version has many called, but those who are called either will not come (to the original feast) or are not worthy (of the second feast) but reject the invitation altogether. So in the first set of stories, many are called but nobody responds. In the third go-around, many are called and do show up, but a few—one man only—are unready. So the triplet is rather odd.

But the point is clear: the Kingdom of Heaven is at hand. Jesus is the son. People reject the invitation to the marriage feast, that is, the Kingdom of Heaven. The invitation is repeated: everything is ready. The invited people now reject the invitation violently and are themselves unworthy. In the third go-around there is no choice about coming; people are dragooned. Now the kingdom is at hand and people must enter. Some are ready, some not. All are judged in accordance with their condition at the moment of the invitation—ready or not.

That is the point at which the Rabbinic version of the same story—the story about the king who made a feast and invited people—intersects with the Christian use of the parable. But to examine it in its context, we have to consider the text that utilizes the parable, not just the parable, which is not freestanding. If the context of the parable as Jesus utilizes it is the Kingdom of Heaven and its sudden advent, the context in the Rabbinic version is everyday life, the here and now and the death that comes to everyone. That is what happens without warning, for which people must be ready. The text commences with generalizations: one should repent one day before he dies, meaning every day. One should be ever ready. This is linked to a verse in Qoh. 9:8, "Let your garments be always white and don't let your head lack ointment," which is taken to refer to keeping one's body in the condition of a corpse—that is, dressed in white garments, the color of death in the Rabbinic writings, and properly anointed, as the corpse is anointed for burial.

The compositor of the construction of the Talmud of Babylonia has then added the parable of the king who invited people to a banquet. He set no specific time. Some kept themselves in readiness, some did not. Now the parable illustrates the teaching that one should be ready for the banquet that God will call at any moment—which is to say, one should be ready for death through a life of perpetual repentance:

b. SHABBAT 153A/*m. SHABBAT* 23:5K-M I.44-45[1]

I.45   A. *We have learned in the Mishnah there:* R. Eliezer says, "Repent one day before you die" [*m. Abot* 2:10D].

B.   His disciples asked R. Eliezer, "So does someone know just what day he'll die?"

C.   He said to them, "All the more so let him repent today, lest he die tomorrow, and he will turn out to spend all his days in repentance."

D.   And so, too, did Solomon say, "Let your garments be always white and don't let your head lack ointment" (Qoh. 9:8).

I.46   A. ["Let your garments be always white and don't let your head lack ointment" (Qoh. 9:8)]—said R. Yohanan b. Zakkai, "The matter may be compared to the case of a king who invited his courtiers to a banquet, but he didn't set a time. The smart ones among them got themselves fixed up and waited at the gate of the palace, saying, 'Does the palace lack anything?' [They can do it any time.] The stupid ones among them went about their work, saying, 'So is there a banquet without a whole lot of preparation?'

B.   Suddenly the king demanded the presence of his courtiers. The smart ones went right before him, all fixed up, but the fools went before him filthy from their work. The king received the smart ones pleasantly, but showed anger to the fools.

C.   He said, 'These, who fixed themselves up for the banquet, will sit and eat and drink. Those, who didn't fix themselves up for the banquet, will stand and look on.'"

The passage bears a gloss, as follows:

D.   R. Meir's son in law in the name of R. Meir said, "They, too, would appear as though in attendance. But, rather, both parties sit, the one eating, the other starving, the one drinking, the other in thirst: 'Therefore thus says the Lord God, behold, my servants shall eat, but you shall be hungry; behold, my servants shall drink, but you shall be thirsty; behold, my servants shall rejoice, but you shall be ashamed; behold, my servants shall sing for joy of heart, but you shall cry for sorrow of heart' (Is. 65:13-14)."

A further treatment of the base verse, Qoh. 9:8, transforms the emphasis upon the attitude of repentance in preparation for death to the practice of the faith, with the reference to garments now alluding to show-fringes, and the reference to the head to phylacteries:

140

E.   Another matter: "Let your garments be always white and don't let your head lack ointment" (Qoh. 9:8)—

F.   "Let your garments be always white": This refers to show-fringes.

G.   "And don't let your head lack ointment": This refers to phylacteries.

Clearly, we have moved a long way from the triple banquet that Jesus has the king hold, and the parable serves remarkably disparate purposes. All that is shared is the common motif, the king who gave a feast and was disappointed in the result because people were unready. There are some corresponding developments, specifically, (1) diverse responses to the invitation, and (2) consequently, some are ready when the hour strikes, some not. Otherwise the versions of the parable scarcely intersect, as the following comparison shows:

JESUS	YOHANAN BEN ZAKKAI
"The kingdom of heaven may be compared to <u>a king who gave a marriage feast</u> for his son,	"The matter may be compared to to the case of <u>a king who invited his courtiers to a banquet,</u> but he didn't set a time.
and sent his servants to call those who were invited to the marriage feast; but they would not come. Again he sent other servants, saying, 'Tell those who are invited, Behold, I have made ready my dinner, my oxen and my fat calves are killed, and everything is ready; come to the marriage feast.'	
But they made light of it and went off, one to his farm, another to his business, while the rest seized his servants, treated them shamefully, and killed them. The king was angry, and he sent his troops and destroyed those murderers and burned their city. Then he said to his servants, 'The wedding is ready, but those invited were not worthy. Go therefore to the thoroughfares, and invite to the marriage feast as many as you find.'	

And those servants went out into the streets and gathered all whom they found, both bad and good; so the wedding hall was filled with guests.

The smart ones among themselves fixed up and waited at the gate of the palace, saying, 'Does the palace lack anything?' [They can do it any time.] The stupid ones among them went about their work, saying, 'So is there a banquet without a whole lot of preparation?'

But when the king came in to look at the guests, he saw there a man who had no wedding garment; and he said to him, 'Friend, how did you get in here without a wedding garment?' And he was speechless. Then the king said to the attendants, 'Bind him hand and foot, and cast him into the outer darkness; there men will weep and gnash their teeth.'

Suddenly the king demanded the presenceof his courtiers. The smart ones went right before him, all fixed up, but the fools went before him filthy from their work.

For many are called, but few are chosen."

The king received the smart ones pleasantly, but showed anger to the fools. He said, 'These. who fixed themselves up for banquet, will sit and eat and drink. Those, who didn't fix themselves up for the banquet, will stand and look on.' "

The upshot is simple: the parable shared by Christianity and Judaism concerns a king who gave a banquet with unhappy results—that alone. But that shared motif (for all we have in common is a motif, not a fully executed tale) suffices to validate comparing the ways in which the two religious worlds have utilized the motif. And that produces striking contrasts, which turn our attention from the detail—the case at hand—toward the large-scale systems that have imposed their respective paradigms upon the detail of the (proto-)parable: the shared motif of the king who gave a banquet for people who were unwilling or unready to attend, the shared lesson that one has to be ready on the spur of the moment, and the common conviction that that for which one must be forever prepared is nothing less than entry into God's kingdom. But what is that kingdom? On that the two heirs of the common Scripture differ radically.

Contexts of Comparison

What do we learn from the contrast? We may speak of religious systems represented in the detail of a parable and gain perspective on the whole from the part. Christianity, in the case at hand, defines God's kingdom around the advent of Jesus Christ. The formulation in the Gospels concerns itself with the rejection of Jesus and the kingdom he inaugurates. People do not wish to respond to the invitation. Or people are not ready to respond. At stake is God's rule, which is at hand, but which comes when least expected. But the net result is the same. Christianity in the statement of the Gospels then sets forth a religious system focused upon the figure of Jesus in the advent of God's rule. Rabbinic Judaism, in the case at hand, centers its interest on the moral conduct of everyday life. That is where God's kingdom is realized, in the quotidian world of the here and the now. How does one accept God's rule, together with the unpredictable occasion at which God will exercise his dominion? People living in ordinary times must engage in a constant process of repentance, to be ready for the event—God's intervention and assertion of his dominion—that is inevitable but unpredictable, death.

Through working on the same motif of the king and the banquet and the guests who are not ready, and through insisting upon the same message, which is that one has to be ready every moment for the coming of the kingdom, the two systems say very different things. Perspective on the character and emphases of each is gained from the contrast with the other, made possible by the shared motif, which generates two comparable but contrasting parables. The humble detail—a few lines of narrative in the respective documents—proves to contain within itself much of what we require to differentiate the one reading of the shared Scripture from the other.

"Our sages of blessed memory" read Scripture as the account of how God's kingdom on earth is to take shape, how holy Israel is to realize the rules that govern the everyday and the here and now of the Kingdom of Heaven in which, through obedience to the Torah, priests and the holy people are to make their life, so declaring every morning and every night with the rising and setting of the sun, the regularity of nature, in the recitation of the Shema proclaiming God's rule. Jesus Christ received the same heritage as an account of not the enduring present but the now-realized future: the climax is at hand, and the Kingdom of Heaven marks not a lasting condition, matching nature with supernature in Israel's obedience, but the acutely present moment. And obedience is to the king, who has made a banquet—in Judaism, for his courtiers (= Israel, or all humanity, for that matter), and in Christianity, for his son (= Jesus Christ). Where else but at the intersection of like parables could we have encountered so jarring a collision: everyday Israel versus Jesus Christ! At every point likeness underscores difference, but only diachronic comparison sustains the encounter, synchronic reading forbidding it.

True, we end up just where we started, but now enlightened on where we stand. The reciprocal reading of the rabbis' and the Gospels' parables, like the comparative-contrastive reading of much else, yields two religions, each constructing upon, but asymmetrical to, the same foundation—buildings remarkable for their symmetry, but also for their utter incongruity.

Comparing Gospels and Rabbinic Writings: A Halakhic Instance

What we see when we turn to Halakhic compositions for comparison and contrast is that the same topic, healing on the Sabbath, for example, makes one point in the Gospels, but in the Halakhah of the Mishnah and the Tosefta makes an entirely different point, and when treating the same subject the two bodies of tradition simply part company. But that fact affords striking insight into the issues that inhere in the two religious systems, respectively.

Matthew 12:9-14 (// Mark 3:1-6; Luke 6:6-11) shows Jesus challenged with regard to healing on the Sabbath. Mark has, "Is it lawful on the Sabbath to do good or to do harm, to save life or to kill?" In Matthew he answers, "What man of you, if he has one sheep and it falls into a pit on the Sabbath, will not lay hold of it and lift it out? Of how much more value is a man than a sheep. So it is lawful to do good on the Sabbath." The premise throughout is whether it is lawful on the Sabbath to save life, as, indeed, the law of the Mishnah and the Tosefta and the exegetical readings of the pertinent passages in the Written Torah all concur is the fact. But saving life is not at issue in the story, only doing good.

And that brings us to the specific premise in the version of Matthew, whether one may lift a sheep out of a pit on the Sabbath. The Tosefta (among many documents) is explicit that one saves life on the Sabbath, and any show of piety is hypocrisy:

TOSEFTA SHABBAT 15:11-12

T. *Shabbat* 15:11: They remove debris for one whose life is in doubt on the Sabbath. And the one who is prompt in the matter, lo, this one is to be praised. And it is not necessary to get permission from a court. How so? [If] one fell into the ocean and cannot climb up, or [if] his ship is sinking in the sea, and he cannot climb up, they go down and pull him out of there. And it is not necessary to get permission from a court.

T. *Shabbat* 15:12: If he fell into a pit and cannot get out, they let down a chain to him and climb down and pull him out of there. And it is not necessary to get permission from a court. A baby who went into a house and cannot get out—they break down the doors of the house for him, even if they were of stone, and they get him out of there. And it is not necessary to get permission from a court. They put out a fire and make a barrier against a fire on the Sabbath [cf. *m. Shab.* Chap. 16]. And one who is prompt, lo, this one is to be praised. And it is not necessary to get permission from a court.

But that brings us to the Halakhic premise of the statement of Jesus: what about the animal in a pit?

TOSEFTA SHABBAT 14:3

L. For a beast which fell into a pit they provide food in the place in which it has fallen, so that it not die, [and they pull it up after the Sabbath].

The rule is given anonymously; it is not subject to dispute but is normative. But then how are we to understand the certainty with which Jesus asks, "What man of you, if he has one sheep and it falls into a pit on the Sabbath, will not lay hold of it and lift it out? Of how much more value is a man than a sheep. So it is lawful to do good on the Sabbath." The Halakhic definition of doing good on the Sabbath is feeding the beast in the pit, not raising it up.

Clearly, the synoptic picture of Jesus deems the critical issue to concern whether or not it is lawful to do good on the Sabbath, and the answer is, it is indeed lawful to do good, and the Pharisees do not understand the law. But what if, to the framers of the Mishnah,[2] the Sabbath involves other issues entirely, so that when they speak of the Sabbath they use a theological language that simply does not intersect with the language of doing work on the Sabbath or doing good on the Sabbath? After all, even the parallelism—to do good or do harm, to save life or kill—hardly is commensurate. Sages concur that one must save life, and everyone knows that one may never murder, not on a weekday, and not on the Sabbath. So the framing of the question, sensible in the setting of Jesus' teaching, proves disingenuous in the setting of the sages' system. But then in what context do sages consider healing on the Sabbath? It is not a matter of (excess) labor—and the story strikingly does not represent Jesus as having done an act of labor, for no labor is involved in the healing. Jesus tells the man, "Come here." He said to the man, "Stretch out your hand." He stretched it out, and his hand was restored. In fact, Jesus has done nothing; *labor is not the issue.*

What defines the issues of the Sabbath for the Rabbinic tradition of the Torah? With regard to the Sabbath, the Halakhah of the Mishnah, Tosefta, and Talmuds concerns three matters, (1) space, (2) time, and (3) activity, as the advent of the Sabbath affects all three. The advent of the Sabbath transforms creation, specifically reorganizing space and time and reordering the range of permissible activity. First comes the transformation of space that takes effect at sundown at the end of the sixth day and that ends at sundown of the Sabbath day. At that time, for holy Israel, the entire world is divided into public domain and private domain, and what is located in the one may not be transported into the other. What is located in public domain may be transported only four cubits, that is, within the space occupied by a person's body. What is in private domain may be transported within the entire demarcated space of that domain. All public domain is deemed a single spatial entity, and so too all private domain, so that one may transport objects from one private domain to another. The net effect of the transformation of space on the Sabbath is to move nearly all permitted activity to private domain and to close off public domain for all but the most severely limited activities. People may not transport objects from one domain to the other, but they may transport objects within private domain, so the closure of public domain from most activity, and nearly all material or physical activity, comes in consequence of the division of space effected by sunset at the end of the sixth day of the week.

When it comes to space, the advent of the Sabbath divides into distinct domains for all practical purposes what in secular time is deemed divided only as to ownership, but united as to utilization. Sacred time then intensifies the arrangements of space as public and private, imparting enormous consequence to the status of what is private. There, and only there, on the Sabbath, is life to be lived. The Sabbath assigns to private domain the focus of life in holy time: the household is where things take place then. When, presently, we realize that the household (private domain) is deemed analogous to the Temple or tabernacle (God's household), forming a mirror image to the tabernacle, we shall understand the full meaning of the generative principle before us concerning space on the Sabbath.

Second comes the matter of time and how the advent of sacred time registers. Since the consequence of the demarcation on the Sabbath of all space

146

into private and public domain affects, in particular, transporting objects from one space to the other, how time is differentiated will present no surprise. The effects concern private domain, the household. Specifically, what turns out to frame the Halakhic issue is what objects may be handled or used, even in private domain, on the Sabbath. The advent of the Sabbath thus affects the organization of space and the utilization of tools and other objects, the furniture of the household within the designated territory of the household. The basic principle is simple. Objects may be handled only if they are designated in advance of the Sabbath for use for the purpose for which they will be utilized on the Sabbath. But if tools may be used for a purpose that is licit on the Sabbath, and if those tools are ordinarily used for that same purpose, they are deemed ready at hand and do not require reclassification; the accepted classification applies. What requires designation for Sabbath use in particular is any tool that may serve more than a single purpose, or that does not ordinarily serve the purpose for which it is wanted on the Sabbath. Designation for use on the Sabbath thus regularizes the irregular, but is not required for what is ordinarily used for the purpose for which it is wanted and is licitly utilized on the Sabbath.

The Sabbath, then, finds all useful tools and objects in their proper place. That may mean that they may not be handled at all, since their ordinary function cannot be performed on the Sabbath; or it may mean that they may be handled on the Sabbath exactly as they are handled every other day, the function being licit on the Sabbath; or it may mean that they must be designated in advance of the Sabbath for licit utilization on the Sabbath. That third proviso covers utensils that serve more than a single function, or that do not ordinarily serve the function of licit utilization on the Sabbath that the householder wishes them to serve on this occasion. The advent of the Sabbath, then, requires that all tools and other things be regularized and ordered. The rule extends even to utilization of space within the household that is not ordinarily used for a (licit) purpose for which it is needed on the Sabbath. If guests come, storage space used for food may be cleared away to accommodate them, the space being conceived as suitable for sitting even when not ordinarily used for that purpose. But one may not clear out a storeroom for that purpose. One may also make a path in a storeroom so that one may move about there. One may handle objects that, in some way or another, can serve a licit purpose, in the theory that that purpose inheres. But what is not made ready for use may not be used on the Sabbath. So the advent of the Sabbath not only divides space into public and private, but also differentiates useful tools and objects into those that may or may not be handled within the household.

Third, we come to the generative problematics particular to the Sabbath. The effect upon activity that the advent of the Sabbath makes concerns constructive labor. In a normal way one may not carry out entirely on one's own a completed act of constructive labor, which is to say, work that produces enduring results. That is what one is supposed to do in profane time. What is implicit in that simple statement proves profound and bears far-reaching implications. No prohibition impedes performing an act of labor in an other-than-normal way, for example, in a way that is unusual and thus takes account of the differentiation of time. Labor in a natural, not in an unnatural, manner is prohibited. But that is not all. A person is not forbidden to carry out an act of destruction, or an act of labor that produces no lasting consequences. Nor is part of an act of labor, not brought to conclusion, prohibited. Nor is it forbidden to perform part of an act of labor in partnership with another person who carries out the other requisite part. Nor does one incur culpability for performing an act of labor in several distinct parts, for example, over a protracted, differentiated period of time. The advent of the Sabbath prohibits activities carried out in ordinary time in a way deemed natural: acts that are complete, consequential, and in accord with their accepted character.

What is the upshot of this remarkable repertoire of fundamental considerations having to do with activity in the household on the holy day? The Halakhah of *Shabbat* in the aggregate concerns itself with formulating a statement of how the advent of the Sabbath defines the kind of activity that may be done by specifying what may not be done. That is the meaning of repose, the cessation of activity, not the commencement of activity of a different order. To carry out the Sabbath, one does nothing, not something. And what is that "nothing" that one realizes through inactivity? One may not carry out an act analogous to one that sustains creation. An act or activity for which one bears responsibility, and one that sustains creation, is (1) an act analogous to one required in the building and maintenance of the tabernacle, (2) that is intentionally carried out (3) in its entirety, (4) by a single actor, (5) in the ordinary manner, (6) with a constructive and (7) consequential result—one worthy of consideration by accepted norms. These are the seven conditions that pertain, and that, in one way or another, together with counterpart considerations in connection with the transformation of space and time, generate most of the Halakhah of *Shabbat*.

Like God at the completion of creation, so is Israel on the Sabbath: the Halakhah of the Sabbath defines the Sabbath not to mean to do no more, but instead to do nothing. At issue in Sabbath rest is not ceasing from labor but ceasing from labor of a very particular character, labor in the model of God's work in making the world. Then why the issues of space, time, and activity? Given the division of space into public domain, where nothing much can happen, and the private domain of the household, where nearly everything dealt with in the law at hand takes place, we realize that the Sabbath forms an occasion of the household in particular. There man takes up repose, leaving off the tools required to make the world, ceasing to perform the acts that sustain the world. The issue of the Sabbath is the restoration of Eden, the realization of Eden in the household of holy Israel.

On that issue, the matter of how much effort is involved in saving the beast proves monumentally irrelevant. Nor can sages have grasped what someone meant in saying, "The son of man is the Lord of the Sabbath." When set alongside the Gospels' framing of issues, we realize, the two pictures of the Sabbath and the issues that inhere therein scarcely intersect. But knowing that fact affords perspective on both the figure of Jesus and the Torah of the sages that seeing each on its own does not provide. Small details turn out to recapitulate large conceptions, and that, in the end, ought to define the hermeneutics and the consequent exegetics of the next phase of study of both the Gospels and the Mishnah.

The Rabbinic literature as well as the early Christian writings may be read in their own terms and framework. But when the two bodies of writing are drawn into a relationship of comparison and contrast, both of them take on deeper meaning. The differences are sharpened. The details of each, emerging as part of a coherent and cogent system, make sense as part of a whole. The Gospel asks the Sabbath to serve as a medium to express the dominion of Jesus Christ over the Torah, and the Rabbinic Halakhah expresses the theology of the restoration of the perfection of Creation that animates much of the Rabbinic system. The two readings of the same matter intersect and part company.

NOTES

Chapter 1. What Is Rabbinic Literature? Why Is It Important?

1. Summarized here are the pertinent chapters of my *Introduction to Rabbinic Literature* (N.Y.: Doubleday, 1994). The state of the question studies by Guenter Stemberger, together with bibliographies, mark the starting point for all future inquiry; see H. L. Strack and G. Stemberger, *Introduction to the Talmud and Midrash* (Minneapolis: Fortress, 1992). See also John Bowker, *The Targums and Rabbinic Literature: An Introduction to Jewish Interpretations of Scripture* (Cambridge: Cambridge University Press, 1969); Hyam Maccoby, *Early Rabbinic Writings* (Cambridge: Cambridge University Press, 1988), in the series Cambridge Commentaries on Writings of the Jewish and Christian World, 200 BC to AD 200 (eds. P. R. Ackroyd, A. R. C. Leaney, and J. W. Packer; vol. 3); Shmuel Safrai, ed., Peter J. Tomson, Executive Editor, *The Literature of the Sages, Volume 1: Oral Tora, Halakha, Mishna, Tosefta, Talmud, External Tractates*, in the series Compendia Rerum Iudaicarum ad Novum Testamentum, Section Two: The Literature of the Jewish People in the Period of the Second Temple and the Talmud (Assen/Maastricht and Philadelphia: Van Gorcum and Fortress Press, 1987). These articles are briefly summarized at the chapters that deal with their topics. The entries on each document in *Encyclopaedia Judaica* (N.Y. and Jerusalem: Macmillan and Keter, 1971). These are cited under the names of the various authors and cover every document treated here. The entries by M. D. Herr are noteworthy for their consistent plan; the others are haphazard and not always illuminating.

2. Before the Common Era (BCE); in the Common Era (CE).

Chapter 2. The Oral Torah

1. Among the innumerable translations into English are the following: C. Taylor, *Sayings of the Jewish Fathers* (Cambridge, 1877) and J. Goldin, *The Living Talmud: The Wisdom of the Fathers* (N.Y.: New American Library, 1957). This writer's

translation is *Torah from Our Sages: Pirke Tractate Abot: A New American Translation and Explanation* (Chappaqua: Rossel/Behrman House, 1983).

2. For further reading and bibliography on the topic of this chapter, see the following: Bowker, pp. 87ff.; Judah Goldin, "Abot," *Encyclopaedia Judaica* 3:983-84: unique among Mishnah treatises, lacking law; provides credentials of sages in chain of tradition; sages are given sayings: "these sayings reveal the convictions which shaped the Pharisaic and the early dominant tannaitic schools." The fifth chapter may have been part of the original core. The work is recited in the synagogue. M. Bialik Lerner, "The Tractate Abot" (name, contents and structure, literary characteristics, Perek Kinyan Tora, the textual criticism of tractate *Abot* [by S. Sharvit]), in Safrai, *Literature of the Sages*, pp. 263-82. Maccoby, pp. 31, 39, 40, 125 ("Tractate *Abot* restricts itself to ethic surrounding the Rabbinic emphasis on the religious duty of study and education; Tractate *Abot* is unique in that it is a treatise on education which not only enjoins study and teaching as a feature of the religious life, but seeks to isolate the moral and spiritual characteristics necessary for good teaching and good studying."). Selections: pp. 124-26; Strack and Stemberger, pp. 120-21, 137 (bibliography).

3. The first translation into English of Version A is Judah Goldin, *The Fathers According to Rabbi Nathan* (New Haven: Yale University Press, 1955). The second, and the first form-analytical translation of the same version, is this writer's *The Fathers According to Rabbi Nathan: An Analytical Translation and Explanation* (Atlanta: Scholars Press for Brown Judaic Studies, 1986). The only translation of Version B is A. J. Saldarini, *The Fathers According to Rabbi Nathan (Tractate Abot deRabbi Nathan) Version B: A Translation and Commentary* (Leiden: E. J. Brill, 1975).

4. For further reading and bibliography: Bowker, pp. 87-88. Judah Goldin, "Abot de-Rabbi Nathan," *Encyclopaedia Judaica* 3:984-86: description of the document, its two versions, no certain date, "in language and content, and style there is virtually nothing to compel a late dating. No *amoraim* are quoted ... the flavor of the work is tannaitic." M. Bialik Lerner, "The External Tractates," in Safrai, *Literature of the Sages*, pp. 369-79 on tractate *Abot deR. Natan*: name and character, structure and contents, versions A and B, date of redaction of versions A and B, bibliography. Maccoby, pp. 39, 128 (ARN is to tractate *Abot* as *Tosefta* is to the *Mishnah*). A. J. Saldarini, *The Fathers According to Rabbi Nathan (Tractate Abot de Rabbi Nathan) Version B: A Translation and Commentary* (Leiden: E. J. Brill, 1975). *Studies in Judaism in Late Antiquity,* ed. Jacob Neusner, Volume XIII. Strack and Stemberger, pp. 245-47: bibliography; text; translations; "The use of a version of Abot which diverges from M suggests that the core of ARN is to be dated no later than the early third century ... The widely accepted dating of the final version between the seventh and ninth centuries ... is essentially based on the fact that ARN is regarded as one with the minor tractates. However, the language, substance and the cited rabbis do not justify such a late date." This writer's translation of the document is *The Fathers According to Rabbi Nathan: An Analytical Translation and Explanation* (Atlanta: Scholars Press for Brown Judaic Studies, 1986); his systematic introduction to, and analysis of, the document, both in relationship to tractate *Abot* and also in its own terms, is *Judaism and Story: The Evidence of The Fathers According to Rabbi Nathan* (Chicago: University of Chicago Press, 1992). Further studies relevant to the same problem are in *Form-Analytical*

Comparison in Rabbinic Judaism: Structure and Form in The Fathers and The Fathers According to Rabbi Nathan (Atlanta: Scholars Press for South Florida Studies in the History of Judaism, 1992).

5. Judah Goldin, "Tractate Abot de-Rabbi Nathan," *Encyclopaedia Judaica* 3:985.

Chapter 3. The Rabbinic Canon: Law (Halakhah)

1. The two systematic, complete translations of the Mishnah into English are H. Danby, *The Mishnah* (Oxford: Oxford University Press, 1933), and this writer's *The Mishnah: A New Translation* (New Haven: Yale University Press, 1987). The Hebrew text most commonly consulted is H. Albeck, *Shisha Sidré Mishnah* (Tel Aviv and Jerusalem, 1954-1958), in six volumes. The definitive study of the text of the Mishnah is J. N. Epstein, *Introduction to the Text of the Mishnah* (Jerusalem: Magnes Press of the Hebrew University, 1948, 1964), in Hebrew.

2. For further reading and bibliography, see the following:

Baruch M. Bokser, Joel Gereboff, William Scott Green, Gary G. Porton, and Charles Primus, "Bibliography on the Mishnah," in *Study of Ancient Judaism*, I (New York: KTAV, 1981), pp. 37-54.

Bowker, pp. 46-48: the Mishnah's origin in exegesis; pp. 53-61.

Abraham Goldberg, "The Mishna—A Study Book of Halakha" (origins and development, Rabbi Aqiba and his pupils, the four layers, principles of editing, arrangement, the more important teachers, language, text, reduction to writing, authority, bibliography, manuscripts by Michael Krupp), in Safrai, *Literature of the Sages*, pp. 211-62.

Maccoby, pp. 30-35; selected passage, pp. 49-133.

Neusner, "The Modern Study of the Mishnah," in *Study of Ancient Judaism*, I, pp. 3-26.

Strack and Stemberger, pp. 119-66: bibliography in general and by tractates; explanation of terms; survey of contents; is the structure of the Mishnah original; origin of the Mishnah; biblical interpretation as the origin of the Mishnah; prehistory of the Mishnah; redaction of the Mishnah; text: manuscripts, editions, translations; the interpretation of the Mishnah.

Ephraim E. Urbach, "Mishnah," in *Encyclopaedia Judaica* 12:93-109: the sources of the Mishnah; how the Mishnah was produced and arranged; how the Mishnah was published (orally or in writing); the division of the Mishnah; the text of the Mishnah; editions, commentaries, and translations.

Among this writer's studies, the following are the most important: *Judaism: The Evidence of the Mishnah* (Chicago: University of Chicago Press, 1981; second edition, augmented: Atlanta: Scholars Press for Brown Judaic Studies, 1987); *The Economics of the Mishnah* (Chicago: The University of Chicago Press, 1989); *Rabbinic Political Theory: Religion and Politics in the Mishnah* (Chicago: The University of Chicago Press, 1991); and *Judaism as Philosophy: The Method and Message of the Mishnah* (Columbia: University of South Carolina Press, 1991). *A History of the Mishnaic Law of Purities; of Holy Things; of Appointed Times; of Women; and of Damages* (Leiden: E. J. Brill, 1975-1984), in 43 volumes, provides a systematic translation of the Mishnah and the Tosefta side by side, showing the relationships of the two documents and descriptions of the history and system of the Mishnah pertaining to its principal categories.

3. The complete translation is J. Neusner, *The Tosefta: Vol. 1: Zeraim, Moed, and Nashim; Vol. 2: Neziqin, Qodoshim, and Tohorot* (Peabody: Hendrickson Publications, 2003).

4. For further reading and bibliography see the following:

Bowker, pp. 61-64.

Abraham Goldberg, "The Tosefta—Companion to the Mishna" (character and date; arrangement and contents; structural layers; commentary and supplement to the Mishna, the Tosefta, and the Baraitot in the Talmuds; editing; Tannaite prominent in the Tosefta; bibliography: editions, commentaries and translations, introductions and research, Tosefta manuscripts [by Michael Krupp]), in Safrai, *Literature of the Sages*, pp. 283-302.

Moses David Herr, "Tosefta," in *Encyclopaedia Judaica* 15:1283-85: structure, editions, and commentaries; the Tosefta was not edited before the end of the fourth century; "The compiler did not add, omit, or change his material in any way, but collected the material that was at his disposal. . . . The aim of this anonymous compiler and redactor was obviously to produce a collection that would serve as a supplement to the Mishnah."

Maccoby, pp. 35-36; selected passages, pp. 133-47.

Strack and Stemberger, pp. 167-81: general bibliography; the relationship of the Tosefta to the Mishnah and the Talmuds; name, structure, contents, origin; the text of the Tosefta; printed editions; translations; commentaries.

This writer's *History of the Mishnaic Law* (in 43 volumes) presents the Tosefta unit by unit in relationship to the corresponding Mishnah passages and comments on the whole. The results are briefly summarized in *The Tosefta: Its Structure and Its Sources* (Atlanta: Scholars Press for Brown Judaic Studies, 1986). See the reprise of pertinent results in *Purities* I-XXI, and *The Tosefta: An Introduction* (Atlanta: Scholars Press for South Florida Studies in the History of Judaism, 1992), which provides a systematic account of the document.

5. The only complete translation into any European language is this writer's *Talmud of the Land of Israel: A Preliminary Translation and Explanation* (Chicago: University of Chicago Press, 1984-1993), I-XXXV.

6. For further reading and bibliography, see the following:

Baruch M. Bokser, "An Annotated Bibliographical Guide to the study of the Palestinian Talmud," in Neusner, *Study of Ancient Judaism*, II, pp. 1-120.

Bowker, pp. 64-5.

Abraham Goldberg, "The Palestinian Talmud" (Tannaim and Amoraim; Palestinian and Babylonian Talmud; importance of the Palestinian Talmud, the Palestinian Amoraim, and the Mishna; relationship to Mishna, Tosefta, and Baraitot; editing, authority, bibliography; manuscripts of the Palestinian Talmud [by Michael Krupp]), in Safrai, *Literature of the Sages*, pp. 303-22.

Maccoby's introduction does not make reference to this document at all, though he does treat documents of its period.

Louis I. Rabinowitz, "Talmud, Jerusalem," in *Encyclopaedia Judaica* 15:772-79: contents; characteristics; acceptance of the two Talmuds; editions; commentaries.

Strack and Stemberger, pp. 182-207: terms; the name; contents and structure; the absence of many tractates; repetitions within the Palestinian Talmud (numerous, literal repetitions of long sections); origin of the Yerushalmi; redaction, probably circa 410-420, in Tiberias; nature of the redaction; sources; the Mishnah of the Yerushalmi; midrashic material in the Yerushalmi; Babylonian traditions in the Yerushalmi; the text; manuscripts; printed editions; translation.

This writer's introduction to the Yerushalmi is in *The Talmud of the Land of Israel: A Preliminary Translation and Explanation. Vol. XXXV: Introduction, Taxonomy* (Chicago: University of Chicago Press, 1985). On the place of the Yerushalmi in the history of Judaism, see *Judaism in Society: The Evidence of the Yerushalmi: Toward the Natural History of a Religion* (Chicago: The University of Chicago Press, 1983; second printing, with a new preface: Atlanta: Scholars Press for South Florida Studies in the History of Judaism, 1991); and *Judaism and Christianity in the Age of Constantine: Issues of the Initial Confrontation* (Chicago: University of Chicago Press, 1987). Further discussion is in *The Yerushalmi. The Talmud of the Land of Israel: An Introduction* (Northvale: Jason Aronson, Inc., 1993).

7. The first complete translation of the Talmud of Babylonia is Israel Epstein, ed., *The Babylonian Talmud* (London: Soncino Press, 1948), reprinted in eighteen volumes. The second complete translation—the only one based on the principles of form analysis—now in print is this writer's *The Talmud of Babylonia: An American Translation* (Missoula, Chico, then Atlanta: Scholars Press for Brown Judaic Studies, 1984-1993), in seventy-five volumes. Further translations into English are presently underway, but none has as yet come close to completion.

8. For further reading and bibliography, see the following:

Eliezer Berkovits, "Talmud, Babylonian," in *Encyclopaedia Judaica* 15:755-68: methods of study; scope of the Babylonian Talmud; Mishnah and Gemara; interpretation and application; development and conclusion of the Babylonian Talmud; style; text; minor tractates; commentaries; manuscripts; authority, influence; translations.

Bowker, pp. 65-67.

David Goodblatt, "The Babylonian Talmud," in Neusner, *Study of Ancient Judaism*, II (New York: KTAV, 1981), pp. 120-99.

Abraham Goldberg, "The Babylonian Talmud" (the Halakhic tradition in Babylonia; the Babylonian academies and generations of sages; the Babylonian approach to the Mishnah ['The Mishna is lacking and thus the Tanna teaches']; relationship to Tosefta, Baraitot, and Palestinian Talmud; the Aggada in the Babylonian Talmud; the *sugya*; the Saboraim; redaction; authority; bibliography; manuscripts of the Babylonian Talmud [by Michael Krupp]), in Safrai, *Literature of the Sages*, pp. 323-66.

M. B. Lerner, "The External Tractates," covering *Derekh Erets, Semahot, Kalla, Sofrim*, and the Seven Minor tracts, in Safrai, *Literature of the Sages*, pp. 367-403.

Maccoby's introduction ignores this document entirely. But see "Tannaitic passages in the Talmud [= Talmud of Babylonia only] (Baraitas)," pp. 182-85.

Zeev Safrai, "Post-Talmudic Halakhic Literature in the Land of Israel," in Safrai, *Literature of the Sages*, pp. 404-10.

Strack and Stemberger, pp. 208-44: structure and contents; origin; redaction; sources; Baraitot; Midrashim; Palestinian sources from the Amoraic period; amalgamation of the Tradition; the contribution of the Saboraim; Geonic additions; the text; manuscripts; printed editions; translations; the authority of the Babylonian Talmud; commentaries; introductions to the Talmud; the Talmud in controversy.

This writer's monographic studies include the following: *The Bavli and Its Sources: The Question of Tradition in the Case of Tractate Sukkah* (Atlanta: Scholars Press for Brown Judaic Studies, 1987); *The Talmud: Close Encounters* (Minneapolis: Fortress Press, 1991); *Tradition as Selectivity: Scripture, Mishnah, Tosefta, and Midrash in the Talmud of Babylonia: The Case of Tractate Arakhin* (Atlanta: Scholars Press for South Florida Studies in the History of Judaism, 1990); *Language as Taxonomy: The Rules for Using Hebrew and Aramaic in the Babylonian Talmud* (Atlanta: Scholars Press for South Florida Studies in the History of Judaism, 1990); *The Bavli That Might Have Been: The Tosefta's Theory of Mishnah-Commentary Compared with that of the Babylonian Talmud* (Atlanta: Scholars Press for South Florida Studies in the History of Judaism, 1990); *The Rules of Composition of the Talmud of Babylonia: The Cogency of the Bavli's Composite* (Atlanta: Scholars Press for South Florida Studies in the History of Judaism, 1991); *The Bavli's One Voice: Types and Forms of Analytical Discourse and Their Fixed Order of Appearance* (Atlanta: Scholars Press for South Florida Studies in the History of Judaism, 1991); *The Bavli's One Statement: The Metapropositional Program of Babylonian Talmud Tractate Zebahim Chapters One and Five* (Atlanta: Scholars Press for South Florida Studies in the History of Judaism, 1991); *How the Bavli Shaped Rabbinic Discourse* (Atlanta: Scholars Press for South Florida Studies in the History of Judaism, 1991); *The Bavli's Massive Miscellanies: The Problem of Agglutinative Discourse in the Talmud of Babylonia* (Atlanta: Scholars Press for South Florida Studies in the History of Judaism, 1992); *Sources and Traditions: Types of Composition in the Talmud of Babylonia* (Atlanta: Scholars Press for South Florida Studies in the History of Judaism, 1992); *The Law Behind the Laws: The Bavli's Essential Discourse* (Atlanta: Scholars Press for South Florida Studies in the History of Judaism, 1992); *The Bavli's Primary Discourse: Mishnah Commentary, Its Rhetorical Paradigms and Their Theological Implications in the Talmud of Babylonia Tractate Moed Qatan* (Atlanta: Scholars Press for South Florida Studies in the History of Judaism, 1992); *The Discourse of the Bavli: Language, Literature, and Symbolism: Five Recent Findings* (Atlanta: Scholars Press for South Florida Studies in the History of Judaism, 1991); *The Bavli's Intellectual Character: The Generative Problematic in Bavli Baba Qamma Chapter One and Bavli Shabbat Chapter One* (Atlanta: Scholars Press for South Florida Studies in the History of Judaism, 1992); *Decoding the Talmud's Exegetical Program: From Detail to Principle in the Bavli's Quest for Generalization: Tractate Shabbat* (Atlanta: Scholars Press for South Florida Studies in the History of Judaism, 1992); *The Principal Parts of the Bavli's Discourse: A Final Taxonomy: Mishnah-Commentary, Sources, Traditions, and Agglutinative Miscellanies* (Atlanta: Scholars Press for South Florida Studies in the History of Judaism, 1992); *The Torah in the Talmud: A Taxonomy of the Uses of Scripture in the Talmuds: Tractate Qiddushin in the Talmud of Babylonia and the Talmud of the Land of Israel. I. Bavli Qiddushin Chapter One* (Atlanta: Scholars Press for South Florida Studies in the History of Judaism, 1992); *The Torah in the Talmud: A Taxonomy of the Uses of Scripture in the Talmuds: Tractate Qiddushin in the Talmud of Babylonia and the Talmud of the Land of Israel.*

II. Yerushalmi Qiddushin Chapter One. And a Comparison of the Uses of Scripture by the Two Talmuds (Atlanta: Scholars Press for South Florida Studies in the History of Judaism, 1992); *The Bavli's Unique Voice: A Systematic Comparison of the Talmud of Babylonia and the Talmud of the Land of Israel* (in seven volumes); and *Talmudic Thinking: Language, Logic, and Law* (Columbia: University of South Carolina Press, 1992).

9. There are two complete translations of the Midrash compilation, and one partial translation. The first translation is Jacob Z. Lauterbach, *Mekilta de-Rabbi Ishmael: A Critical Edition on the Basis of the Manuscripts and Early Editions with an English Translation, Introduction and Notes* (Philadelphia: The Jewish Publication Society of America, 1933), I-III. The partial translation is Judah Goldin's, of the tractate *Shirata*, in his *The Song at the Sea: Being a Commentary on a Commentary in Two Parts* (New Haven: Yale University Press, 1971). The second complete translation, and first analytical one, is this writer's *Mekhilta Attributed to R. Ishmael: An Analytical Translation* (Atlanta: Scholars Press for Brown Judaic Studies, 1988), I. *Pisha, Beshallah, Shirata, and Vayassa,* and II. *Amalek, Bahodesh, Neziqin, Kaspa and Shabbata.* This translation closely adheres to that of Lauterbach in all matters of philology and text criticism.

10. This attribution cannot be evaluated. The "Ishmael" here is presumably the colleague of Aqiba, a master in the Land of Israel at the turn of the second century. But we have no dependable historical information in the Rabbinic literature on any authority, and attributions of documents to named authorities cannot be shown to be reliable. To the contrary, the documents accepted as authoritative or canonical are uniformly anonymous; after the fact attributions do not change that fact. For an account of why Rabbinic literature contains no biographies, personal letters, signed books formulated in a personal style, and equivalent marks of individuality, see my *Why No Gospels in Talmudic Judaism?* (Atlanta: Scholars Press for Brown Judaic Studies, 1988). The same observation applies to the other compilations that bear attributions, for example, *Pesiqta deRab Kahana*; in no case can we verify that the named authority wrote or compiled the document or any of its principal parts. Nor do we know why some documents bear attributions of authorship and some do not. Efforts within Rabbinic literature itself to assign books to named figures, for example, the Mishnah to Judah the patriarch, persuade only the believers in the inerrancy of these writings; others tend to take a position of suspended judgment. In any event there is no point in narrating the life and times of Ishmael when we open this Mekhilta, since there is no established correlation between stories about, and sayings assigned to, Ishmael, and the character and contents of this document in particular.

11. For further reading and bibliography , see the following:

Bowker, pp. 69-71.

M. D. Herr, "Mekhilta of R. Ishmael," *Encyclopaedia Judaica* (Jerusalem: Keter, 1971), 11:1269: the name; coverage in Exodus; division of the work; special characteristics; language; first printed editions.

Maccoby, pp. 148-72: extensive selections with commentary.

Strack and Stemberger, pp. 274-80: the name; contents and structure; character, origin, date ("an account of the origin of Mek can only proceed from the individual sources...The form of the individual traditions, the cited rabbis and the historical allusions suggest a date of final redaction in the second half of the third century..."); the text, manuscripts, and printed editions.

This writer's introduction is *Mekhilta Attributed to R. Ishmael: An Introduction to Judaism's First Scriptural Encyclopaedia* (Atlanta: Scholars Press for Brown Judaic Studies, 1988).

12. Moshe D. Herr maintains that the work was "probably compiled and redacted in Erez Israel not earlier than the end of the fourth century." The prevailing scholarly consensus assigns to the present document a place within the "Halakhic Midrashim," or the "Tannaitic Midrashim," that is to say, compilations of exegeses of verses of Scripture that pertain to normative behavior, on the one side, and to the period of the authorities who produced the Mishnah (that is, the first and second centuries of the Common Era) on the other. The two current discussions are as follows: Ben Zion Wacholder, "The Date of the Mekilta de-Rabbi Ishmael," *Hebrew Union College Annual* 1968, 39:117-44, who rejects the received date and proposes one in medieval times; and Günther Stemberger, "Die Datierung der Mekhilta," *Kairos* 1979, 31:81-118, who systematically proposes to refute Wacholder's position. In Wacholder's behalf, however, we have to note that if *Mekhilta Attributed to Rabbi Ishmael* belongs to the classification of Tannaitic Midrashim and of Halakhic Midrashim, as we shall see, it is quite different from the other books in those categories, *Sifra* and the two *Sifrés*, in the indicative traits of rhetoric, logic, and topical exposition.

13. The word means "the book," and refers to the first Rabbinic commentary on the book of Leviticus.

14. The only translation into English is this writer's *Sifra: An Analytical Translation* (Atlanta: Scholars Press for Brown Judaic Studies, 1988), *I. Introduction* and *Vayyiqra Dibura Denedabah* and *Vayiqqra Dibura Dehobah*; *II. Sav, Shemini, Tazria, Negaim, Mesora*, and *Zabim*; *III. Aharé Mot, Qedoshim, Emor, Behar*, and *Behuqotai*.

15. For further reading and bibliography , see the following:

Bowker, p. 71.

Moses D. Herr, "Sifra," *Encyclopaedia Judaica* 14:1517-19: the name; construction (outline); language; source; editing; additions to the document; editions.

Maccoby, pp. 172-77 (selections, no introduction or analysis).

Strack and Stemberger, pp. 284-89: the name contents and structure; character, origin, and date; manuscripts, printed editions, translations, commentaries; a Mekhilta on Leviticus?

This writer's introductions are two, one in relationship to the Mishnah, the other in regard to the document's rhetorical, logical, and topical traits and program. The first is *Uniting the Dual Torah: Sifra and the Problem of the Mishnah* (Cambridge and New York: Cambridge University Press, 1989) and the second is *Sifra in Perspective: The Documentary Comparison of the Midrashim of Ancient Judaism* (Atlanta: Scholars Press for Brown Judaic Studies, 1988). The latter conducts "comparative Midrash," treating this document in comparison with other Midrash compilations of its class. That kind of comparative Midrash has been worked out only in the books of mine summarized in this introduction.

16. The word *sifré* corresponds to the Hebrew *sefarim*, "books." It is explained

by Moses D. Herr, in the article cited in the next note, as follows: "As early as amoraic times the word *sifré* was employed as the designation for a collection of halakhic *beraitot* [legal rulings not found in the Mishnah but enjoying authoritative status], and also used for a collection of *beraitot* containing *halakhot* [legal rulings] derived from exegesis of biblical verses."

17. The sole complete translation into English is *The Components of the Rabbinic Documents: From the Whole to the Parts. XII. Sifré to Numbers* (Atlanta: Scholars Press for USF Academic Commentary Series, 1998), *Part I: Introduction. Pisqaot One through Eighty-Four. Part II: Pisqaot Eighty-Five through One Hundred Twenty-Two. Part III: Pisqaot One Hundred Twenty-Three through One Hundred Sixty-On. Part IV: Sifré to Numbers: A Topical and Methodical Outline.*

18. For further reading and bibliography, see the following:
Bowker, pp. 71-72.
Moses D. Herr, "Sifrei," *Encyclopaedia Judaica* 14:1519-21: coverage of Numbers, distinction from *Sifré* to Deuteronomy; *Sifré* to Deuteronomy; characteristics; origin in the school of Aqiba; commentaries; critical editions.
Maccoby does not introduce this document.
Strack and Stemberger, pp. 290-93: translation; the name; contents and structure; character, origin, date (after the middle of the third century); manuscripts, printed editions, commentaries.
This writer's introduction is in *Sifré to Numbers. An American Translation.* II. *59-115* (Atlanta: Scholars Press for Brown Judaic Studies, 1986).

19. This is the argument of my *The Perfect Torah* (Leiden: E. J. Brill, 2003).

20. There are two complete translations into English, Reuven Hammer, *Sifre: A Tannaitic Commentary on the Book of Deuteronomy: Translated from the Hebrew with Introduction and Notes* (Yale Judaica Series XXIII; New Haven and London: Yale University Press, 1986), and this writer's *Sifré to Deuteronomy: An Analytical Translation* (Atlanta: Scholars Press for Brown Judaic Studies, 1987), *I. Pisqaot One through One Hundred Forty-Three: Debarim, Waethanan, Eqeb, Re'eh,* and II. *Pisqaot One Hundred Forty-Four through Three Hundred Fifty-Seven: Shofetim, Ki Tese, Ki Tabo, Nesabim, Ha'azinu, Zot Habberakhah.* The only difference between them is that Hammer's has no analytical reference system of any kind and lacks a systematic introduction to the document.

21. For further reading and bibliography, see the following:
Bowker, pp. 71-72.
Moses D. Herr, "Sifrei," *Encyclopaedia Judaica* 14:1519-21: coverage of Numbers; distinction from *Sifré* to Deuteronomy; *Sifré* to Deuteronomy; characteristics; origin in the school of Aqiba; commentaries; critical editions.
Maccoby, pp. 177-81 (selections, no introduction or analysis).
Strack and Stemberger, pp. 294-99: contents and structure; critical edition, translations; character, origin, date (late third century); commentaries.
This writer's introduction is *Sifré to Deuteronomy: An Introduction to the Rhetorical, Logical, and Topical Program* (Atlanta: Scholars Press for Brown Judaic Studies, 1987).

Chapter 4. The Rabbinic Canon: Theology (Aggadah)

1. Translation: *The Components of the Rabbinic Documents: From the Whole to the Parts. IX. Genesis Rabbah* (Atlanta: Scholars Press for USF Academic Commentary Series, 1998). *Part I: Introduction. Genesis Rabbah Chapters One through Twenty-One. Part II: Genesis Rabbah Chapters Twenty-Two through Forty-Eight. Part III: Genesis Rabbah Chapters Forty-Nine through Seventy-Three. Part IV: Genesis Rabbah Chapters Seventy-Four through One Hundred. Part V: A Topical and Methodical Outline of Genesis Rabbah, Bereshit through Vaere, Chapters One through Fifty-Seven. Part VI: A Topical and Methodical Outline of Genesis Rabbah, Hayye Sarah through Miqqes, Chapters Fifty-Eight through One Hundred.*

2. For further reading and bibliography on the topic of this chapter, see the following:

Bowker, pp. 72-77: the homiletic Midrashim: a number of works which have made a collection of synagogue sermons; *Midrash Rabbah* (= Pentateuch, Song of Songs, Ruth, Lamentations, Ecclesiastes, and Esther), pp. 77-78. *Genesis Rabbah,* pp. 780-79.

Moses D. Herr, "Genesis Rabbah," *Encyclopaedia Judaica* 7:399-401: the title, structure, language, redaction, later additions, editions; apparently edited at about the same time as the Talmud of the Land of Israel, not later than 425 CE.

Maccoby, pp. 226-29 (sample passage).

Strack and Stemberger, pp. 300-308: the name, contents and structure; sources of *Genesis Rabbah*; redaction and date (after 400 CE); the text: manuscripts, Genizah fragments, printed editions, translations, commentaries.

This writer's introductions to the document are in *Comparative Midrash: The Plan and Program of Genesis Rabbah and Leviticus Rabbah* (Atlanta: Scholars Press for Brown Judaic Studies, 1986); *Genesis and Judaism: The Perspective of Genesis Rabbah. An Analytical Anthology* (Atlanta: Scholars Press for Brown Judaic Studies, 1986); and *Confronting Creation: How Judaism Reads Genesis. An Anthology of Genesis Rabbah* (Columbia: University of South Carolina Press, 1991).

3. Those responsible for compiling the compositions that are made into the composite document as a whole. Since some materials were formulated on their own prior to inclusion in the document in which they are now located, we have to distinguish between the author of a composition, whole and complete in its own terms, and the authorship of a composite of such compositions. On the formation of compositions prior to their inclusion in composite documents, see *Making the Classics in Judaism: The Three Stages of Literary Formation* (Atlanta: Scholars Press for Brown Judaic Studies, 1990); and on the distinction between composition and composite, note *The Rules of Composition of the Talmud of Babylonia: The Cogency of the Bavli's Composite* (Atlanta: Scholars Press for South Florida Studies in the History of Judaism, 1991).

4. Translation: *The Components of the Rabbinic Documents: From the Whole to the Parts. X. Leviticus Rabbah* (Atlanta: Scholars Press for USF Academic Commentary Series, 1998). *Part I: Introduction. Leviticus Rabbah Parashiyyot One through Seventeen. Part II: Leviticus Rabbah Parashiyyot Eighteen through Thirty-Seven. Part III: Leviticus Rabbah. A Topical and Methodical Outline.*

5. For further reading and bibliography on the topic of this chapter, see the following:

Neusner, *Study of Ancient Judaism*, pp. 55-106.

Bowker, pp. 80-81.

J. Heinemann, "Leviticus Rabbah," *Encyclopaedia Judaica* 11:147-50: fifth century in the Land of Israel, description of the document and its contents, survey of a *parashah*, construction of the *parashiyyot*, relationship to *Pesiqta deRab Kahana*.

Maccoby does not explain why, while he includes *Genesis Rabbah* in "early Rabbinic writings," he excludes *Leviticus Rabbah*, which I do not find mentioned in his introduction.

Strack and Stemberger, pp. 313-17: text, the name, contents and structure, redaction and time of origin (400–500 CE).

This writer's introductions to the document are as follows: *The Integrity of Leviticus Rabbah: The Problem of the Autonomy of a Rabbinic Document* (Chico: Scholars Press for Brown Judaic Studies, 1985); *Comparative Midrash: The Plan and Program of Genesis Rabbah and Leviticus Rabbah* (Atlanta: Scholars Press for Brown Judaic Studies, 1986); and *Judaism and Scripture: The Evidence of Leviticus Rabbah* (Chicago: The University of Chicago Press, 1986).

6. *Pisqa* yields "chapter," so the plural can be rendered, "chapters attributed to R. Kahana."

7. Translation: *The Components of the Rabbinic Documents: From the Whole to the Parts. XI. Pesiqta deRab Kahana* (Atlanta: Scholars Press for USF Academic Commentary Series, 1998). *Part I: Introduction. Pesiqta deRab Kahana Pisqaot One through Eleven. Part II: Pesiqta deRab Kahana Pisqaot Twelve through Twenty-Eight. Part III: Pesiqta deRab Kahana. A Topical and Methodical Outline.*

8. For further reading and bibliography on the topic of this chapter, see the following:

Neusner, *Study of Ancient Judaism*, pp. 55-92.

Bowker, pp. 74-76.

Maccoby omits this document from his introduction.

Bernard Mandelbaum, "Pesikta deRav Kahana," *Encyclopaedia Judaica* 13:333-34: the identification of the document, the original structure of the document and manuscript evidence, the manuscripts of the document; the original order followed the cycle of the Jewish calendar from the New Year through the Sabbath before the next New Year.

Strack and Stemberger, pp. 317-22: translation; the name, contents and structure, redaction and date (various).

This writer's introduction is *Pesiqta deRab Kahana: An Analytical Translation and Explanation. II. 15-28. With an Introduction to Pesiqta deRab Kahana* (Atlanta: Scholars Press for Brown Judaic Studies, 1987*); From Tradition to Imitation: The Plan and Program of Pesiqta deRab Kahana and Pesiqta Rabbati* (Atlanta: Scholars Press for Brown Judaic Studies, 1987).

9. Translation: *The Components of the Rabbinic Documents: From the Whole to the Parts. IV. Lamentations Rabbati* (Atlanta: Scholars Press for USF Academic Commentary Series, 1997).

10. For further reading and bibliography on the topic of this chapter, see the following:

Bowker, p. 84.

Moses D. Herr, "Lamentations Rabbah," *Encyclopaedia Judaica* 10:1376-78: the name (*Eikha Rabbati*), the structure, language, date of redaction (at about the end of the fifth century); editions.

Maccoby omits this document from his introduction.

Strack and Stemberger, pp. 308-12: text, the name, content and redaction; the date (early origin, in Palestine); the *petihot* (proems).

This writer's introduction is *The Midrash Compilations of the Sixth and Seventh Centuries: An Introduction to the Rhetorical Logical, and Topical Program. I. Lamentations Rabbah* (Atlanta: Scholars Press for Brown Judaic Studies, 1990).

11. *The Components of the Rabbinic Documents: From the Whole to the Parts. V. Song of Songs Rabbah* (Atlanta: Scholars Press for USF Academic Commentary Series, 1997). *Part I: Introduction and Parashiyyot One through Four. Part II: Parashiyyot Five through Eight and a Topical and Methodical Outline of Song of Songs Rabbah.*

12. For further reading and bibliography on the topic of this chapter, see the following:

Bowker, p. 83.

Moses D. Herr, "Song of Songs Rabbah," *Encyclopaedia Judaica* 15:152-54: the name of the compilation, definition, language, sources, date: Land of Israel, middle of the sixth century.

Maccoby omits this document from his introduction.

Strack and Stemberger, pp. 342-44: text, translation.

This writer's introduction is *The Midrash Compilations of the Sixth and Seventh Centuries: An Introduction to the Rhetorical Logical, and Topical Program. IV. Song of Songs Rabbah* (Atlanta: Scholars Press for Brown Judaic Studies, 1990).

13. Translation: *The Components of the Rabbinic Documents: From the Whole to the Parts. III. Ruth Rabbah* (Atlanta: Scholars Press for USF Academic Commentary Series, 1997).

14. For further reading and bibliography on the topic of this chapter, see the following:

Bowker, p. 83.

Moses D. Herr, "Ruth Rabbah," *Encyclopaedia Judaica* 14:523: the name, the structure, the language, redaction, editions; the work was redacted in the Land of Israel, not prior to the sixth century.

Maccoby omits this document from his introduction.

Strack and Stemberger, pp. 344-45: text, translation, bibliography.

This writer's introduction is *The Midrash Compilations of the Sixth and Seventh Centuries: An Introduction to the Rhetorical Logical, and Topical Program. III. Ruth Rabbah* (Atlanta: Scholars Press for Brown Judaic Studies, 1990).

15. Translation: *The Components of the Rabbinic Documents: From the Whole to the Parts. II. Esther Rabbah I* (Atlanta: Scholars Press for USF Academic Commentary Series, 1997).

16. For further reading and bibliography on the topic of this chapter, see the following:

Bowker, p. 84.

Moses D. Herr, "Esther Rabbah," *Encyclopaedia Judaica* 6:915-16: definition of the work, redacted in the Land of Israel not later than the beginning of the sixth century. *Esther Rabbah II* (covering Esther 3–8) is eleventh century.

Maccoby omits this document from his introduction.

Strack and Stemberger, pp. 346-47: it must be dated to 500 CE, in Palestine.

This writer's introduction is *The Midrash Compilations of the Sixth and Seventh Centuries: An Introduction to the Rhetorical Logical, and Topical Program. II. Esther Rabbah I* (Atlanta: Scholars Press for Brown Judaic Studies, 1990).

Chapter 5. Rabbinic Literature and the Hebrew Scriptures

1. For the theology of the Aggadah and the Halakhah, see, respectively, the following present systematic accounts: *The Theology of the Oral Torah: Revealing the Justice of God* (Kingston and Montreal: McGill-Queen's University Press, 1999 and Ithaca: Cornell University Press, 1999); *The Theology of the Halakhah* (Leiden: E. J. Brill, 2001).

2. I hardly need repeat that this definition of "Israel" cannot be confused with any secular meanings attributed to the same word, e.g., nation or ethnic entity, counterpart to other nations or ethnic groups.

Chapter 6. Rabbinic Literature and the Christian Scriptures

1. A medieval treatment of the same verse in Qohelet completes the exposition by referring to the trilogy, commandments, good deeds, and Torah study:

> Does Scripture speak literally about garments? But how many white garments do the pagans have? And if Scripture literally speaks of good oil, how much good oil do the pagans have! But Scripture speaks only of the performance of the commandments, good deeds, and the study of the Torah. (*Qohelet Rabbah* 9:8)

Here we see how the medieval documents of Rabbinic Judaism clearly continue and carry forward with great precision the teachings of the classical writings. Nothing has intervened in the unfolding of the Rabbinic system, which amplifies and refines the initial statement, and absorbs new ideas and naturalizes them, but which continues an essentially straight path from antiquity forward.

2. The role of Pharisees before 70 CE in the framing of Rabbinic Judaism afterward sets forth its own set of problems, which I have discussed in *Eliezer ben Hyrcanus: The Tradition and the Man* (Leiden: Brill, 1973, I-II).

APPENDIX:

THE CONTENTS AND DIVISIONS OF THE MISHNAH, TOSEFTA, AND TALMUDS

Division	Tractate Mishnah (chapters)	Tractate Tosefta	Gemara Palestinian Talmud	Gemara Babylonian Talmud
Zera'im *Agriculture*	Berakhot (9)	X	X	X
	Pe'ah (8)	X	X	
	Demai (7)	X	X	
	Kila'yim (9)	X	X	
	Shebi'it (10)	X	X	
	Terumot (11)	X	X	
	Ma'aserot (5)	X	X	
	Ma'aser Sheni (5)	X	X	
	Hallah (4)	X	X	
	Orlah (3)	X	X	
	Bikkurim (3)	X	X	
Mo'ed *Appointed Times*	Shabbat (24)	X	X	X
	Erubin (10)	X	X	X
	Pesahim (10)	X	X	X
	Sheqalim (8)	X	X	
	Yoma (8)	X	X	X
	Sukkah (5)	X	X	X
	Besah (5)	X	X	X
	Rosh Hashanah (4)	X	X	X
	Ta'anit (4)	X	X	X
	Megillah (4)	X	X	X
	Mo'ed Qatan (3)	X	X	X
	Hagigah (3)	X	X	X
Nashim *Women*	Yebamot (16)	X	X	X
	Ketubot (13)	X	X	X
	Nedarim (11)	X	X	X
	Nazir (9)	X	X	X
	Gittin (9)	X	X	X
	Sotah (9)	X	X	X
	Qiddushin (4)	X	X	X

Neziqin *Damages*	Baba Qamma (10)	X	X	X
	Baba Mesi'a (10)	X	X	X
	Baba Batra (10)	X	X	X
	Sanhedrin (11)	X	X	X
	Makkot (3)	X	X	X
	Shebu'ot (8)	X	X	X
	Eduyyot (8)	X	X	X
	Abodah Zarah (5)	X	X	X
	Abot (5)			
	Horayot (3)	X	X	X
Qodashim *Holy Things*	Zebahim (14)	X		X
	Menahot (13)	X		X
	Hullin (12)	X		X
	Bekhorot (9)	X		X
	Arakhin (9)	X		X
	Temurah (7)	X		X
	Keritot (6)	X		X
	Me'ilah (6)	X		X
	Tamid (7)		X	
	Middot (5)			
	Qinnim (3)			
Tohorot *Purities*	Kelim (30)	X		
	Ohalot (18)	X		
	Nega'im (14)	X		
	Parah (12)	X		
	Tohorot (10)	X		
	Miqva'ot (10)	X		
	Niddah (10)	X	X	X
	Makhshirin (6)	X		
	Zabim (5)	X		
	Tebul Yom (4)	X		
	Yadayim (4)	X		
	Uqsin (3)